CELTIC'S LOST LEGEND

First published 2007
This edition first published 2019
by Black & White Publishing Ltd
Nautical House, 104 Commercial Street Edinburgh EH6 6NF

1 3 5 7 9 10 8 6 4 2   19 20 21 22

ISBN: 978 1 78530 246 6

Typeset by Ellipsis, Glasgow
Printed and bound by CPI Group (UK) Ltd, Croydon CR0 4YY

CELTIC'S LOST LEGEND

THE GEORGE CONNELLY STORY

GEORGE CONNELLY
with **BRYAN COONEY**

BLACK & WHITE PUBLISHING

PUBLISHER'S NOTE

We first published *Celtic's Lost Legend: The George Connelly Story* in 2007 and are proud to publish it again in 2019. For Celtic fans in particular, and football aficionados in general, George Connelly's remarkable career remains something of an enigma – and so it feels fitting to return to his story to mark George's 70th birthday in 2019. We have retained the original text for its authentic perspectives upon George's life at the time it was written, and added a short postscript to help bring George's story up to date.

For Helen

CONTENTS

PROLOGUE

How many men can look in the mirror and approve of what is staring back at them? After years of running away from reality, I feel I am at last equipped to peer in that mirror and confront the demons that have tormented me for years.

I suppose, in many ways, I've had one hell of a life, touching the heights one minute, plumbing the depths the next. Now, I need to put those roller-coaster years into perspective and tell a story that is probably way overdue. With alcohol having played a leading role in how I've lived, there are perhaps gaps in my memory and I apologise for them. However, those closest to me – my wife, my son and my dearest friends – have kindly helped to bridge some of them and I hope their contributions will let you understand someone who is both straightforward and extremely complex at the same time.

This, then, is what fifty-eight years of living has done to a guy from High Valleyfield in Fife – a guy who might have been a football king if he'd only had the strength of character.

1

BREAKING POINT

There are some parts of your memory that are very much like a fine day when it's possible to see as clearly as Johnny Nash. With no rust clinging to your recall, you remember every detail as if it happened only a couple of minutes ago. This is one of those moments in my life when I've been blessed or perhaps cursed with clarity. The year was 1973 and Scotland were pretty good at international football in those days – in my opinion, even better than they are today under Alex McLeish. They had fine players, plenty of self-belief and just about the right degree of arrogance. They had just placed both feet in the World Cup finals that were due to take place in West Germany the following year. The motivational skills of manager Tommy Docherty had kick-started the team's chances in the competition but, with The Doc having agreed to go to Manchester United, Willie Ormond had been handed the responsibility of sealing qualification. I was there the night we did it on 26 September of that year. We beat Czechoslovakia 2–1 at Hampden Park and I stood alongside big Jim Holton to destroy the best-laid plans of the imaginative Czechs in a game that obviously will receive the attention it deserves later in this book. That night brought deep joy all round! If everything went according to plan, I was going to become part of that World Cup dream – I'd travel to West Germany the following year to join a circus of great football performers.

On a domestic level, the gods were equally generous and, whenever the sun shone, I seemed to be under it. I was established in the Celtic side and the Scottish press had voted me their current Player of the Year. People were talking very warmly about me and, indeed, were placing me on pedestals – ones that probably were far too high for my ability or, in some ways, for my liking. Of course, nothing really fazed me in a professional sense in those days. I was at ease with a football at my feet and, even from a distance, could pass the ball to a teammate without too many things going pear-shaped. And yet there was room for exaggeration – Jock Stein later likened my abilities to those of the captain of West Germany, Franz Beckenbauer, the imperious Kaiser. Now this was nosebleed territory, right enough. Embarrassing or what? Sure it was in many ways but I suppose, deep down, it's only right to elbow aside the hypocrisy and get real because it was also enormously flattering at the same time. From a professional point of view, it doesn't really get any better than that, does it?

In a material sense, the family Connelly wasn't doing half badly, either. In 1973, I wasn't on a fortune at Parkhead – remember, this was a time when the biscuit-tin mentality tended to dictate Celtic's every move – but I owned a nice house in Blantyre, if you conveniently forgot the fact that it was mortgaged to the hilt, and I also had another, more modest home in Kincardine – a bought-and-paid-for one this time. I had a childish love of cars in those days and there were three cars in and around the garage – an Audi 100LS, secured on the live-now-pay-(a-lot)-later scheme of hire purchase, a Vauxhall VX 4/90 (a World Cup sponsored car) and an Austin 1100, my wife's little runabout. It was nice work for a twenty-three–year-old who didn't possess a shred of sophistication or understanding of the world and wouldn't have known where to put his finger on these things even if he'd been given written directions to them.

Still, I had arrived as a footballer. I worked with great names like Kenny Dalglish, Davie Hay and Danny McGrain, members of the so-called 'Quality Street Gang', I was managed by the legendary Jock Stein and I had played alongside some of those wonderful Lisbon Lions. You don't need a degree in detective work to see that I had my finger pressed hard down on the button of the big time. So, if you assumed that I should have been lapping it all up, no one would blame you. But the trouble was that I wasn't – not for one minute. The situation wasn't right. Something was wrong – so dreadfully wrong that, in many ways, it defied all logic. However, as you will discover, there are some things in life that have got nothing whatsoever to do with logic – not where George Connelly is concerned.

Anyway, let's get back to that day in 1973. There I was travelling through the town of Kincardine on a bright Scottish morning on the way to visit my folks in Valleyfield. It was my day off and, by rights, I should have been pumped full of the joys. Most people, in fact, would have been glad to be alive that morning but the sunny weather did not fit with my dark mood. Funny things were going on inside my head and that was about par for the course in those days. It felt as if my brains had spent the night in a tumble dryer, scrambling up a dangerous mixture of fears and prejudices.

Then something happened to put it all my confusion into perspective – a very sad perspective, when I peer over my shoulder at my past life. I looked out of the car window and glimpsed this guy standing beside a pub. He was calmly reading a paper and looking as if the cares of the world had avoided him and gone on to annoy someone else. He might have been a night-shift worker or maybe he was on the dole or the sick or something but there he was, probably studying the runners and riders of that afternoon's horse racing, just waiting for the mid-morning pub doors to swing open. I looked at that guy again and knew instinctively that I was deeply jealous and resentful of that complete stranger. I wanted to be that man who seemed to be without a care or a responsibility to drag him down into the place I was now occupying.

Now, for all I knew, he might have had his own crosses to bear – he might have been suffering from some terminal disease; he may have been experiencing heartache at his workplace; he may have had a mother-in-law who gave him serious earache at any excuse. On the other hand, he might have been the happiest bunny in a field of rabbits. Who knows? I certainly didn't but one thing I did know was that I would have happily swapped shirts with him. I wanted to be standing on a corner, thumbing through the racing statistics, waiting for that unmistakable sound of the bolts being drawn back on the pub doors, anticipating the first taste of alcohol. In fact, I wanted to be anywhere other than where I was.

What could make a top footballer want to swap places with a man he's spotted on the street? I sometimes wonder if there are there any similar examples today. Do the current crop of top footballers ever wish they were away from it all? Do they think that they are perhaps standing in the wrong place at the wrong moment in time? My thoughts that day show you exactly where I wanted to be. Oh, the envy which came at me like a tidal wave wasn't because I was desperate for a drink – those days would visit me with a vengeance soon enough but not right then. No, it was just that, on the surface anyway, there were no complications surrounding this guy. He was about to have a light refreshment and that seemed to be the beginning and end of his worries. As far as I could tell, his most pressing concern was whether to choose a lager tops or something stronger.

And, when I contrasted that with my lot . . . the clear sky of that Kincardine day was replaced by the great, black cloud of my depression. All I had to look forward to was another day's training at Celtic Park and, after that, attempting to please the huge crowds that flocked to the Park and the various away venues. To most folk, that must seem like an awful attitude. If someone had penetrated my private thoughts that day, they'd have called me worthless and ungrateful and I don't suppose I could have put up an argument to that assessment. But the thing was that I couldn't help it – it was just the way I felt. And this wasn't just an off day. To give you an indication of how I was feeling back then, let me tell you I used to wake up most mornings and want to pull the blankets over my head. I needed to hide from the world. Most people are delighted to see the dawn and involve themselves in the situation of another day, another dollar – but not me. I dreaded the dawning of a new morning. I'd peek out from the comfort of those blankets and say to myself, 'Oh, God, no. Not again!' Come to think of it, if you had been able to buy invisibility at the chemist's I'd have been at the front of the queue seeking a lifetime's supply! In fact, that isn't as far-fetched as it may sound because, before long, I was doing disappearing acts at Parkhead – walking out in the middle of training and things like that.

So, I can hear you quite rightly wonder how a man of twenty-three who has the world at his feet comes to be in a position like that. What, you may ask, makes him want to turn his back on reality? Why does he keep walking out on football and frustrating everyone surrounding him, including a genius like Jock Stein? A lot of analysis has been thrown at those questions over the years, particularly after I'd quit the professional game for the last time some three years later, but none of it really came close. Some people said it was all down to the drink. Well, I suppose, latterly, when things pulled me right down, that's true – alcohol did have more than a few fingers around my throat – but not in 1973. The extremes of what alcohol would do to me were still to come. At that time, it was a long way from being the real culprit.

Others said that my wife was having an affair. As far as I know, that wasn't true – not at that time, anyway. Mind you, my marriage was in such a shocking state that, if she had been playing away, I wouldn't have cared – indeed, the way I felt then, I'd probably have held the door open for her. Those claims were double-edged as it was also being said that I had become a womaniser. That was so far from fact that the distance could not have been measured. When you're a well-known footballer, there are countless women willing to jump into bed with you for no other reason than to play the fame game with you. There were plenty of women I could have hooked up with if I'd cared to but I didn't want any other involvement – I had enough on my plate with the one I had.

No, the real reason for the black moods, for the anger, for the paranoia was that my marriage was a disaster. People often say it's good for young men to get married so maybe I was just very unlucky. Whatever, it almost turned me into a basket case, a man who almost became frightened of his own shadow, a man terrified of being part of the social whirl. There were times I could have screamed for a year and still wouldn't have been content with things.

To let you understand fully what I mean, we need to go back another few years from that day in Kincardine. The year 1969 was when the full horror of what my life had become dawned on me.

I was still in my teens and just beginning to make my way with Celtic. As far as the opposite sex was concerned, I was a right novice and, if they had pinned a big red letter L on my back, I could not have complained. OK, I played football in Glasgow but I was just a country boy at heart. I started going out with a girl from Falkirk but the relationship didn't last long.

After that, I lost my swagger – if I'd ever had one to start with. The way I reasoned it, Falkirk was a foreign land and I shouldn't really be making treks to foreign lands. 'Sod this for a game of soldiers,' I thought. 'I'll get someone from my own village.' There spoke a boy of vision.

Valleyfield in Fife is where I was born. It wasn't an intimidating or threatening place – on the contrary, it offered protection and comfort. So I started going out with a local lassie called Christine and, before long, she fell pregnant. I felt obliged to do the right thing by her. *Obliged*? I'll address that word in a minute. Even now, I sit myself down and ask the vital question – Why?

My folks were dead set against the idea. My mother raised the strongest objections. It wasn't that she was in any way snobbish – our roots were in coal mining and there's no room for snobbery in that community – but she felt that we were poles apart – too far apart, indeed, to mould as a unit. I'll put it as diplomatically as I can – she thought that my girlfriend's family placed their priorities on different things and that they loved their social life more than their home life. Her father, according to Mum, didn't have a brain in his head. But, there again, he was in good company as neither my wife-to-be nor I had a brain between us. Christine didn't know her way around life and she was in good company. We were just village idiots. Anyway, at nineteen years of age, I ignored the pleas of my parents. What did they know, anyway? Young men and women know best, don't they? They are blessed with vision denied to their elders, aren't they?

But I had a far more persuasive reason to ignore what they were saying – my mother-in-law-to-be swore that, if I did not marry her daughter, she'd take a knife to my throat! This, even before the *Godfather* films, was an offer I could not refuse. Look, that woman was fantastic with her own children but she was a horror to me – a battleaxe that I had no intention of facing on the field of combat. So, yes, I was obliged to marry the girl. Things were different in those days and I had to do what I thought was my duty. Is that not frightening? Even now, when I think about the whole scenario, it makes me shudder and I try to turn away from the embarrassment of that memory. How could anyone be so bloody stupid?

Anyway, I told Jock Stein, the Celtic manager, that I was getting married and that I needed a house. Buying property back then wasn't as fashionable as it is today but something told me that, if nothing else, I needed a bit of security. The place I had in mind was scarcely built along the lines of Buck House. It was, in fact, a room and kitchen in Kincardine – still, it was cheap. I'm not sure whether Stein joined in the general disbelief that I was embarking on such a course of action as marriage but, if he did, he pretty much kept it to himself. What I do remember is that he asked how much the house I had my eye on cost. That was on the Tuesday and, when I walked into Celtic Park on the Friday, he handed me a cheque for £750. It was a generous gesture. I think I had to pay it back at around £10 a week but it was interest free. Lovely biscuit tins! Later I bought a bigger house down the road from the first one in Kincardine. I actually kept the first one – it was to come in handy later on – so I had two feet on the property ladder and was beginning to climb but keeping my balance in my marriage was another thing.

As it happened, my wife suffered a miscarriage. Her waters were breaking and the doctor took her to hospital in the back of his car. We had married for the sake of a baby and now we'd lost it. Later we would have two daughters, Susan and Sharon, within two years of one another but even those children, as lovely as they turned out to be, could not bind us together. We were too young and too inexperienced. We had nothing in common and we couldn't get on with each other at all. Don't get me wrong, I couldn't just point the finger at her – there was blame on both sides. I simply didn't have enough maturity to deal with the situation. Maybe, deep down, I was resenting the fact that I'd succumbed to a shotgun marriage and now I was regretting my loss of freedom. Whatever, I must confess that I grew to really dislike Christine and, I wouldn't be surprised if she disliked me intensely me in return.

To put it in a nutshell, I think it might have been better if we'd just stayed in our own locality where we felt comfortable but, when we moved to Blantyre in 1973, I sorely needed someone to take me on to another level, someone to provide advice and encouragement – none of which was forthcoming, I'm afraid. Christine wasn't the answer. Everything was wrong, even the physical contrast between us – I was that big and I thought she was awfully wee. I was very conscious of the way I looked – I was gawky, had goofy teeth and ears that stuck out like wing mirrors on a car. She was not an unattractive girl but it felt odd being with her. I just wasn't comfortable.

Now I don't think of myself as being big-headed. Well, maybe I have been without knowing it but I would like to have been with someone who was giving me more encouragement – someone who would tell me I had to get a move on and not squander the talent I had been given. People say I was a very good footballer and that I could have become a great one but I'm telling you now that I don't think people saw the half of what I could do. Granted I got plenty of motivation from Jock Stein but, if only I could have counted on the same level of motivation from my wife, perhaps it would have done the trick.

By this time, we'd moved up the property ladder again and were living in Blantyre. I wasn't loving it in Blantyre and my mind wasn't really on my football. With a marriage that was

running along the lines of a disaster movie, I found it so difficult to concentrate on anything else. I went to work every day
but I was constantly thinking on what I would be going back
home to. It wasn't even that we were having huge rows or
anything like that – it was just that I felt I couldn't enjoy the
success that was coming to me. And, somehow, I got it in my
head that I couldn't go anywhere and nor could I take Christine
anywhere.

What I'm going to say may seem like absolute madness.
There I was a staunch Celtic supporter, with my brothers all
Celtic supporters. I used go up to the Park and watch the
games, fascinated by the likes of Billy McNeill, Stevie Chalmers,
John Divers, Bertie Auld and Jinky Johnstone – I idolised all
of them. Yet, all of a sudden, I was sitting in a dressing room
alongside them and then, later, playing beside them but I
couldn't allow myself to get friendly with them. In one of Jinky's
books, he said I didn't mix. He was *so* right. What he didn't
know was that I was too scared to mix. I would rarely go into
the city with her – I just didn't need that kind of hassle. It was
a horrible time. It would have been easier if we'd known our
way around but neither of us had a map or a compass.

They say that getting together with your team-mates for social
events fosters friendship and togetherness but, because of the
way things were at home, I just wasn't getting into any of that.
With my wife offering me no support or encouragement as far
as my career was concerned and finding myself unable to enjoy
the kind of motivation colleagues would usually provide, you
might say my life, at that time, was rather abnormal. The most
I'd ever say to her was, 'Come on, we'll go through to Kincardine
or Alloa.'

We never arranged to go out anywhere else. Communications
between us were sparse to non-existent. The only times we
were all right together was when we were having a drink

together. That was tolerable for then you could forget everything that was going on. To make matters worse, I was on the offensive all the time with people. They'd say, 'Do you fancy coming out here with me?' and I'd answer in the negative straightaway. They must have thought me very rude. No sooner was a night out mentioned than I'd change the subject so I'm sure the other players wondered what was wrong with me. The really strange thing about it was that they were the people I wanted to be with – I've already it mentioned how much of a supporter I'd always been and here was my chance to spend time with them yet I was rejecting it at every turn.

I can remember one night sitting in Kincardine (it was our second house – the one we had before we moved to Blantyre), all ready to go to the function in my honour where I was to be presented with another Player of the Year award through in Glasgow. But I never went and never even phoned to tell them I was bottling out. They were not pleased. Yet their displeasure didn't really register with me – fear of being out in public with my wife had me by the testicles. At a rough estimate, I suppose my marriage represented about 90 per cent of my problems at the time.

Bizarre behaviour such as this had begun far earlier in our marriage. I'll give you another example which occurred when we were staying in the tiny house Stein's money had helped us buy. It was the close season and, for once, I was out on the razz one Friday. I met Arthur Walsh, the nephew of the former Celtic player, Jimmy Walsh. I'd been at school with Arthur and we arranged to meet on the Sunday. I was relaxed and not experiencing too much pain at the time but, when I sobered up and realised what I had committed myself to, I started panicking. I knew that Arthur was bringing his wife and would be expecting me to bring mine to our night out. I was determined it wasn't going to happen so I thought up an elaborate plan. I chapped on a neighbour's door and asked him if I could put my car in his garage on the Sunday evening. I told him that there was a guy coming round for me but I didn't want to go out with him and so it would be better if he thought I was out. Then I told my wife the same thing. I wanted to go out all right but not with her. Anyway, when Arthur duly came round, he started blasting his horn. Just imagine, while all this was going on, I was lying on a bed in a darkened room, hiding from reality.

If this had happened in today's football world, someone would have zeroed right in on what was going on and they'd probably have been able to iron out most of the difficulties. But this is the early 70s we're talking about and people in football weren't as clued up about the kinds of problems I had as they are nowadays. As it was, Celtic recommended that I go to a psychiatrist. I wasn't too keen on that. However, I went along a few times just to see if there would be any improvement but there wasn't. The guy was attempting to get to the bottom of a well. However, what with my fractured marriage and so forth, it seems as if that particular well was bottomless. I don't remember too much about it, really, although the guy told me I had the same kind of problems as some university professors suffer from and I suppose he meant it was like some kind of mental overload. He also said that I'd done well getting as far as I had done in my career while feeling like this. But, those meetings apart, things just weren't set up to help those with problems.

You may well be wondering, if a psychiatrist couldn't help me with my problems, couldn't Mr Stein? After all, here was a man who seemed to know everything and who was so talented in so many areas. But I can't blame him. First of all, I wouldn't open up to him about my problems. And secondly, probably nothing in football had equipped him to deal with someone like me. Besides, while I was happy to approach Stein about buying a house, there were two things that I found too difficult to approach him about – one was my wages, which weren't all that clever, and the other was my marriage. I bottled up all the problems and just kidded on that everything was all right. Talk about cover-ups – I was the expert at that.

In fact, no one really knew what was going on because I refused to take anybody into my confidence. Of course, maybe they were smarter than I thought and maybe I was a whole lot less smart that I imagined myself to be. So maybe they did know or at least suspected that things weren't right with me.

A man like Stein knew everything, of course, so maybe I'm sorely underestimating him. But what is for sure is that they didn't know the half of it! Stein certainly never said anything to me about my marriage. And, believe me, I was too ashamed to talk about it to anyone else. I kept it from my closest friends, Davie Hay and Davie Cattenach, I kept it from my brothers and sisters and I kept it from my father and mother. I held on to that terrible secret myself. The way I looked at it was that it was my problem and I was stuck with it.

Do you know, I kept it all inside me until just a short time ago and, even then, I didn't exactly grab a loudhailer and tour the streets. It was a bit subtler than that. One night, at the back end of 2006, I was able to sit down and tell my son David, from my second marriage, all about it. I was amazed at myself that, after thirty-odd years, it all came pouring out like water from a kettle. You have no idea how much that helped me – how much of a relief it was to tell somebody my side of affairs. I'd been dying to get it off my chest for so many years but I'd never allowed myself to open up before.

I wasn't drinking at the time so I think that helped a lot. I thought David would just say, 'Aw, Dad, shut up! Away up the stairs to your bed!' I thought it would have been embarrassing for both of us but not a bit of it – it was so relaxed. We sat there for about an hour and a half and it helped me so much. He wasn't disgusted with me – he just listened intently and no doubt he was amazed by the things I was coming away with about a career and a marriage that had collapsed all because two silly misfits had tied the knot.

Of course, with all those years under my belt, it is a bit easier to analyse my part in it all. What did I do wrong? Was I difficult to live with? Well, maybe I was at the time although I can't remember being that way. Christine and I did have some slanging matches and I would give her the verbals a few times. Of course I was George Connelly of the Celtic and you get away with these things just because of who you are, don't you? But it stayed at verbals – I never hit her or anything like that. I would never lift my hand to a woman. No way! I can't even remember if there was an attempt at reconciliation, if I ever sat down and talked to her about our problems. When something doesn't suit you, people have a capacity for being able to blot things out. But I know I wasn't even able to tell her how much I hated being in the marriage.

If matrimony was one torment, let's now turn to another. You know, all my life I have been tormented by this suggestion that I wanted to be a long-distance lorry driver instead of a top-class footballer. Sure I maybe sent out a few mixed signals to some of my colleagues back then but, I'm telling you, someone, somewhere got their lines crossed. I may have said this in jest to someone at Celtic Park and they then translated it into a statement of serious intent. Do me a favour! I may have been seriously naive back in those days and I might have visited a psychiatrist but I wasn't terminally stupid. No, sitting in the cab of an articulated lorry for hour after mind-numbing hour was never for me.

The point is that things come into your mind but they're not long-term lodgers and they exit just as quickly – like the feeling that came over me in Kincardine that day. The feeling that I wanted to swap shirts with that guy outside the pub probably lasted only a few minutes before reality engaged gear again but it was a very powerful emotion at the time. I wanted just to be out of the pressure-cooker existence of having to please thousands upon thousands of people every week of my life. For somebody who had lived in a village and had limited horizons to be suddenly catapulted into the big smoke of a city like Glasgow, it's a major thing – it's impossible to adequately describe what it does to you. But it blows you away and you just hope your brains stay intact. Unfortunately for me, mine were scrambled for what seemed an eternity. That day in Kincardine summed up so much about my life. I had come to a crisis point in my relationship not only with Celtic but also with football in general.

Of course, in my moments of clarity, I would have hoped to join Willie Ormond's exodus to West Germany but soon that dream was going to evaporate, like so many of my other dreams. Over the next couple of years, I staged several walkouts from the club – disappearing acts that Harry Houdini would have approved of – and my relationship with my once-beloved Celtic would begin to show ominous cracks. Up until then, Stein had always been very nice to me but there was to come a point when he would no longer look at me as if I was the favourite apple in his barrel.

If I'd only had the courage or perhaps the common sense to tackle the problems at their roots, there would have been time to do something about the situation. But, when it came to something as basic as looking reality in the face, I was just as stubborn as I was when my mother had been begging me not to get married.

I was in this dark place all on my own and I didn't even

15

want to reach out and grab a torch. What a contrast to my childhood. Then, I'd never thought there was any darkness in life when I was learning the ropes in Valleyfield. Then it was only light and laughter.

2

THE EARLY DAYS

Born on a mountain top in Tennessee
Greenest state in the land of the free
Raised in the woods so he knew every tree
Kilt him a b'ar when he was only three
Dav-y, Davy Crockett
King of the wild frontier

Before we get to the nitty-gritty of a life thrown into the dustbin, let me tell you about the good days and, believe me, there were plenty of them, particularly before the pressures of professional football promised to cave my head in. So let's go right back about fifty years or so to the times you couldn't escape Davy Crockett even if you drove a souped-up Morris Minor and had an unlimited amount of petrol. The year was 1955. The Crockett thing was a phenomenon that simply bowled everyone over. The replica 'coonskin hats of the uncrowned king of America's wild frontier seemed to be on the heads of every young boy who had more than two ha'pennies to rub together. His song was on the lips of everybody. Aye, if you weren't singing or whistling 'The Ballad of Davy Crockett' in that baby-booming year, you weren't quoted. The record was not so much a hit as an explosion. I'm told it sold over ten million copies worldwide.

In 1955, I was six years of age and just setting out on the

grand adventure of life and I wasn't on any mountaintop in Tennessee but in a small, tight-knit mining community in Fife. High Valleyfield was my home and had been ever since I came into the world on the first day of March 1949. I didn't have enough money to buy a 'coonskin hat in those days but really I didn't need one. Football satisfied every need I had. It made me happy and I wanted nothing else.

The youngest of eight children – three girls, five boys – in that year of the Davy Crockett craze, I was a pupil at the local primary school. Sadly, as far as I was concerned, the beautiful game wasn't part of the school's curriculum but that was no deterrent. Football was my game – the game that I loved – and there was simply no stopping me from playing it at every opportunity. Every break, every evening, every weekend, every holiday, I was out there playing with my pals either in the playground or on the waste ground. I didn't miss an opportunity to hone the skills that would eventually take me into the professional game.

The playground was particularly great because it was right next to the place where the local miners would wait for the buses to take them to the outlying pits. It was like having your own audience. Some days, there weren't a lot of miners around but, at other times, there would be quite a few and that's when I came into my own. By the time I was eleven and had put in a few years of practice, I was right up for a bit of showing off. If I could see that I had a big audience, I would try a lot harder, I'd put myself about more and strut my stuff. I was getting a bit of a name for myself by then and, I suppose, enjoying the small chunk of celebrity that was attached to being a good player.

My dad was a quiet-spoken man from the Tollcross district of Glasgow. He had moved through to Fife to pursue his life below ground. He was called Dan and he had four brothers –

George, Oor Tommy, Jimmy and Josie – and he called his five sons after his brothers. Like my dad, my brothers were all miners and I can remember how three of those brothers would come racing home from the pit as the first in got the biggest dinner!

My three sisters were called Ellen, Annie and Jane. A big family? Maybe but nothing compared to my mother's. She was one of a brood of nineteen from Blantyre. Ach, it was more of a host than a family. The Greenhorns were a formidable firm, in numbers anyway. Mum was quite formidable, herself. She wasn't fat or thin but I'm comfortable with the description 'well made'. She was quite a good cook, as I remember. Not much found its way past her and my father wasn't far behind her in that respect. They were quite strict parents and we were kept well in line.

One blessing is that they never argued so you didn't need to keep clapping your hands over your ears like so many kids had to do in those days when rows could be an everyday event in the family circle. In fact, the only time I remember any arguments breaking out was when my mum would say, in a voice that cancelled any thoughts of a comeback, 'Well, who's contradicting you, then?' No, there was never any response to that. I suppose my dad knew when to keep the peace – in that instance, anyway.

He was a stubborn soul, mind you – really set in his ways. He had pyorrhoea of the gums and had to get all his teeth pulled out but he just wouldn't put in his false teeth – he was like that, my dad. And he wouldn't take aspirins for headaches or anything – he just didn't believe in any form of drugs. Neither, if I mind right, did he fancy us getting our clothes wet. No, you couldn't go out and get wet. That was forbidden. If you did, retribution came quickly. To avoid getting a sore one because of the state of my clothes, I've seen me hiding from him in the flats across the road until I'd watched him going out. Then it was time to sneak into the house and take off the garments that would have offended him so much.

So it was a mostly happy regime but a disciplined one. In spite of our numbers and the obvious temptation to have a bit of a carry-on in bed at night, we just couldn't misbehave. If we did, it would be time for corporal punishment – we'd get the belt or the dog's lead and the amount of pain inflicted depended on which end of those weapons was handiest.

The clan had got so big that we had to move to a bigger house in another part of High Valleyfield but my oldest sister, Jane, eased the situation by moving out. She went to Glasgow to learn to be a ballroom dancer. My other two sisters, Annie and Ellen, had no such fancy notions. They were mill workers and, as far as I know, content with their lots. There were four of us in one room, in two sets of bunk beds, three in another bedroom and Mum and Dad in the other. There was a coal fire on all the time and, as often as not, the radio would be blaring in the background. I mind Billy Cotton coming on, crying, 'Wakey! Wakey!'

There was a wee sitting room downstairs that sometimes was used as a bedroom. It's funny the things that stick in your mind and refuse to move but I can remember being parked there in a chair in 1963 and the announcement coming over the airwaves that President Kennedy had been assassinated. I can remember feeling sad, only I didn't really understand why.

The house was spotless but never fancy. You sat on old chairs and a sofa. This was Britain in the late 50s and early 60s and there were no posh leather suites for us in those days, nothing as grand as that. We were miners and the comforts of home were few and far between. Once, my mother bought new covers for the suite but the trouble was that they didn't fit the shape of the furniture. Problem? Nae problem! Well, not at first, anyway. I found Mum sawing the wings off that sofa but she sawed too much and the back of the thing collapsed.

She had better luck with her music, though. She was the tuneful one, I think. She played the piano. On a Friday or Saturday, there would regularly be a party and a sing-song back at the house. It was all very sociable. My mum's preferred choice, at one stage, was 'Puppet on a String' but she would sing anything and my sisters were the same. You'd often hear the familiar refrain of 'Gaun yersel!'

But that kind of upbringing served me well in other ways. For instance, the grub was plain but good and consequently I can eat anything nowadays. I'm not fussy and nor was I encouraged to be that way in those early years. You would get a scud around the ear if it looked as if you were in any way being choosy. Did it do us any harm? Not a bit of it! Any danger to health came from our location. Where we stayed was right next to the pit – well, about a quarter of a mile away from it and there was a big pit lum that used to spew out coal dust like nobody's business. Particles would get in your hair all the time. It was also in your clothes and on the car. In the summer, you could see it lying like sand on the roads.

The distance from the pits was certainly handy for Dad in the mornings as it meant he didn't have far to go; but think of the damage that working there must have inflicted on his lungs. It was no surprise that Dad had a chronic chest infection – it was really bad and, to make matters worse, he smoked all the time. I remember him lying puffing in his bed before he got up. He was a smoker and a cougher. He died at sixty-nine and that's not really very old, is it? Towards the end of his life, he had begun to seriously deteriorate. We used to stay on a flat road, between two hills. He was so bad that he'd get on the bus at the bottom of one hill, get off at the top and walk down, rather than get off in the middle and walk up. He just wasn't fit enough to climb up the distance between two bus stops.

I felt sorry for him, I suppose, but that was it. If you ask whether I was really close to my parents, the fact is I don't think I really was. I can't be bothered with all that stuff about people who always go on about loving the bones of their mothers and their fathers. I was never brought up with that sort of sentimentality. There wasn't a lot of touching, holding and kissing like there is nowadays. I'd ask you not to hold that against me, though. It's not that I'm unfeeling – it's just the way I was brought up. I'm just a product of the times. Then again, I was lucky. My folks were strict enough but some way from being tyrants. I was not required to go my mum's messages and things like that – not me. I wasn't domesticated. I had other things to occupy my mind or, rather, my feet with.

Soon, I was making some good pals at my new home. Like me, they were mostly the sons of miners. There was a spare piece of ground at the back of our houses and someone with a bit of brainpower suggested that we should clear it of rubble and burn the debris that was left. It was here that we would play a lot of football over the next five years. Sometimes, there would be just half a dozen of us but, at other times, it would be games with twenty-a-side. There was no limit. Numbers didn't matter. If you wanted a game, you were on. Of course, we did occasionally take wee breaks from football. Was it time for cricket? Behave yourself! During that time, we would often have card schools. These games were popular in the 60s and we would play here, there and everywhere about the village. It was during those sessions that I honed my skills at three-card brag – skills that were to come in useful in later life when I met up with guys like Lou Macari and Davie Hay!

When I was twelve years old, I began attending St Margaret's School in Dunfermline. On one hand, it was undoubtedly an exercise in real learning and one I didn't fancy much at all. On the other, I fancied it like mad because at last there was some structure to my football. The school team played games all over

Fife on Saturday mornings. That was more my style. But, of course, the great part of school is learning and this is where I fell apart. I couldn't bear books and studying – I just wasn't at ease with them and I felt my only option was truancy – I played that almost as well as I played football. If my Dad was on day shift, I would creep back into the house and have a few hours of freedom. If, on the other hand, he was on night or back shift, he would make sure I went to school. Well, the ever-present threat of corporal punishment would see to it that you attended.

As I got older and moved into the third year, I was making a name for myself as a keepie-uppie specialist, as well as being someone earmarked to go places in the football world. Maybe I didn't like poring over schoolbooks but put that ball at my feet in the back garden and away I went. Bob, bop, bop, thud, thud, thud, ping, ping, ping – I was able to keep the ball up for more minutes than I care to remember. But it wasn't all Circus Boy stuff – I could play the game too.

Our gym teacher was W. J. Mullen. He was a top referee in the professional game and later he took charge of a few of my games at the top level. I remember him standing in front of the school team and announcing that he had plans for me. I also remember my cheeks colouring fairly rapidly. I was beginning to understand the meaning of embarrassment. But there were two parts to me even then. I might have suffered a red face when someone mentioned my name in despatches, but put me on the sporting stage and another George Connelly lived and breathed quite easily.

Keepie-uppie was a speciality with me and my brothers and we would have competitions out in the back garden to see who was best. Only one of my brothers went into the pro game – Josie was scoring regularly for Oakley United (wearing a pair of Billy McNeill's old boots, incidentally) before going on to play for East Stirlingshire and Cowdenbeath.

There were other ways of developing my skills, though, and I wasn't slow to utilise them. To put a bit more money in the Connelly trouser pockets, I got a job delivering the evening newspapers. The ball came with me on my paper round – it was my closest and most constant companion. I'd hit it against walls and against pavement kerbstones as I walked along delivering the news. It came from all angles yet I wanted to be its master. Sometimes, I'd stop and put in a spontaneous burst of ball skills. There were going to be rewards for all this practice.

By the time I was fourteen, I was playing in the five-a-sides at Bowhill, Fife. Funnily enough, I can even remember the team – Campbell Young, Davy Sinclair, Ian Downie, Tam Barrowman and me. Davy Sinclair's son went on to play for Raith Rovers and Falkirk. None of us had a pair of football shorts so we all played in our long trousers. Yet, we won the tournament. Campbell Young, the goalkeeper, didn't have particularly good sight and, on losing a goal, threw the ball up the park and hit the referee on the back of the head. The official was not best pleased!

One Saturday morning in the autumn of 1963, a few of the boys and I had been down the lane playing cards. We were standing outside my front gate just after dinner time, debating what we should do next. It was around one o'clock when this man came running over the field from the bypass road. He was all breathless but managed to explain to me that he wanted me to come and play a game for the local junior club, Tulliallan Thistle. The man's name was Charlie McTaggart and he was a member of the team's committee. He revealed later that my brother Dan had kept telling him about me. He'd told Dan that he would give me a shout if they were stuck. And bingo! Here they were, strapped for players! Picture the scene: I was just fourteen years and a few months old at the time; I didn't even possess a pair of football boots although one of my pals performed a rescue act by offering to lend me his pair; and here was the local juniors club wanting me to turn out for them.

So, that day, the real part of the adventure began. Dressed to kill? I wasn't even dressed to knock someone over! I was wearing white jeans that were ripped at the knee and only partially sewn together (see, I was an unwitting trendsetter even then), I didn't have a jacket and I was carrying someone else's football boots. Nevertheless, away I went to play for Tulliallan against Nairn Thistle in Kirkcaldy which, at the time, felt like travelling across the world as far as I was concerned. If you accept that I was a very bashful boy and incredibly self-conscious, you'll appreciate that Tulliallan hadn't chosen Britain's most confident player that day. But, after sitting on the Kirkcaldy-bound bus, with my nerves playing a rare old tune in my belly, I didn't let those nerves get me down. I created what was to be the decisive goal five minutes from time in a 3–1 victory and, on the coach ride home, I was asked to sign for the club. There was no team of agents, accountants and lawyers in those days. Tulliallan had my signature in about one minute flat – and without a signing-on fee, mind. At that time, we played for expenses only so sometimes I pocketed about half a crown while, at others, I would be slipped five shillings.

I had played about half a dozen games for Thistle when my dad called me into the living room of our house and told me that a football scout called Charlie McGuinness had talked to him and he wanted me to go through to Celtic Park for possible signing talks. That was on the Sunday. The next morning I was told that the Dunfermline manager, Jock Stein, was coming up to the house to talk about signing for him. This episode and my ongoing relationship with Stein are dealt with in more detail later in this book, but let's just say I did one of my tradi-tional body swerves around Stein and ended up signing schoolboy forms for Celtic, after talking to their manager Jimmy McGrory and his assistant, Sean Fallon.

This time there was a signing-on fee (£20) and the wages were to be £2 a week. But the perks didn't end there – if I wanted tickets for any of the big games, I just had to phone up and they would be mine. It was also determined that I would start at the Park as a ground-staff boy in the summer of '64. There was no discontent that summer. I was now on £14 a week, plus my bus or train fares through from Fife.

Football had me in its clutches in those days – I played for the school on Saturday mornings and Thistle in the afternoons. Soon, though, the demands of being at Celtic meant that I started giving my school strip to someone else on Friday afternoons and playing only for the juniors the next day. In fact, I continued playing for them for another season as Mr Fallon reckoned that it would only give me some much-needed experience.

Neilly Mochan, who became a Celtic trainer, lived in Larbert in those days and we used to travel through to Glasgow together on the train. The large crowds of the city were too much for me. I always tried to keep my eyes on Neilly and stay close to him. It was difficult because he was quick off the mark and I'd almost have to run to keep pace with him. At other times, we'd get the bus through to Glasgow. He'd start singing and I'd get so embarrassed. Why, I don't really know. He was a right good fella and a proper character.

Celtic changed so much in my life, even my attitude towards schooling. At this time, my mum bought me my first school uniform and truancy suddenly became a thing of the past. I began attending lessons on a regular basis and managed to become a huge hypocrite in the process. There were several kids in my class who were known to dodge school whenever they could. Now I would ask them to ensure they were in the classrooms on a Friday at the very least so that we could go

home a period early – this was the reward for good attendance!

In my final year at Dunfermline, our sports day was held at
Pitreavie playing fields. In those days, you sat in the grandstand when events had ended and listened to the head teacher
announcing the First, Second and Third Year champions. As
I'd won the Third Year trophy fairly easily, I expected my name
to be mentioned but the head never did call out my name.
Perhaps he believed I had an unfair advantage over my rivals
because of my football training. I don't know – I never got
around to asking him. At the end of the day, I suppose, it didn't
really matter that much. Too many other things were going on
in my life then.

From Tulliallan to Celtic – you couldn't have had a more
dramatic contrast. When I first signed for Thistle, they were
having new changing rooms built but, until then, players had
to put up with the temporary facilities offered by a farmer's
barn. Those who were first in that barn would have to put the
lights on, chase the rats and tell them it was time to get out of
town, if only on a temporary basis. When we finished training,
we used to wash up in an old tin bath. Then, suddenly, there
I was with Celtic and all the best facilities of a professional
football club.

The day I started as a ground-staff boy stands out clearly in
my memory. My dad took me through to Glasgow and we got
there for about ten o'clock. We sat in the foyer waiting to see
either Mr Fallon or Mr McGrory. In the end, it was the latter
who met us. He was a true gentleman. After I had signed for
him, he took Dad and me into Glasgow to catch the bus home.
He stopped on the way to show us the building in the Calton
where Celtic were first formed. My dad was a quiet man and
it really made his day. But he couldn't stop laughing on the
way home. I asked him why. While we were sitting in that

foyer, we had watched Mr McGrory taking a couple of people on a conducted tour around the place. He had apparently taken them into the dressing rooms and the trophy room and then on to the pitch. They were just about to leave when one of the men turned round to Mr McGrory and said, 'What was your name again?'

Now we are talking about one of the most decorated players in football – a Celtic legend and one of the most famous men alive at the time! Consider the McGrory record: 550 goals in first-class matches; 410 in 408 league games; seven caps for Scotland; and twenty years as Celtic manager. No wonder my father found the man's ignorance hilarious. Yes, as they say, football is a funny old game – and so it was even back in 1964.

3

PARADISE FOUND

If you know anything at all about me by now, it's that I've never been one of life's pushy people. I've never put my shoe in anyone's door to prevent it from slamming in my face and breaking my nose. I came from nothing and was accompanied, no doubt, by an inferiority complex the size of a small country. As I said earlier in the book, I imagined myself to be a physical misfit so I could never hope to be compared with a painting to be hung in an art gallery. And yet here I was, at fifteen, a Celtic player, taken to the Park by the combined efforts of the manager, Jimmy McGrory, and his assistant, Sean Fallon. I signed schoolboy forms in 1963 and professional forms two years later. I was right, smack in the centre of the field of many people's dreams, particularly my own, surrounded by men who were considered football giants – Billy McNeill, Jimmy Johnstone, Ronnie Simpson, Tommy Gemmell, Stevie Chalmers . . . the list was endless.

As I said earlier, I come from a very long family line of Celtic supporters. I just had to hear the opening bars of Glen Daly's 'Celtic Song' and the hairs at the back of my neck would rigidly stand to attention, as if they were on some sort of army parade ground. So there was no doubting my love of the club and yet I started having qualms only a short time after I had signed the schoolboy forms. I was fifteen and doing every odd job that you could imagine from painting fences to carrying bottles in off the terracing. I suppose it would not have taxed the brain of a dunce, let alone an intellectual but, even then, I went home and said to my mum that I didn't want to go back. I told her I'd rather be walking one of our neighbour's greyhounds – a part-time job that I'd taken on earlier. That, I hope, gives some kind of indication of the problems to come – I thought walking the dogs was preferable to walking among giants! I think I was just overcome by nerves and what was going on around me in the big smoke. Maybe I was just homesick and wanted to run about the village rather than Glasgow. This was how I was feeling very early into my time with Celtic – after some weeks rather than months.

Luckily for me, my dad was a bit more pushy than my mum in this instance and he put his foot down so hard the earth around us shook. He'd played a very important part in me signing for Celtic and he had no intention in seeing that invest-ment of time and thought going down the tubes. 'You're stayin' put and that's it!' he told me. I might as well have gone and argued with the nearest lamp post – I told you he was thrawn. There was never going to be any way of changing his mind about this.

So I returned to the regime. I'd be in at nine and then take all the training gear down to the dressing rooms. Next the other apprentices and I would go into the boot room, taking the boots and shoes with us. Mondays were the days for cleaning the boots from the Saturday games and putting all the jerseys, shorts and socks away to the laundry. Fridays were for packing the hampers for the away games. We would normally train with the players on Mondays, Tuesdays and Wednesdays. After one midweek game, the boots were still soaking on the Friday. Being on my own at the time, I put them up to the drying room but somehow forgot all about them and went home as usual at around one o'clock. On the

Monday, I went in with my heart occupying a large section of my mouth. The boots had been well and truly scorched and it was just as well there was no big game that weekend. I fully expected to be reprimanded but nothing was said. I didn't know it at the time but I had just used up one of the many lifelines Celtic were to throw me!

Before long, the man I had turned down when he was manager of Dunfermline was walking into Celtic Park as the big boss man. Jock Stein had left East End Park to have a successful spell at Hibs but he could not refuse the call to Parkhead. I suppose, at the time, I had my own misgivings about his arrival, given my rejection of him a couple of years previously, but someone else had more to fear. I remember talking to Ronnie Simpson – yes, the fabulous Ronnie Simpson – and I said to him something along the lines that we were getting a great manager. Ronnie turned round and replied, 'Oh, yeah? Well, that's me out of the door!'

Simpson was just basing his assessment on earlier impressions. Stein had, after all, let him go to Celtic from Hibs as cover for John Fallon but, in reality, his football life was only just beginning. He went on to become a Lisbon Lion and, arguably, Celtic's best-ever goalkeeper. Apart from that prediction about Stein having no time for him, I always listened to anything Ronnie said about football. I got closer to him than just about anyone else in those early days. He was like a father figure to me – in fact, he was always helpful to new players and constructive about the game in general. Something I'll never forget is the time he saved my bacon sandwiches in an Old Firm match at Parkhead when I was nineteen. I had made a very slack back-pass and a Rangers player – I forget who it was – picked the ball up and whipped it past Ronnie in a crowded penalty area. Somehow, I don't know how to this day, Ronnie threw himself back and stopped it right on the line. That photograph of him, with his hand on the ball on the line, was on the front of the *Wee Red Book* the following year, 1969.

I was gradually bedding myself in and becoming accustomed to the sights and sounds of Glasgow and the proximity of my heroes. One of them was Jinky Johnstone. What a man! As I have explained elsewhere, I could never allow myself to get close to my heroes but sometimes I had my moments with Jinky. I marvelled at his brilliance, for instance, and wondered how he managed to keep his feet on the ground. One day, I told him what was on my mind. 'You were brilliant in that situation but you're no' even big-headed about it,' I said.

He didn't go in for a big explanation. Sometimes, short is good. 'Listen, son,' he said, 'football is simple. You can either dae it or you can no' dae it.'

You might have looked long enough but there just wasn't an arrogant bone in Jinky's body. He could be nippy sometimes, though. And he was as hard as nails. I saw first-hand evidence of this. When I was a fifteen-year-old on the groundstaff, he'd come down to the gymnasium, grab a medicine ball and ask me to bounce it off his stomach. I didn't like to at first because I thought it would hurt him. Some chance! If it did, he wasn't letting on. He'd just lie there and I'd bounce it off his belly! His muscles were rigid. No wonder the big fellas in football got such a shock when they tried to shoulder him off the ball – they had encountered an object that liked to think of itself as immovable!

If I couldn't allow myself to really relax in Jimmy's company, my pal Davie Cattenach was able to pick up that baton and run with it. He arrived at the Park from Stirling Albion when he was seventeen and we became friends. He has often told me about his first day. He says he was shaking like a leaf when Billy McNeill and then John Hughes first walked past him. He went outside and was standing on the track waiting for the first day's training to begin, looking, I suppose, for an ally. He found one soon enough. Wee Jimmy tapped him on the shoulder and a great friendship began.

In fact, when they went over to Lisbon for the European Cup, they were the only single players making the trip. Davie's fiancée, Janice, wasn't allowed to travel – perhaps because of the absence of a marriage certificate – and Jimmy's wife, Agnes, was expecting her first child so she wasn't there, either. Apparently, after the victory over Inter Milan, the two of them were out the whole night in pubs all over Lisbon, having sing-songs with the fans. The Wee Man was doing his Rod Stewart thing and Davie was giving it Sinatra to anyone who would care to listen. Seemingly, they had been out till about eight in the morning and the bus to take them to the airport was sched-uled to leave at ten. They had about an hour's sleep when their alarm call came. They were struggling and Davie had been sick but they managed to climb on to the coach. They were sitting at the back when Big Jock came up to them and asked them how they were doing. The conversation between them went something like this:

Jinky: 'Aye, fine, smashin', boss!'

Stein: 'Watch whit ye're daen!'

Jinky: 'Aye, we're OK, boss!'

Stein: 'No, you're no'! Watch whit ye're daen!'

Jinky: 'We've just won the Cup!'

Stein then put his arm round Johnstone like a father but, by this time, his voice had softened. He whispered, 'You've still got to watch whit ye're daen!'

It was the first time Davie had seen the tolerant side of Mr Stein. The Big Man could see they'd been having a carry-on and were still drunk from the night before but he didn't go over the top with them. He was just letting them know that he knew – a better tactic than reading the Riot Act. What a tactician that man was – both on and off the pitch!

So, where was I when the Lions were roaring in Lisbon? My memory tells me I was parked on my mother's settee in Valleyfield, watching the game on the television. I was eighteen at the time and, when I wasn't watching telly or playing football, I was trying, but probably failing, to dedicate myself to fashion. I can mind going about in glasses and wearing some funny trousers. I had a wee car too – a car among the miners, eh? Was I getting above myself?

The night of victory over Inter Milan was great. It was going to be some homecoming. I remember Mr Stein saying that, if anyone wanted to watch the Lions' return, they could go through to the Park but I never went. But that's me in the smallest of nutshells. Who could fathom me? Call me an enigma and I won't be offended enough to want to fight you. I was too over-awed by the occasion to go and that's just the sort of person I was at the time – still am, if I'm being honest. You cannot assume arrogance if you're not really like that. At the same time, I know I'm playing myself down. I should have gone and enjoyed what was, by all accounts, the mother and father of celebrations. It was another thing I was to miss out on – and I've missed out on so much in my life.

The one thing I wouldn't have minded missing out on, though, was Celtic's trip to South America not long after Lisbon. It was the World Championship sort-out against Racing Club of Buenos Aires and, believe me, it was some sort-out. Celtic had won the first leg 2–1 at Parkhead and were counting the bruises to prove it. We had to travel over there for the second leg. I don't think I was considered for what was to be an unscheduled double-header – I was really just taken along to drink in the experience but there was nothing pleasant about the taste. First, I had to suffer those awful flights to and fro across the Atlantic, with my nerves playing a rare old tune. Then, from a place of protection in the stands, I had to watch games in Buenos Aires and then Montevideo that had very little connection with football.

The second leg hadn't even begun when Ronnie Simpson went down clutching his head. He had been hit by something thrown by the crowd and had to be replaced by John Fallon. Later, I asked him about the incident and he told me he had been felled by a piece of metal. If it had hit the wrong spot, he could have been killed! Me? I just sat there and watched the madness of it all around me. There was more confetti thrown by the fans than you'd get in a lifetime of Scottish weddings. And those fans were something else. Talk about excitable! The club were so shocked by the behaviour of the Argentinian players in the first game, which the hosts had won 1–0, that Bob Kelly, the chairman, was all for upping sticks and flying home. But I believe Mr Stein insisted on keeping our commitment and playing a decider. It all ended in mayhem, with four of our players – Bobby Lennox, Jimmy Johnstone, John Hughes and Bertie Auld – and two of theirs getting their jotters. Soldiers hefting swords were summoned, not to quell uprisings in the stands but to stop the free-for-all on the pitch. Ah, so this was international football . . .

My career with the club, for some of the time at least, was beginning to motor on just about all cylinders. Stein had watched me at close quarters and he knew that, even if I was shy in terms of meeting people and putting myself forward, I had the balls for the big occasion. At sixteen, I'd had one season at outside right before being played in many different positions to give me experience.

You know, I almost feel sorry for that young guy, Wayne Rooney. Oh, I know he's built like a middleweight boxer but he's getting pitched in there and really he's only a wee laddie.

It's a very demanding game and there are so many areas where you can get found out. One night I was sitting watching a Man United game on the television when I remember thinking to myself, 'Who's that old guy with the bald head?' It was Rooney. I didn't mean it in a cheeky way but that's the way he sometimes comes across to me. He was really struggling that night. I think he needs to be sitting there on the bench for two or three games, to come on in the last fifteen minutes or so. In my opinion, he's played too much too early. I think the same has happened to Michael Owen as well, with another perfect example being Norman Whiteside – that was a real shame.

To my way of thinking, they should have been given the benefit of my upbringing. That's why Celtic were so good. Kenny Dalglish and Davie Hay were nursed along and so too were John Gorman and Vic Davidson. The same was true for Lou Macari. These guys played here and there in the first team and then were back out again so that, when they came into the side again for real, they were men. They weren't just young boys coming in and trying to make an impression – they were hardened men who'd completed their trade. I analyse all the young players who come into football that way because I know how well I was looked after. I felt at times I was getting pushed by Stein but I didn't complain because I knew it was all designed with my own good at heart.

So I just did the things he asked me to do. Early on in my career, I was only about 5ft 10in and 10st. Then, when I was seventeen or eighteen, I couldn't train hard because I was growing so fast. Stein would just let me go training in the mornings. There were no afternoon sessions for me even in the pre-season – he knew it would take too much out of me. I think it was John McKenzie of the *Daily Express* who wrote that the manager was undecided about playing me in two games in the one week – Wednesday and then Saturday – because I would need time to recover. I can only judge Rooney and Co. by what I went through myself. I had a great man who brought me up through it all gradually. I knew I was being nursed along and shouldn't be rushed. Whiteside, Rooney, Owen, in my opinion, all played too much too soon.

Many players have been flung in as kids. It has even happened at Celtic. Just look at Paul McStay for example – Celtic were playing him in the first team when he was sixteen and seventeen and that's why, in my opinion, he never became a world-class player. Just imagine what those games must have been like for him, playing against mature men at midfield in the mud. You might think the skill factor will level things up – I mean, Maradona and Pelé got away with it – but they came from huge countries and you're guaranteed one or two exceptions will come through from millions like that. But how many like them do you get to the pound? Rooney might just get away with it because of his strength. Hopefully, he'll be OK.

The way I see it, the best way of handling youngsters is as follows: you have them sitting in the stand for a couple of weeks; you get them coming in in the morning to have a bath and a walk around the track and sometimes that's enough; maybe, at times, you tell them they won't be playing for another fortnight and they should be away out enjoying themselves – at that age, you can afford to let them do it.

But, just thinking of how much money Manchester United paid for Rooney, maybe they can't afford to let him rest. Maybe they're just going to grind him out – next please! Maybe he's an exception and he'll grind it out himself. We'll see. But that's the way it seems to be. Whiteside was out of the game at twenty-seven but hadn't he played in the World Cup in Spain as a seventeen-year-old?

I can certainly remember when I was that age – I was struggling every game, even in the reserves. Apart from anything else, there are the seasoned pros to contend with – they're probably not too amused by some cocky kid coming in and hoping to make a fool of them. This is where Stein's experience mattered – he would play me at outside right where I'd get a bit of protection because there was nobody on the other side of me. Oh, I know it made for some funny comments. For instance, they used to say, 'Was Big Geordie playing?' and someone would respond with, 'Aye, he was on the park.' OK, I may have seemed a bit lazy but I was growing and I wasn't experienced so I was trying to gain some knowledge and understanding of the professional game. I think I was reading the game and making mental notes of why I should be going here and going there. As people say, the game is made simple by great players.

Anyway, around my late teens, I was covering four key roles – on the wing, inside-forward, wing-half and even centre half. The wing could be fun. I had Stevie Chalmers sometimes playing in the reserves or maybe John Divers. I was playing deep and would make runs behind the full back. I would just flick it up in front of Chalmers and Divers. I was playing a sort of David Beckham role. It was the role I made my first-team debut in and it was the role I would play in the 1969 Scottish Cup final.

First, that debut. It was a League Cup double-header against Rangers and we were playing at their place first. Now, never mind Argentina or Uruguay, Ibrox can offer as much intimidation as a man could wish for. I was in a daze as I wandered into that dressing room. The lost sheep found a shepherd, though. Tam Gemmell told me to go into a corner and get stripped. It was all a bit unreal. My memories of that day are not all that sharp but I do remember Willie Wallace scoring twice. If I've got my brains together correctly, I think I flung a ball through and it went under John Greig's feet to set up one of those goals. The game ended 2–0. I was taken off early and there was Jim Steele with a tot of whisky to calm me down. I played again in the next game and Wallace again put the skids under Rangers. But there were even greater things on the horizon.

The date was 26 April, the venue was Hampden Park, the attendance was 133,000 and the score? Celtic 4 (McNeill, Lennox, Connelly, Chalmers), Rangers 0! I was credited with the assist for Bobby Lennox's goal and then came my own one. They say it was a great goal but it really was a simple one for me. I had become a good reader of a game. I was immediately able to weigh up what was going on with Rangers and they fell into the trap. As soon as Norrie Martin's goal kick went to John Greig, I knew Willie Mathieson was standing there. I never looked properly but I could see him out the corner of my eye – you're talking about split seconds with these situations. I was thinking that the only choice Greig had was either to pass the ball back to Martin or give it to Mathieson. Willie wouldn't have known me in those days – being only twenty, I was the dark horse. Up until then, I had gone for everything on Greig's right foot and made myself look stupid but, this time, I waited until the last split second just before he passed it. I stuck out my foot and it worked – I had the ball. On the park I was learning all the time but I was a fox even then. The ball just fell nicely. I knew Martin wasn't fast so I just did the natural thing, going by him and putting it into the net. That was it. Maybe if the situation had recurred when I was twenty-five or twenty-six, I wouldn't have done it like that but youth knew no fear that day. It was just a thing that happened in a game and I took full advantage of it.

I don't know if I could ever have been a striker, though, but that's where Stein played me in the reserves sometimes. He was pushing me right, left and centre. The only thing they didn't really push my way was real money, but that's another story.

You could have called me the man for all positions in those days. I didn't mind. It taught me most of what I needed to know about my trade and that was a big bonus. I had a season on the right wing and also a season at inside right, in an old-fashioned 4–2–4. It was all a learning process for me. Then I had one term at centre half. I must admit I didn't like that – there was just too much responsibility in that position.

Believe it or not, despite my height, I wasn't great in the air. By now, I was over 6ft so, playing against someone as forceful and fearless as Finn Dossing, of Dundee United . . . well, bugger that! I'd be standing there one minute, minding my own business, and he'd come out of the skies at me, arms flailing. It was a bit too physical for my taste.

Still, I was starting to get a wee game here and a wee game there but I was always one of these types of guys who went into a trance whenever he walked into the dressing room and saw a Celtic jersey – especially a first-team jersey. I had grown up just thinking of the jersey. I just used to stare at the fabric, even when I was in the reserves, and be overawed by it. The whole caboodle of being a Celtic player was just amazing for me. I remember one game at Dundee, David Cattenach and I went to watch a Scottish Cup tie from the terracing and, the next day, we were training with them. It was like being a supporter one day and running about with them the next.

As I said, centre half was not the position of my dreams but that's where I was stuck when we playing Aberdeen's reserves one time and they thrashed us 3–0 at Parkhead. Aberdeen had some great laddies at the time. It was the Eddie Turnbull era and youngsters like Arthur Graham, Martin Buchan and Tommy Craig wore the red jerseys with pride. This guy from Kincardine, Pat Miller the baker, had taken me through for the game. He couldn't stop laughing afterwards.

'You should see your face,' he said.

I suppose it was a picture. You could have placed Laurel and Hardy in front of me for an hour and I wouldn't have cracked a smile. I was mad at getting beat – it was really getting me down. I suppose, looking back, there was a bit of credit in that because I thought about the game very deeply in those days. But the unhappiness did not evaporate overnight. I knew I had to do something about it. I was tied to the position of centre half and, in my eyes, I might as well have been tied to a goalpost. You couldn't move. I'd heard the other players saying they were going in to see the gaffer to ask where they weren't playing so I decided to follow suit – but for a totally different reason.

Now, this was not as straightforward as it might have seemed. Stein was quite an awesome character. When his voice sounded, eleven players listened. I saw him lose his temper plenty of times, especially with Jinky, and it was a sight to behold. When he blew his top, there was so much steam around you might have been forgiven for thinking that the *Flying Scotsman* was coming your way! They say he swore a lot. He didn't need to swear to put the fear of God into me. Anyway, that day, it was a case of eyes down, charge in!

I told him that I couldn't do anything about the defeat because I'd been scared to desert my post and then we would have been naked at the back. Mr Stein listened. There was not a harsh word to be heard from him. Instead of shouting at me, he took in what I'd had to say and began to think of a new position for me – and soon he had introduced one. He made me sweeper, with a licence to attack on occasions. I used to love going forward – that was the Celtic tradition. (Well, it was – they don't always seem to play that way so much nowadays.) So sweeper it was – I think he started getting it into his head that this is where I would be most effective.

The trouble was I didn't get it right at first so, if I remember it properly, he put Bobby Murdoch there one time and told me to watch what he did. Bobby was good with both feet and that's how I learned it – well, most of it. Stein was clever. He knew Murdoch could whack the ball from right to left or vice versa. And that's when I began to fling it about. I could pass the ball quite well anyway and Bobby just showed me what was possible. I was mostly right-footed but I used to work on the left. Sweeper was the ideal position for me – a bit of defending plus a wee bit of attacking. Rampaging centre forwards? Billy McNeill could deal with that kind of thing. He was amazing to play alongside. He never moved. I played with his defensive partner, John Clark, when I was centre half in the reserves. He would not let you move. He went here, there, everywhere, depending on where the ball was, but you had to be the immovable object.

By the end of that season, I had learned lots from my spells in the first team and in the reserves. Playing at sweeper gave me a chance to stand back and see how the game developed around you. It also taught me a lot about making – and taking – a tackle. I felt I had matured but I knew it wouldn't break my heart if I didn't get a regular first-team spot right away. I had plenty of patience in those days. The 1969 Scottish Cup final gave me a terrific boost – not just because I won a medal but also because I proved I could slot into the first team without too much rehearsal. I was a stone overweight when I came back from the close-season break but that happened every summer. It only took a few days on the Parkhead track to sweat it off.

Then, in the late summer of that year, we were off to France for a pre-season friendly with St Etienne. I was always a fan of John 'The Voice' McKenzie and his writing in those days. No wonder I felt flattered when the squad flew to France, minus Jinky, and he wrote:

> Jimmy Johnstone stayed at his Hamilton pub observing a discreet silence. What has he done to incur Jock Stein's wrath? No one knows. But Stein at the moment prefers the certainty of George Connelly to the uncertainty of Jimmy Johnstone.

But what was that he wrote about certainty? If he'd only known, would he have committed that to paper?

4

THE GANG'S ALL HERE

DAVID CATTENACH'S STORY

A back garden on a Sunday morning somewhere in North London. A sizeable stretch of grass, mind you. There's a small football pitch marked out and two sets of goal nets. A few familiar faces are playing five-a-side football but it couldn't be *them*, could it? Weren't these guys playing Manchester United at the Emirates Stadium only yesterday? Take a closer look. Yes, it's *them*. It is not a case of mistaken identity, after all. There's Gaël Clichy, Philippe Senderos, Abou Diaby, Robin van Persie . . . and, yeah, there's that clever little bugger Cesc Fabregas. A friendly five-a-side? It doesn't look too friendly from this distance – they're getting stuck in like tomorrow has been cancelled. They're at each other's throats – blood is flowing.

The scenario above is all a pure fiction, scooped from my mind, of course. Now, I don't know what the young players of Arsenal FC do with their Sunday mornings – if they ever meet up and get it on in such a fashion – but, believe it or not, that's just what used to happen in the back garden of my house in Booth Place, Falkirk, almost four decades ago. The difference was the players didn't hail from all points on the compass – they were Scots through and through. Some were famous, some were going to be famous, others less so. But how's this for a line-up? Davie Hay, John Gorman, Davie Cattenach, Jimmy

Quinn, Kenny Dalglish, Vic Davidson, Danny McGrain, Tony McBride, Lou Macari, my wee brother Edward Cattenach, Alex Smith . . . and, of course, George Connelly. In other words, the Quality Street Gang, plus extras.

It was a big house – four or five bedrooms – and we used to have wee Saturday nights there. All the boys would come through from Glasgow and we'd go to the Polmont Bank Hotel because the proprietor looked after us. We had a private room where nobody could see us and we'd have a wee drink and a good laugh. There were maybe ten couples. Then we'd retire to my house at Booth Place, where we'd have some more drink and, in all probability, listen to a few records and have a wee sing-song before retiring for the night – we even brought in a disc jockey. There was a fair chance that most of us were steamin'.

Then, the next morning, we got down to the real business of the weekend – the five-a-sides. The day before, we might have played Rangers but, see on that Sunday, there we were, arguing about corner kicks and shies. It was taken very seriously. If, say, on a Monday following one of these weekends, Lou, Vic or Kenny hadn't made it through to Falkirk, the first thing they'd ask was, 'Catt, what was the score?'

They wouldn't be interested in talking about the Rangers game or whatever – they were more fascinated by what happened in the five-a-sides. What memories! My mother, Katey was her name, lived across in Melrose Place and she'd come across to make the breakfast. We took that at half-time. 'Right,' she'd shout, 'who's wanting rolls and egg? Who's wanting sausage?'

My mam would then bring out the rolls and bacon and sausage and whatever at half-time. We'd eat them, drink our tea and wait for the second half. We were all arguing about what had gone on. It was tasty – we'd think nothing of kicking and booting each other. The first time Danny McGrain came out, he looked on askance. I was one captain and Alex Smith, who was to become my partner in the Caledonian Club in Stirling, was the other. The formation of my team generally depended on how much you had to drink the night before. It wasn't so much my ball as my hoose, so it was generally my decision and I'd have Davie Hay, Geordie Connelly, Gorrie (John Gorman) and, if wee McBride was there, he was in.

There was a lot of fun and a lot of banter. I wouldn't want you to think it was bevvy all the time but Saturday nights and Sunday mornings were set aside for a real bit of recreation. It happened once or sometimes twice a month. You know, it got kind of famous. Folk actually used to come and watch the games. And then they would want autographs. But, principally, it was fun. I don't suppose you would get that happening today. Professional football is too much business and too much money. What would Jock Stein have thought about it? Hey, he knew all about those games. But I suppose his logic would have been that they're taking it seriously and getting the drink out of them. And, believe me, it was serious. I've seen stand-up fights and people kicking each other. It wasn't just a piece of nonsense on a Sunday morning. We would argue about the least little thing. I know that sounds crazy but that's what happened.

So where did Big Geordie fit into all this carry-on? Very nicely, as it happens. He could look after himself all right – whether it was those Sunday morning affairs or the real thing. I would say, in fact, that the dirtiest combination for booting folk was me and him. George, being George, did it in a very clever, subtle way. But he was hard – oh, he was hard! Magnificent on the ball, he could suddenly ping a fifty-yard ball right to your feet. On the other hand, when he was coming about you, the skies were growing dark and there was a rumble of physical thunder. He was able to handle situations. Davie Hay,

Geordie and I were the three kind of anchor men. Assassins, did I hear you say? Aye, I wouldn't quibble with that. But the poetry was Geordie, especially when it got to the real thing of competitive matches. He would take it on his chest, it would roll down to his feet, he would look up and he'd just go bump and the ball would travel forty, fifty yards, no problem. He was some player. Dear me! What a case he was!

All this was wrapped up in a keen sense of humour. That humour didn't kick in so much when he was playing centre half, though – he had a bit of an aversion to playing in that position and, in fact, always liked to be on the left-hand side. Although he was right-footed, he liked the left, just off the centre half. So, around this time, we were all playing in the reserves. We had some team and had just won everything. I think it was the end of the 1967–68 season and we played Dundee United at Tannadice, before travelling up to Aberdeen to finish up. Geordie and I were playing at the back and United had this player called Alex Reid, who had red hair and this big, red beard. Geordie and I were standing looking at him before the game began and someone, I think it was Kenny Cameron, turned round to Reid and said to him, 'All right, faither.'

Well, I don't know why but the big man and I started laughing and we just couldn't stop. We were in hysterics and Geordie had the kind of laugh that you hear from donkeys. It was a big, stupid laugh – so distinctive. I can hear it now. So, there we were, standing on the park, roaring our heads off and Sean Fallon, emerging from the dugout, was going mental. 'What the f*** are youse daen', you bastards?' he screamed.

Did that persuade us to stop? Not a bit of it. Right then, this Alex Reid came down the park, with that great red beard of his. Geordie took one look at him and went into further convulsions. He was making whooping noises. Anyway, all the hilarity did not make one scrap of difference to the result. We had beaten them 6–0 in the first leg of the Reserve Cup final and, in this, the second leg, we beat them 6–2.

My own sense of humour was cut short that day, however, when I got sent off. As I said earlier, Geordie, Davie and I were quite hard and quite dirty, to be honest. So, when Kenny Cameron came in and gave me a clip, I turned round, gave him a bit of the 'F*** you!' treatment and punched him in the mouth. As captain of the reserves, I wasn't setting a good example but I couldn't help myself. Sean was out of the dugout again and, this time, he was giving me pelters for an altogether different reason.

But the smile was back on my face when we went up to Aberdeen soon afterwards. It was April and the last game of the season, we'd won the league and nobody had beaten us all season. The pitch was quite bumpy. The ball was played back to me. I controlled it and took a couple of steps forward but, when I went to play it up the line, it bounced and went right up into the stand. There was nobody near me. I just made a hash of it. The big man started again, whooping with laughter. 'Whit are ye daen', Catt? Oh-o-o!'

And away we went again. Do you think you could stop us laughing that day? George had a brilliant sense of humour. We were so close and so fond of each other. This was the late 1960s and a bond had been formed between a few of us. We had this esprit de corps. It was hard to beat us because we were all pals, and, if anyone even started a wee bit of a carry-on, they just got dumped – simple as that.

But there were storm clouds gathering even then. Wee Tony McBride came from Castlemilk and had some ability. Big Geordie, Davie and I used to talk about him because he had a lot of skill and it was reckoned he could be the next Jimmy Johnstone. We were training one day at Celtic Park. We ran around really on a kind of wee jog. Tony was only eighteen years old and he'd only done half a lap when he started being sick. I was looking at him boss-eyed – I'd seen this happen a couple of times. I drew him aside and asked him if he'd been drinking. He said he did like a wee bevvy so I told him straight, 'Son, you've got a lot of ability. Stop that! Never mind what anybody says. Stop drinking!'

The next day, we were going to Aberdeen. Sean had said to me that he was going to play wee Tony in that game but that a lot depended on it because they were thinking of releasing him. I knew how important it was for Tony if he was going to prevent this from happening so I told him that he was playing and should get himself sorted out. The rest of us were going out that night – we'd been given the green light by Sean – but I told Tony he couldn't come as he had to be on his best behaviour. I found out later he had gone out and got blitzed.

I said to him, 'What were you doing? You let me down, never mind Celtic!'

He stammered, 'I love you, Catt . . .'

I replied, 'That doesn't work. You've flushed your career down the toilet 'cos you're getting released now. He's no' going to play you.'

He said, 'Youse were oot last night.'

I gave him a look and said, 'Aye but we've all done it. We ken what we're daen' . . .'

But did we really know? The day of the Aberdeen match, George was drinking on the train. I warned him about the drink but he said, 'What, with the team we've got?'

He then said that they (the Aberdeen players) were never going to get near him. And, to be honest, he was right – they never did get near him. We were so hard to beat in those days but, with the drinking, it just shows you what can go on. Look at what happened to wee Tony, for example, and – although it was some time away – what was to happen to George.

I was able to get closer to George than those Aberdeen footballers. We used to share a car into the Park – his car one week, mine the next. We were really close friends. When I had the place in Stirling, George would come across with his first wife, Christine. But, although we were really good mates, I could never understand him on those nights – or, especially, when he was nominated for one of the the the Player of the Year awards in 1973 and never turned up for the presentation. He could come across to the Caley and sit right at the bottom door, with his back to everybody. He didn't want anyone to recognise him. It took my breath away that he behaved in such a way. I just couldn't understand what was going on with him.

However, he was easier to understand the time Celtic beat Rangers 4–0 in the 1969 Scottish Cup final. To explain, although we were all friendly in the Quality Street Gang, we had our own even tighter little circle – Davie Hay, Jimmy Quinn, Gorrie, me and Geordie. If any of us were playing in the first team, the others went to support him. There was never any jealousy, never any 'we're better than him' stuff. That didn't happen. We were just good friends and wanted to play for Celtic. So, all of a sudden, the big man was picked to play against Rangers in the Cup final and he was only twenty.

Alex Ferguson was playing up front for Rangers in that final and I can also remember a New Year's Day Old Firm game at Parkhead when I was marking him. We were already pals at this time and, at one stage during the game, Celtic were awarded a corner. Just as the corner was about to be taken, Alex said to me, 'Where are we gaun tonight?'

I said, 'I don't know. We cannae go out in Glas . . .' At that point, the ball came over and Fergie elbowed me! That's friendship for you – professional football style!

Despite that, Alex and I remain very friendly and I still have a carry-on about the elbowing incident with him. By the way, he's still the same today as he was then – he's never changed a bit.

Anyway, back to that final. Big Billy McNeill came up for a corner and Fergie was supposed to be marking him but Alex didn't pick McNeill up and Billy just went boomp. Goal! That mistake finished Alex at Rangers as they held it against him that Rangers lost the final to Celtic. Later in the game, when Big Geordie took the ball off John Greig and went round the goalie to score, we were up there with the birds!

We were going out that night and we decided to go to the Mauritania Hotel in Clackmannan. There were ten of us. We had a good wee drink to ourselves then went back down to George's house in Kincardine. We had more drink and, about three in the morning, we decided to go outside and have a three-a-side game with a ball. The trouble was one of the neighbours phoned the polis, who arrived with lights flashing. What a carry-on!

The policeman asked what was going on. He then looked around in amazement and said, 'George Connelly, Davie Hay, John Gorman, Jimmy Quinn, Davie Cattenach . . . can I get your autographs?'

That policeman ended up in the house having a laugh and a carry-on and, yes, getting our autographs. It was so funny. Those things don't happen today. They would think it a feather in their caps if they caught players like that and very likely they'd be on the phone to the newspapers. But that didn't happen then. The policeman was a Celtic man and he was so pleased with the result from the day before.

We had some laughs in those days. Once, for instance, we were playing in Tel Aviv. Mr Stein was there and that meant recreation was severely limited. Even though it was the close season, he didn't let us go out and enjoy ourselves. As it happens, we were there for a week and played the Israeli national team in what was our only match on the first Monday. We beat them and then we had a week's holiday although we knew we'd have to be careful what we got up to with Stein around. Anyway, one night, Jimmy, Geordie and I were out having a daft night and a good drink. In fact, the night was so daft that it turned into day and there we were, at seven in the morning, standing on the beach, right across the road from the hotel. As we closed in on the hotel, we spotted Big Jock in the foyer. Stations were set at panic! Big George – big, quiet George – organised things immediately. He pointed at the swimming pool, which was outside the front of the hotel, and ushered us into a clump of bushes.

'Right, boys, get your clathes aff!' he said.

Next thing was we were down to our underpants, with our clothes hidden in the bushes, and heading over to the swimming pool.

Jimmy Quinn wailed, 'I cannae swim!'

George's response was quick and pointed. 'You'll swim now!' he said and the three of us jumped in the pool.

Seconds later, Big Jock came through the doors. 'Mornin', boys!'

'Mornin', boss,' we chorused.

I added, 'We always like a swim before breakfast!' and it looked as if everything was fine.

I think our all-nighter was on the Tuesday or the Wednesday and we arrived back in Scotland the following Monday. As we got off the plane, Mr Stein came up to us. 'By the way, Catt, Quinn, Connelly,' he said, 'I knew you'd just come in that morning!'

We were all quite young at the time and going away to Israel had been a big thing for us. Up until then, we'd always thought of Stein as a bit of a strict disciplinarian and that was the first time he'd shown us that there was another side to him – one with some humour.

George, of course, could be two different people. Give him a ball and he was magnificent – the best sweeper I ever saw, a man oozing confidence – but, without the ball, it was another story – he could be so introverted, the guy who would sit with his back to the crowd.

Tragically, Jimmy Quinn died of a heart attack in 2002. His funeral was held at Croy chapel and, after the service, we went to the Celtic Club in Croy. Geordie wasn't drinking at this time and I think he just went home not long after we arrived. We arranged that he should come up and see me at my restaurant near Falkirk every Monday and he did this for four or five Mondays in a row – no problem. We had a laugh.

Then, one day, he said, 'It's coming up six months.'

'What's that?' I asked.

'I'm coming up six months without drinking. Next Monday – if I can reach that, it'll be great.'

He never turned up the following Monday so I suppose he was saying, if he could do six months off, then he could have a drink. That seemed to be a landmark with him – a sad landmark. I don't mean that in a bad way. I love George Connelly and always will. He is a man who wouldn't do you a bad turn even if he could organise one.

I'd left Celtic Park by the time George's troubles had started but I couldn't understand it when he finally walked out. In the early 70s, my cousin John Dick was a Celtic fanatic. He lived Celtic – a bit too much, to be honest. It was his life. I used to coach Grangemouth International and I told John I would get the big man down to the club and George lapped it up. We had a smashing team, full of great wee laddies. John Colquhoun played up front. My young brother Edwin – he's dead now –

was also some player. He just scored goals, simple as that. We didn't care about winning cups and stuff like that. I just loved to take those laddies through and get them into the senior ranks. We won more than we lost. Big Geordie came down and coached alongside me.

We worked well together. At set pieces, he'd birl the ball around the wall into the back of the net and I'd tell the goal-keeper that his positioning had been wrong. The two of us would have been really good together as a management team. I'd indicate to him where I'd want him to put the ball and he did it without hesitation. It was a big, heavy ball then but it made no difference. He would hit it from twenty-five, thirty-five yards – no problem. Then he would stand there keeping the ball up. He just loved doing that. He was still at Celtic – still only a youngster himself – but, when he came down, the laddies' mouths fell open as if they were catching flies. Those lads hero-worshipped him. I would tell them to look and learn. We would sit and have them in the palms of our hands. As long as a football was there, life was OK for him.

I knew nothing of his troubles at that time. If he *had* come to me and confided in me, I'd like to think I might have sorted them out for him. I'm not surprised, though, that I didn't know that his marriage was in trouble. Geordie was as deep as an ocean but, if anyone could have told him what to do, it would have been me. I got on smashing with Christine. I always found she was great. She was a very, very good-looking lassie. A lot of people said that she went out with other people but I never found her like that. I'm not daft – I'm sure I would have got the vibes if she was that way but I never saw it.

It makes me so sad to think of what George's lifestyle has been over the last few years. George's second wife, Helen, is fantastic – I really don't know where he'd be without her – considering what she's had to put up with. I remember going down to their house to see him one day and his son, David, answered the door. The Big Yin was drinking at the time and he was sitting there not with a glass of vodka and coke but a great big mug of it. As I said, though, I love George dearly and it doesn't matter what he does. He's really different class as a man.

Sometimes we don't keep in touch although that's not my fault – I often phone him to see if we can meet up. In December 2006, I phoned him and asked him to come up for his dinner at a cabaret night. I told him my wife Janice would be there and that he should bring Helen with him. He agreed and said he would see me later on – nae problem. He didn't come.

Was George universally popular with the other players? I really don't know what, for instance, his relationship with Billy McNeill was like. If there was any animosity, it was probably more on George's side than Billy's. Maybe George kind of imagined that Billy didn't like him but I'm sure that's all it was – George's imagination – because Big Billy was a magnanimous man. For instance, he came to Jimmy Quinn's funeral and, when I thanked him very much for attending, he said, 'David, I was captain of Celtic and Jimmy was one of my laddies – I wouldn't *not* be here.'

However, Tommy Gemmell wasn't there, John Clark wasn't there, in fact, there was a squad of them not there but Billy was. No, I think there must have been something between Big Billy and Geordie but, if there was, Geordie has never said what it was. As for the others, I would say that everyone respected his ability.

Everybody liked me – I guess I just have that kind of person-ality – but it wasn't the same for George. He always held himself back a wee bit. People would say, 'There's the Catt!' but it was never a case of, 'There's Big Geordie!' I'd say only Davie Hay, Jimmy Quinn, John Gorman and I got to know

George. Apart from us, people didn't really know him at all. It wasn't that he was distant – it was just that he lacked the confidence to communicate. The reverse side of the coin was when you gave him a ball. The change in him, then, was startling.

I suppose Davie Hay and I were his best friends and, when he and I met up a few months ago, we spent most of the time speaking about the big man and his amazing skill. George loved his fitba' and fitba' loved him back. If life had just been about fitba', then the world might have known a different George Connelly.

5

ON THE ROLLER COASTER

Anyone who saw that Beatles film, *A Hard Day's Night*, will understand the meaning of hysteria without going to the bother of thumbing through a dictionary. Do you remember the chaotic scenes at Euston Station when our Scouse heroes were confronted by hordes of excited and emotional teenage girls? Those who witnessed the scenes in Central Station on an April afternoon in 1970 will also be familiar with the word. That was when the Celtic team came back to Glasgow after beating Leeds 1–0 in the European Cup semi-final, the first leg of the initial Battle of Britain. That's when thousands of fans (estimates said 5,000 but, believe me, it looked more) turned up to hail the conquering heroes – heroes who ended up having to be virtually smuggled out of the station in a police van. Undignified or what? But who cared?

Jock Stein was naturally delighted with the result but he managed to control that delight as we sat huddled together on top of the kit hampers, behind the metal grilles of that police wagon, and made our way back to Parkhead to pick up our cars. There was this tight, little smile playing at the corner of his lips as he turned to me and said, 'This is all your fault!' – a typical example of the understated Stein humour.

It had been some match and, as I had scored the only goal of the game, I suppose he was right – if there *was* any 'fault', it was mine. We hadn't had the best of results in the run-up to the first leg, though. We were on our way to our fifth Scottish League title in a row but had been mugged 2–1 by Aberdeen before eventually clinching the championship with a 0–0 draw with Hearts. Our preparations, however, were imaginative – we stayed at Troon, ran along the beach on the Sunday and put on a practice match in the grounds of the hotel. There were lots of holidaymakers watching us and there was no admission fee. They loved it. When we made the train journey to Leeds (from Kilmarnock), we had a carriage to ourselves and that dedicated Rangers fan, Lex McLean, then a popular comedian, entertained us with his machine-gun-like patter. It was a relaxing journey and there was no time to be bored, that's for sure.

We stayed at Harrogate and Davie Hay, Lou Macari and I were so overwhelmed by pre-match nerves (I don't think) that we stayed up till the early hours playing three-card brag. That did nothing to take the shine off us – we were as fit as butchers' dogs and straining at the leash to get at Leeds.

It was to be the night of socks-gate! Both teams traditionally wore white and Don Revie decided to wage psychological warfare by insisting that we changed ours so, eventually, we wore red stockings. Revie's tactic didn't work because, under the floodlights, they actually looked orange, which pleased Mr Stein no end. However, we could have been wearing multicoloured socks that night. Our team had been assembled for just over £40,000 – Can you believe that? – whereas, at £300,000, the Leeds side was Bank of England stuff. It was only numbers, after all.

Talking of numbers, the Celtic fans had been allocated 6,000 tickets but 10,000, maybe more, of them travelled to Leeds. They said nothing like this had happened in Yorkshire since the Roman legions had been there. For some reason, though, I didn't feel there was a fantastic atmosphere in the ground.

I can remember thinking, when we went on to the park, 'Where's the carnival?' Maybe I had become accustomed to the vast crowds and noise factories of Celtic and Hampden.

Perhaps it was the cold night that removed the edge from the atmosphere at first but Leeds soon found out that there was something special in town and it was wearing green-and-white jerseys. The pitch was a wee bit slippery but, forty seconds into the match, it might have been the Cresta Run for all I cared – Celtic were one up and I was sitting pretty on that cloud forever occupied by delighted footballers. It was all over so fast it's difficult remembering everything exactly but I'm sure I remember standing sixteen yards out when the ball came to me. I hit it first time and it skimmed Paul Madeley's shin guard and that was enough to put a spin on the ball and beat Leeds' keeper Gary Sprake. The goalie had committed himself and, once the ball took the deflection, he couldn't get back as it twirled past him.

Leeds, with big Jack Charlton and Co. in defence, were a secure unit in those days and had not lost a goal in Europe all season. But, fifty seconds into the second half, their secure unit had been breached again. Jimmy Johnstone, who was in devastating form, clipped the ball over from the right and I slanted it past Mr Sprake for a second time that evening. I was just about to charter a rocket for the moon again when I noticed the referee blowing his whistle for offside, presumably against Wee Jinky. We all thought Terry Cooper, who had spent the night chasing the Johnstone shadow, had played him onside but we were to be proved wrong as far as the officials were concerned and that second Connelly strike was destined never to show up in the record books.

I played in midfield that night, which was a culture shock considering I had been turning out at centre half in the reserves just before this. I was perpetual motion, running backwards and forwards without worrying whether or not there was a big enough reservoir of energy. But, because of the relatively static nature of centre-half play, I wasn't as fit as I needed to be. Cramp set in and I began to struggle. I took myself off, thinking I would let everybody down if I started hobbling about. I was frightened of what Mr Stein would say if I messed up so off I came. But there was a satisfaction in me that I'd done my job.

In this game and the next, which I'll come to later, there was never a suggestion of any skulduggery. You might have expected it from Leeds because they had a reputation as hatchet men. They had a real bad name down in England – it was said that the other top teams hated them. But Terry Cooper never kicked Wee Jinky that first night and, come to think of it, none of them did anything really dirty which, I suppose, was strange. In the normal scheme of things, it seemed they all tried to outdo each other in the rough-house department. Hunter, Madeley, Reaney, Charlton, Bremner, Giles – they were all tough nuts. But I think, if you examined those games, you wouldn't spot many fouls. The teams showed each other mutual respect and the managers were on friendly terms.

Mind you, we had a few who could dish out the pasta if it was needed. Auld, Murdoch and John Clark were no shrinking violets but Davie Hay was the man you had to watch – he was a real tough cookie on the park and, if he set his sights on you, he wouldn't miss you. And Jinky, even though he was more sinned against than sinning, would put you away if he caught you the right way and he wouldn't think twice about it, either.

The next morning, the Scottish press were predictably, and deservedly, on a similar high to our players'. In his inimitable style, Hugh Taylor wrote in the *Daily Record*, 'It was a victory that should have been accompanied by the pipes of the Scots Guards, a roll of drums and a commentary by Olivier!'

But the trouble with football is that it's much like the wise man said – one day you're a cock rooster, the next a feather duster. And so it was for us when, few days later, we met Aberdeen again, this time in the final of the Scottish Cup in April. We never reached the crazy heights we'd achieved against Leeds and we went down 3–1. Now, I played in that final – well, let's be truthful, I appeared in that final. It was a warm day and I never kicked a ball. I think I was playing because Stein liked me, simple as that. I had No. 10 on my back but I just never got going. And we had to watch as Derek 'Cup Tie' Mackay punctured our balloon.

I think Celtic were beaten in four finals that year but the feeling in the dressing room was that the directors would not have been too disappointed about it because it meant they didn't have to pay out bonuses. I hope I'm not being too cynical or unkind by saying that. Two years later, I remember playing Inter Milan in the European Cup and drawing 0–0 with them – it was the time Dixie Deans missed a penalty – and we never got a penny for that. Do you know what makes me remember that so well? It was Jim Brogan's humour. We were training one day and he was halfway round the track when he shouted out, 'Hey, what about this Inter Milan bonus?' He wasn't shouting at anyone, in particular – he was just making a point. We never got a sausage. But, to be honest, I couldn't have cared less at the time. I didn't devote one second of my time to thinking about the folding stuff in those days. The feeling of injustice on that score would come later – back then, I was just happy to be playing, happy to be breathing the same air as such great players.

Mr Stein, for his part, was not totally impressed by our efforts against Aberdeen. That was something that I remember clearly about him – he would never get in about you after a game but on the Monday morning, after a poor performance at the weekend, that's when you had to watch yourself, that's when the venom would be released.

Now, that particular Monday, Tommy Gemmell had brought Tid Callaghan into the Park. Tid? He was Willie's tiddler brother. Anyway, they turned up late. It was Tommy's fault, no one else's, but the manager took it out on Tid. Davie and I were in the boot room when we heard this awful commotion coming from the home team dressing room. Stein was bawling at Tid for being late. I think he took his complimentary tickets away and just gave him a stand ticket for the second leg against Leeds. After all the tension surrounding the first leg and the cup final, it was a blessed release. Davie and I were peeing ourselves in that boot room. Considering my performance against Aberdeen, I don't know what I was laughing about – I had been so much rubbish I was lucky the bin men didn't come to collect me!

Four days after the debacle, we took on the English again. There was no hangover from the Dons game – we were right up for it. Mind you, who wouldn't rise to the occasion in front of a crowd like that? They say the attendance was almost 137,000 at Hampden Park that night – the game had been switched from Parkhead to accommodate a bigger crowd. You'll never see a game like that in Glasgow again. There was so much electricity in the atmosphere that you could have lit up the city with it. The noise from the crowd was frightening but, because of the way we overturned Leeds, I have to say it was the most enjoyable game of my life.

I was in midfield again but this time I wasn't auditioning for the part of the Invisible Man. Bobby Murdoch, Bertie Auld and I put an armlock on the midfield department and we forced a whole lot of Celtic corners early on. But, as is often the way in football, the opposition took the lead against the flow of play. Billy Bremner whacked the ball from the thirty-yard mark and it careered into the net via the angle of the post and the crossbar. The goal momentarily silenced the crowd but it did not crush their spirit. Soon, they were cranking up the engines of their voice boxes and chanting, 'Cel-tic, Cel-tic, Celt-tic . . .' The opposition were about to be haunted by 130,000-odd Hampden larynxes.

Nil-one at half-time did not accurately reflect the way the game had gone – we had attacked constantly and Leeds cleared off the line a couple of times. Their luck ran out at a crucial time, two minutes into the second half. My pal Davie Hay slipped a short corner to Bertie Auld and he chipped the ball across for Yogi Hughes to head into the net. This set the stage for frenzied activity around the Leeds goal – only their goalie Sprake wasn't around to see it because he was injured in a collision with Hughes. It wasn't long before we were 2–1 up after a Murdoch–Johnstone combination ended with Bobby battering the ball past David Harvey, who had come on for Sprake. Jinky didn't score but his contribution that night had been monumental – he'd turned Cooper and Hunter inside out and outside in so often that they were left with twisted limbs.

Hunter didn't like it and screamed at his colleague, 'Kick him!'

Cooper was unimpressed and yelled back, 'You try and kick him!'

The fact is that no one could get near Jinky that night. And, apart from that verbal exchange between Cooper and Hunter, they still didn't resort to the illegal side of the game. I saw Wee Billy Bremner come into our dressing room afterwards and congratulate us heartily. It was a very sporting moment. Leeds had fancied themselves to win at Hampden all right – Catt was pally with Bremner and he'd told me as much – but they took that defeat well and I don't think I was fouled once. In those days, mind you, not just Leeds but teams in general didn't try to kick me into the middle of next week. Sure, I was Big Geordie, Quiet Geordie, Gentle Geordie at most times but, if trouble insisted on announcing itself, I could handle myself. If someone did me, I didn't believe in instant retribution. I was an opportunist who was prepared to wait as I believed that scores should be settled in the right place at the right time. I used to nab them with my knee into their upper leg while going fairly fast. Doing that at pace could really do damage. How did I feel afterwards if I saw someone lying there and a stretcher coming out? It didn't bother me and I'd kid on that I never did the crime. I'd just be quite pleased that the culprit was out of the reckoning. It was that type of game then. Teams could all dish it out if needs be. You just had to handle yourself or you'd be the one who landed in soapy bubble. I wasn't taught the knee thing or anything like that; I thought of it myself and it just became my own particular weapon.

Professional footballers in general know what to do. Rattling opposition players with my knee was my way of disarming them, frightening them, intimidating them, call it what you like. It discouraged them from coming back into my territory. Did I frighten them deliberately? Well, maybe not – not 100 per cent, anyway – but, then again, I think sometimes I did. It was there as a fallback – something to use when things were perhaps not turning out as you had hoped. Some players had an entirely different approach and would get friendly with players from other teams. I wouldn't do that. I used to see the opposition coming in before games and they'd stand chatting away to some of our guys but I refused to get involved in that. And nor would I involve myself talking on the park. A lot of the others would do it but not me. I didn't believe in it and I was too zoned in for that to happen. Besides, you don't need to talk to a man you are just about to demolish.

The last thing I remember of our beating Leeds at Hampden was the massive crowd giving it plenty of 'Ea-sy, ea-sy, ea-sy!'

And, yes, I suppose it had been fairly simple – it was certainly far less difficult than we could have imagined it to be. I suppose, at the time, we thought we had climbed the highest mountain and that it was going to be a downhill stroll from then on.

Feyenoord lay ahead of us in the final but there's no way you'd have heard our teeth chattering. We weren't intimidated by their past performances or their reputation and yet there was no denying they had an impressive record.

The march of the Dutch towards supremacy in European football was, by this time, well under way. Ajax had reached the European Cup final in 1969 and were only beaten 4–1 by those aristocrats, Inter Milan. Feyenoord took on the champions in the second round of the following year's competition so we should have learned something from that. Taking a 1–0 lead to Rotterdam, Milan had struggled and lost goals to Wim Jansen and then van Hanegem. Having dismantled such famous opposition early on, the Dutchmen were always likely to reach a final that was to be held in Milan. Mind you, you might not have recognised the city in northern Italy that night. It was invaded by 25,000 green-and-white clad Scots and 25,000 Dutchmen wearing red-and-white shirts.

Stein attempted to build us up with a couple of team talks before the game. If I remember correctly, he told us he was going to attack the Dutch with a 4–2–4 formation. I might have been a village idiot but I was quite quick on the football uptake and I said to myself, 'That's me – I'll be out.' I was spot on. (Davie Hay has strong views on that subject which you'll read about later on.)

It really didn't bother me, though – not at the time. I suppose I was just pleased to be there. Besides, I was used to being in and out of the team in those days. I had been really surprised I was playing at Leeds but I kind of half expected to play at Hampden. In another way, I suppose I was still a wee bit star-struck at the time. I was thinking to myself, 'Yogi will be playing and Jinky – just stand back and admire.'

In both semi-finals, we had played the same midfield and we dominated that area. In the Feyenoord game, they were playing 4–3–3. Consequently, with a man extra in midfield, we seemed to be chasing shadows all the time. You knew there was something wrong. When they got the ball, they were passing it five to ten yards; when we got it, we seemed to be wondering who we could pass it to. However, we took the lead through Tommy Gemmell, who was making a habit of scoring from the edge of the penalty area in European Cup finals. But, being outplayed in midfield, our lead lasted only a couple of minutes. The Dutch captain, Israel, headed home a free kick and then Evan Williams, our goalkeeper, was called upon to justify his wages a few times over.

Soon, Celtic took Bertie Auld off and put me on, instead of taking off an attacker and tightening up the midfield. Looking back on it, it was kind of screaming out for that. Without being overly critical of Mr Stein, I think he made a tactical error there but I believe at the time he wanted to hang on to his 4–2–4 formation, rather than go on to the 4–3–3, which was the way the game was going and the set-up favoured by one of Stein's biggest rivals, Eddie Turnbull of Aberdeen. I think, to be fair, he was also hanging on to Yogi and Jinky, his top players. I was young and relatively inexperienced so it would have been easier to tell me that I wasn't playing, rather than one of them. They might have given him a bit of earache and who could have blamed them if they had – they were top-class players.

In spite of the imbalance in midfield, we managed to cling on to 1–1 for the rest of the ninety minutes. Our downfall came in the final seconds of extra time. Then it was a case of sudden death by long ball. A free kick was hoisted all the way from the Feyenoord half into our penalty area. My memory tells me

Big Billy McNeill stumbled and looked as if he punched the ball away but, before the referee could take charge of the situation, Ove Kindvall took the ball round Billy and lobbed it over the goalkeeper into the net.

Oh, I suppose I was disappointed that we had not won that night but, in a way, not really disappointed that I had not played a more important role in the final – I was young and had time as my ally. And, if my chance for European glory had come and gone in 1970, there would be a host of other opportunities to shine, wouldn't there?

6

THE SALAD DAYS

It's at times like these, when I'm trying to dip into the past and sometimes coming up with thin air, that I would dearly like my name to be Leslie Welsh instead of George Connelly. How I wish I had a memory like the guy who became famous on the radio in the 1950s. He was known as 'The Memory Man' and, if you asked him a question about history, geography, mathematics, sport or simply the price of tea in China, before you could clear your throat, you had an answer. Me? I've forgotten a whole lot more about my playing career than I've remembered. I reckon at least some of this is down to the fact that I was never obsessed with myself as a footballer. I just did things and that was it – I just forgot about them and ordered the next drink.

Now I know some people like their facts and figures so I'll try my best to please them but you'll have to bear with me – my name's not Welsh. Here's one fact that might startle you – I started in twenty-one Old Firm games, the first was in August 1968 (which has already been mentioned) and the last was on 15 September 1973. Of course, I made substitute appearances against Rangers after that date but, with my ankle injury, which I'll expand on later, and my home life in freefall, my career against them basically lasted only five years. That's scarcely longevity in anyone's book, is it?

Some of these Old Firm encounters are worth recalling – the

match played on 14 September 1968, for instance. Having experienced the fantastic atmosphere that games between these teams generate, I now had a taste for playing in them. However, this time out, we were beaten 4–2 at home and, in fact, were soon two goals down. On the plus side, I survived the full ninety minutes and helped to make one of the goals. Seven months later, it was back into the Old Firm fires for a Glasgow Cup semi-final. Again we were gubbed, this time 3–4. This was billed as a second-eleven match because of the absence of so many regulars. I remember that Pat McMahon came on as sub in that game – I often wonder what happened to him. Five days later, I was playing in the cup final that was to put my name up in lights. That's been discussed enough elsewhere, so let's move quickly on.

The following season, it looked as if I wasn't going to achieve the kind of destiny this victory seemed to promise. We travelled to Ibrox on 13 August 1969, for a League Cup game, and were beaten 2–1. Jim Baxter had just come back to Scotland from Sunderland at the time. Rangers had signed him in the hope that he would give them a much-needed lift and a bit of encouragement, which they certainly needed considering the league form Celtic were then showing. What a man! I remember coming through the middle and he shouted me to shoot. Nice try, Jim! I was about thirty-five to forty yards out and there was no way I was going to do it.

That was the only time I ever played against Baxter. He was a bit of class that day, as he controlled things from midfield. Another thing I remember is that, on his return to Ibrox, he was Slim Jim no longer. He'd put a bit of weight on. However, there but for the grace of God go I – it wouldn't be long before I would know all about weight problems.

In September of 1970, I played in a landmark league victory (2–0) over Rangers for Jock Stein. It was the twenty-fifth time he'd put a team out against Rangers since he took over and it was his fourteenth win. John Hughes and Bobby Murdoch claimed the goals. Folk said I had a good game that day, both in defence and building attacks, but, as Celtic legend Willie Fernie used to say, 'Self-praise is no honour.' so I shall step back from saying any more.

During the next month of that same year, we faced Rangers at Hampden in the Scottish League Cup final and limped away after suffering a 1–0 defeat. Rangers had just been humiliated by Aberdeen at Ibrox in the league and you could almost see the pain in their eyes – but not for long. They said John Greig wasn't going to be playing and that a young lad called Derek Johnstone was going to be tried out. That gave me so much confidence. He was only sixteen, wasn't he? Surely not a threat . . . I think Willie Johnston crossed and Derek fired it past Evan Williams with a great header. You should never prejudge these things.

Tragically, the second half of season '70–71 began with the Ibrox Disaster. I can't remember too much about what happened but I do know that sixty-six people died and over a hundred were injured when they were crushed on one of the stairways. Rangers were a club in mourning and Glasgow was a city united in grief.

We played Rangers in the Scottish Cup final on 8 May and it ended 1–1. Then, four days later in the replay, we won 2–1. I may have blotted out most of the tragedy of 2 January but, strangely enough, I can remember plenty about those two cup games. The first took place in front of 120,092 fans and soon half of them were appreciating a Bobby Lennox goal. But what was it about cup matches and this guy Derek Johnstone? On the first occasion, he came on as substitute. Willie Johnston – aye, him again – lobbed the ball over from the wing and I was caught on the wrong side of Big Derek. He headed over Evan, who was on his way out of goal at the time. Looking back on it, I took the blame and that's OK, but maybe Evan would have done better to stay on his line. If you come out, you commit yourself and it's up to you to get the ball. But, thinking about it, perhaps I need to see it again to be sure although, I have to say, it was certainly partly my fault.

The replay fascinated the fans, too – so much so that there were only 16,000 fewer present. We scored through a Harry Hood penalty and a Lou Macari goal but an own goal by Jim Craig gave them hope. It was time for that man Johnstone to figure again. He came on as sub at half-time and it had re-kindled their spirit. In fact, when he had a shot blocked by Williams, he tried again and it struck Craig on its way into the net. In both matches, I had Billy McNeill beside me at the back and this was a partnership that was to bring quite a lot of success. My head was high as I left the field. I remember seeing John Greig at the trackside. His head was bowed.

We got Rangers in our League Cup section in August of that year and twice we had the better of them. We travelled to Ibrox first and it was a notable occasion as it was Kenny Dalglish's first Old Firm game. Davie Hay and I were playing in defence but our dominance was so great that we were able to desert our posts and get forward. Jinky opened the scoring, after a heavy bout of pressure, then Yogi was pulled down in the box – a stonewall penalty. Big Billy decreed that young Kenny should take the spot kick – a test of a youngster's mettle and no mistake. Yet, if there were any nerves in him, he didn't show it. He even bent down to lace his boot before putting ball past Peter McCloy! We went a goal better on the second leg, with Dalglish, Tid Callaghan and Bobby Lennox taking the honours.

Then we played Rangers about three times in a month around this time. All the matches were at Ibrox because Parkhead was being reconstructed but playing away didn't seem to be a problem for us. On 11 September, we edged them out 3–2 in the league when our scorers were Macari, Dalglish and Johnstone. At 2–2, I headed the ball back to Evan. When Colin Stein ran in and put his foot up, the referee gave a foul. I was given star rating by the *Glasgow Herald* that day – in fact, I shared it with Tid – and the scribe said I could easily have hit a fly on the wall from fifty or sixty yards, so accurate was my passing. Meanwhile, Tid was complimented for eating up ground with that tremendously powerful stride of his. Seven titles in a row were beckoning and a 2–1 victory, on 3 January 1972, over the old enemy served to make this even more likely. We were all over them during the first half although we could only score one goal – through Jinky. They came at us like bats out of hell in the second period and Stein nabbed a goal back. In the last minute, however, victory was ours when Hood lobbed the ball into the penalty area and Jim Brogan headed it past McCloy.

We were winning league titles for fun in those days and, on our way to our eighth consecutive title, beating Rangers was plenty of fun. I wouldn't have been surprised if they were sick of the sight of us.

On 16 September 1972, goals from Dalglish, Johnstone and Macari gave us a 3–1 win. With a comfortable scoreline, it was time to do a bit of keepie-uppie! No, it wasn't a replica of what I did when we played Dynamo Kiev – nothing really fancy and no flipping the ball on to my head – only my feet and thighs were involved and I probably only did it about half a dozen times before passing it back to the goalkeeper. I think I did it in response to Willie Johnston, who once sat on the ball when Rangers were winning. It was just my way of giving him a taste of his own medicine – but it took a bit of bottle. You would never see it nowadays as anyone trying something like that would find his manager waiting for him with a shovel when he came off the park. But I never got into trouble over it – Stein never even mentioned it – and the Rangers players never said anything either. How could they? They would have remembered what Johnston did and everyone knew that, if you gave it, you also had to take it.

However, on 3 January, in the return league match, they beat us 2–1. I was playing well at the time and went on to become Player of the Year. The late Ian Archer of the *Glasgow Herald* was very complimentary about me. He was a nice fella and I was quite pally with him. He used to lend me money now and then – a fiver here and there. It wasn't drink money – it was just when I was a bit short and, considering the wages I was on, I was often short in those days.

I always played at the back at this time, as the spare man beside McNeill, and I suppose the top moments of my career, as far as I was concerned, came between 1972 and 1973. I was in my prime. But a strange thing happened in the cup final of that year, just after we had taken our eighth league title. By the way, the title run-in was impressive that year – we won seven on the spin, scoring twenty-three goals and conceding only one. At Hampden, before a 122,000 crowd, we were facing a team that had been beaten on their own Ibrox turf by St Mirren and Stenhousemuir but you should never take anything for granted with Rangers. They beat us 3–2 that day, with goals from Derek Parlane, Alfie Conn and Tam Forsyth bettering ours by Dalglish and yours truly, who scored from the penalty spot.

It was the SFA Centenary Cup final and Princess Alexandra was there to meet the teams. They gave us these special tops to be worn over our jerseys. After we were introduced to the princess, I couldn't wait for the action to begin so I unzipped my top to reveal the beloved jersey. But the thing was that no one else had done this and I felt very conspicuous. It completely unnerved me and I felt as if everybody was looking at me. And so I went into that cup final thinking more about protocol rather than football. Apart from the penalty kick, I never kicked a ball in that game. I had no influence on it at all – it just passed me by – and I think I got caught out for two of the goals. I fully believe that, if I hadn't done that stupid thing, I would have been OK and we'd have won. But that's the way it was.

We won a League Cup tie 2–1 against them on 18 August that same year of 1973 but I can't even remember taking the field that day. I do remember, however, the return seven days later. We should have had five, six or seven goals in the first half for we ran over the top of them but, instead, we got just the one through Bobby Lennox. The vibrant talent of Brian McLaughlin was emerging and Steve Murray was blending in well in midfield. Then they came out in the second half, got three chances and stuck them all away. It was unbelievable.

Nine in a row was very much on the cards and this was underlined when we went to Ibrox on 15 September of 1973 and came away with a 1–0 victory. My pal Davie Hay put over a low cross and Jimmy Johnstone scored with a header. I wish I could remember every detail of that match but, sadly, I can't. Why the blanks, you may ask. I haven't got a definite answer – maybe it was because my private life was in such a mess that I wasn't able to concentrate on anything else. My football career certainly didn't get the kind of attention I should have been able to give it. Anyway, that was the last time I would start an Old Firm game.

Apart from the aforementioned, the cup final that stands out most in my memory was the one on 6 May 1972, when we beat Hibs 6–1. Dixie Deans grabbed a hat trick that day, Macari got two and Big Billy weighed in with the other one. It was red-hot that day and the heat we generated matched the weather. I was more than a wee bit surprised at the result because Hibs were a good side at the time. Their full back, Erich Schaedler, and I used to play squash together but this was squash of an altogether different variety!

There are, of course, still some little bits and pieces clinging to the lifeboat of my memory. For instance, I remember fragments from European nights such as the semi-final of the European Cup against Inter Milan in 1972 when we lost on penalties after two 0–0 draws. I nearly scored over there – nearly, but not quite. Then, in the return, they gave us all the ball and let us play up to a point. We had two terrific chances and missed them – we really shouldn't have needed penalties. They had only one man up and I was in my comfort zone. The next year, in the same competition, I had my best-ever night away from the Park, apart from maybe the Leeds game. We played Vejle on 24 October and I remember doing my stuff that evening. Afterwards Jock came up to me and just gave me a nod. That was all the appreciation I needed.

There was no such nod of approval when we played Partick Thistle in the League Cup final of 1971, though. I played in four finals and lost every one – to Rangers, Hibs, Thistle and then Dundee – but it's the Partick one that belongs to the realms of nightmares. Big Billy wasn't playing and I had just got used to being alongside him. That day, I was at centre half and Jim Brogan was beside me. Who did Thistle have up front? A couple of flying machines in Jimmy Bone and Frank Coulston. Bobby Lawrie was outside left and he was fast too. They stretched us and then they stretched us some more. Bone and Coulston were crossing all the time and I could do nothing with them. If Billy had been there, we'd have had a bit of stability and I could have worked round him but they just blew us away in that first half: 4–1. That was it. In the second half, we had about half a dozen chances, but the game was over by then. If I remember rightly, Celtic signed Dixie after that, and about a fortnight later, we beat them 5–1, with Dixie scoring twice.

The memory of one game stands out more than any other, though. Let me take you back to 1968. Jimmy Johnstone had destroyed Red Star Belgrade in the first leg of a European Cup tie at Parkhead. Jinky hated flying and he had got Jock to agree that, if Celtic got a good score behind them in the home leg, he wouldn't need to fly to the former Yugoslavia for the second leg. With the score at 5–1, Jinky had fulfilled his side of the bargain so I was given the No. 7 shirt for the second leg and I've never had an easier night in my life. I'll bet Big Billy can't remember that game and the reason it's all so clear to me is because I stood and watched it at my leisure. I can picture it now. Red Star flung everything at Billy in the first half and he was absolutely fantastic – in the air and on the ground, he was supreme. They scored but then Willie Wallace, who had come on as sub, hit one from about forty yards right into the top corner and that was it. Job done!

That night, of course, I was alongside the players who, the season before, had been dubbed the Lisbon Lions. They were the ultimate professionals and it's my opinion that the guys playing nowadays are not in the same league as them. I think, in many ways, they broke that team up too early but there were so many players coming through that I think Mr Stein felt he had to offload some of them. But, as far as I was concerned, they could have stayed for a wee while longer. I would have thought that some of them were surprised at the speed of their departures. Tommy Gemmell went, Bobby Murdoch followed and then Jim Craig. They were still big players. I never had a lot to do with them, really. I just went in, did my stuff and hit the road. But, although I could never bring myself to get close to them, I do have fond memories of them.

I've told you already about Ronnie Simpson. I only need to add that I loved listening to him because he always spoke so well about fitba. I also got on great with Jim Craig. He's a learned man. When this book came to mind, I thought about him a lot because he used to write down all the details about the trips and the games. Wouldn't having access to that have come in handy for me? I think he took a while to settle down in the team. He was studying dentistry at university so he started as a part-timer and maybe, to begin with, he was more interested in university than football but he ended up a right good player. I used to enjoy playing alongside him because he was good in the air and I wasn't.

Big Tam Gemmell was a very flamboyant character who, unlike me, never missed a day's training. He came across as a great joker but there was a serious man lurking underneath it all. I remember playing Newcastle twice in 1968 at the time Stein first started blooding me. Tam and Willie Wallace, another fine fella and a great footballer, took me to see Julie Christie in *Far from the Madding Crowd*. Whenever I see that film now, I think of Tam and Willie.

Bobby Murdoch was another great character. He had a gift for being able to pass the ball from any angle and I began doing it too. I think he was the best player on the park in Lisbon. If you watch the game again, you'll see that anything worthwhile went through Bobby. He was a tremendous player and Stein thought the world of him, I know that.

To my mind, the Lions had three managers playing for the team – Bobby, Bertie Auld and Big Billy. Bertie, for instance, told me off for running with the ball in training. He said I was running thirty yards and then passing it ten, instead of passing it thirty and running ten. It was good advice and it sank in right away. Bertie was the key to so many things: he scored goals with both feet; he could read the game with ease; he was a great passer of the ball; and he could dig in when it was called for. They were all so knowledgeable. John Clark was a studious one and no mistake. He would study the opposition intently until he knew all about them and, in my opinion, as far as the sweeper's position was concerned, he and Martin Buchan were probably the best in the business at the time.

Joe McBride sustained a bad injury and, of course, didn't play in Lisbon but what a goalscorer he was! He was one of those types that, if you saw him in training, you would possibly have some reservations about him but put him on the park on a Saturday and he would score from anywhere. It wasn't that he didn't train well – it was just that, when he applied himself to business, he was transformed. I think he got thirty-six goals in all competitions before Christmas and his injury, and I believe he was still leading scorer at the end of the season.

Stevie Chalmers – what a great bloke he was! And he was just fantastic in training. He wasn't a drinker and was as fit as any fiddle. Kids would look up to him – he was the perfect role model. You could say the same about Bobby Lennox, another character with as much effervescence as a bottle of champagne. John Hughes, meanwhile, was an absolute gentleman and another idol of mine. Those were the days of the white boots. When he was on song, he was almost unstoppable. He gave Jack Charlton of Leeds a right roasting at Hampden in the European semi-final. He was incredibly nimble for such a big guy and I remember one day we were going to be playing on a soggy pitch. I said I thought the heavy going would suit him. 'No, no,' he replied, 'I can play in any conditions.' And he could. When I was coming through in the reserves and I was starting to play centre half, I was marking Yogi in a practice game. I could do nothing with him. If he went on a run and I went with him, he would lay the ball off. And, if I stood off him, he'd just turn and come at me. I'm convinced to this day that he was getting signals from the gaffer from the sidelines!

On the other wing was Jinky. Was there anyone better than him? I doubt it. Jimmy was consistently brilliant over those nine seasons when Celtic won the championships. You don't need to say any more than that. I'll never forget the day of the great man's funeral. This was the first time I'd been to the Park in almost thirty years – not that I went into the official gathering. Why didn't I join in? Don't you know me by now? I couldn't possibly be so forward. The point was that I didn't duck out. I attended the funeral of a man who did so much for Celtic. I put all my doubts about going through to Glasgow and making a fool of myself through drink to the side – I simply had to be there. This guy drove me through and we stood there in the crowds outside the Park. I just stood there respectfully, with my black tie on and a tear in my eye. Jimmy, bless him, deserved no less.

7

PARADISE LOST

These days, I earn a living driving a taxi at the weekends. One of the main drawbacks of doing that is that it gives me plenty of time to think and, consequently, plenty of time to depress the hell out of myself – I'm sure the same would happen to anyone who was that way inclined. The curtain of depression tends to descend when my thoughts go back to the days when I was winning honours with Celtic. There were more than a few and I certainly couldn't count them on the fingers of two hands – I appeared in five Scottish Cup finals, won four league medals, played in four League Cup finals and picked up two caps for Scotland. I don't need to fantasise or imagine anything – these are the facts. And, by the way, I never argued with referees – I just got on with the game.

Now, I'm not a jealous person and I know you can't turn the clock back. A lot of footballers are getting £30,000 plus a week, with some earning £100,000 a week and more. Well, I say good luck to them and I hope they enjoy their Gucci days, their Prada presents and their Ferrari years. I was just born at the wrong time but I'm not alone in that. What would Bertie Auld have been worth today? Or Billy McNeill, Stevie Chalmers, John Greig, Willie Henderson? The really galling thing is that I know I could have had another ten years of a career and it was my fault it didn't turn out that way – *that*'s the annoying part of it.

Without wishing to seem in any way boastful, I suppose I'm still a famous person yet here I am driving people about at the weekends and, in this game, you never know what is going to come your way next. A variety of horrors is on offer, probably the most irritating of which are the no-shows because they mean you are out of pocket. Then there are the insults and threats of violence (although I've been fairly lucky in that respect), folk running off without paying and, unfortunately, those who vomit all over the back of your car and so temporarily put you out of business. With all these possibilities, I often wonder why I'm doing it. I've learned to cope with most things the job throws at me but there was a time when, if I thought about things too much, it got to the stage where I was tempted to park the car and run away from it all. In fact, there were times when I might even have done something a whole lot worse than that and ended it all. But, in moments like those, common sense takes over and I remind myself of the things that really matter.

When I consider the good things, suddenly the world doesn't look like such a threatening venue, after all. And I really do have much to thank God for – a wonderful marriage, a grounded home life (on the good days) and, when, of course, the drink hasn't taken me on some magical mystery tour, a great relationship with all three of my children. So, when I'm sober, it's remembering all those things that prevents me from doing anything stupid. Anyway, I've done enough silly things to last this lifetime, thanks very much.

I'll take you back to the early 70s to prove my point. My memory of that time is a bit fragmented, particularly when it comes to remembering individual football games, but I'll try to fill in the jigsaw as best I can and there are certain incidents which stand out in my mind. After many years spent proving my worth by playing in just about every position known to man and flitting in and out of the first team, I was, at last, considered a first-team player and had been given the all-important Stein vote of confidence.

By the season 1971–72, I had established myself as sweeper and was playing alongside the great Billy McNeill. In a most unusual way, that role came in particularly useful in a game against Aberdeen at Parkhead, when Jimmy Johnstone was sent off. As Bobby Murdoch escorted Jinky from the park, bottles were thrown and someone chucked a whisky glass on to the park. I instinctively bent down to pick it up. I remember, also, putting my hand up to the area known as the Jungle and shouting at the fans to behave themselves. I mean I was scared of that kind of stuff. Throwing glasses at people was right over the top in my book – although, to my eternal shame, there was to come a day when I was to do the very same myself. Thankfully, the Parkhead commotion stopped and I was quite pleased with myself as it might not have done had I not intervened.

But, if that was one moment of maturity from me, there were several moments when the same certainly was not true. With Celtic going for eight in a row in that next season and losing only three games in the process, the bonuses were dropping into our laps like nobody's business but, at the same time, common sense, I'm afraid, was going out the window. As I said earlier, I had a big mortgage and a couple of cars. Money was coming in but it was going out a whole lot faster. Things might have been all right if my marriage had been working like clockwork but it was not. In fact, very little was right at home and it was beginning to affect my football judgement.

Nevertheless, I was playing well and attracting quite a lot of attention. In October of 1972, for instance, Tommy Docherty picked me to go to Denmark on World Cup qualification business with Scotland. The team flew out minus Mr Connelly, however. We were still living in Fife at that time and my wife had driven me from our Kincardine home through to Parkhead, where Celtic doctor John Fitzsimmons reluctantly advised me not to go. I remember reading in the newspapers: 'Connelly was obviously upset at the verdict. He had arrived at the ground with all his playing gear.'

However, those newspapers, through no fault of their own, did not have their hands on the correct story. Upset? I was delighted not to be going! I was never unfit to play – not in a million years! The reason for me pulling out was simply that I didn't want to go – don't ask me why. I didn't like flying at the time – in fact, I still don't – but it was just general things, most of them stemming from the discord at home which meant that my head was all over the place. When people ask me why I only played twice for Scotland, I just tell them to take the number of call-offs into consideration and make their own minds up. On the other occasions when I didn't turn up for Scotland games, I just sat in the house and said I had the flu or whatever and they believed me. F****** madness, eh? Sure it was but, remember, we're human beings and there are always reasons for such conduct – you only need to look at Garry O'Connor for an example of that kind of behaviour. The one bonus as far as the Denmark time is concerned was that the SFA did not take any action against me. Looking back, I suppose that was the first sign of a crack appearing; before long, however, there would be splits all over the place.

In the June after I'd been named Player of the Year in 1973, I staged another disappearing act with Scotland. This time, I vamoosed when the squad met up at Glasgow to fly to Switzerland, via London, for a World Cup qualifier. When I was quizzed about it later, I said I had been worried about my wife's health as she was expecting our second child at the time. Well, maybe that was part of the reason but, in truth, my head was really messed up by then. So what really happened? It had all become too much and I simply had to get away so I ducked out of Glasgow Airport, jumped in a taxi and went home. We had just moved to Blantyre at the time. I asked the taxi driver to stop at an off-licence and I bought two bottles of Cinzano. I took them up to my bed and drank them while reporters rattled at the door.

My wife couldn't handle the press either. A pack of them had laid siege to my door, offering to pay money for photographs which they wanted to take in the kitchen. I was so angry that I ended up jumping on one of the photographer's cameras and getting done for it – I was fined and had to buy the guy a new camera. Christine was angry too and, by this time, I think she wanted out of the marriage just as much as I did. She probably realised then how much of a complete mismatch it was.

I waited till night came and then proceeded to sneak off to my bolthole in Fife. I'd thrown away another honour. Who knows, maybe if everything had been well and I'd turned up instead of hiding in my bedroom, I'd have loads and loads of international caps instead of only two.

Davie Hay remembers that incident well:

We'd been down at Largs, staying at the famous Queen's Hotel, which is a nice, homely place but not the type that modern-day football teams would normally use. I remember, the day before we were due to leave for Switzerland, we were going out for a few pints in the George Hotel in the town. George didn't fancy it and said he wasn't going. I told him that the Scotland players were all good lads but I think he just felt uncomfortable at the thought of being around virtual strangers. He was slightly more at his ease with the Celtic players but these were internationals and, knowing what George was like, it's not difficult to imagine how uneasy he was at the prospect of being in their company. So, as far as I know, he stayed in that night.

The next morning we were up reasonably early. It wasn't a direct flight as we had to change at London before going on to Berne. We arrived at Glasgow Airport to check in and I'm not sure if George had put his baggage through or not but he turned round and said, 'I'm no' gaun.'

I was amazed. 'What do you mean, you're no' gaun?'

'Exactly that! I'm no' for it!'

He disappeared. I then went to phone his wife, Christine. I said to her, 'George is wanting to come back. If he changes his mind and decides he does want to go, just make out he missed the flight.'

I was trying to protect him. As I was going down the stairs at the airport, I heard one of the journalists, Alex Cameron, inquiring as to his whereabouts. I can't remember my exact reply but it would have been vague and pretty noncommittal. We flew down to London but, as far as I know, nobody apart from Christine and me knew George wasn't on that flight. We got to Heathrow and we had to check in at the Swissair desk to go to Berne. All I heard was the tannoy going bing-bong, followed by, 'Would George Connelly please come to the Swissair desk?' And, suddenly, the smell of a good story was in the air. The journalists' nostrils were twitching and Alex Cameron again asked me where George was. I tried to look as if I knew nothing but it was no good – the press quickly realised they had got hold of something juicy.

His refusal to fly to Switzerland was a sign of the problematic side of George's life. If I remember correctly, the press tracked him down at his home and he reacted quite badly to their attention. Nevertheless, he overcame that hurdle and played on but it had been the first public indication that all was not well.

There were many wonderful qualities about Willie Ormond – the quality of mercy being one of them. I had let him down dramatically by not showing up for the World Cup qualifier against Switzerland and yet he chose me for the all-important game against Czechoslovakia at Hampden in September of 1973. I remember being quite embarrassed before the game when we went down to that wee hotel in Largs, but not for the reasons you might imagine. Maybe my memory is playing games with me but I think they only had about one bathroom to about ten players. When I eventually got in to have a bath, there was this wee bit trickle of water coming out and it was one of the shallowest dips I've ever had. If there was two inches of water, that's all there was. I wondered what Billy Bremner and all the boys were thinking. Would they have been happy with such facilities after enjoying such lavish treatment with their clubs? I wouldn't have thought so.

Anyway, nothing seemed to matter on that night of 26 September. Up until this time, Scotland possessed an embarrassing record as far as World Cup qualification was concerned. To remember the last time we had got through, you had to go back so far in time that Dr Who would have had to provide the transport. But, on this occasion, we hit the Hampden Park sweet spot and, after a Nehoda goal had given the Czechs the lead, goals from Jim Holton and Joe Jordan put us on the road to West Germany. Experience and youth were woven into what was an irresistible package. People said that Denis Law was too old – not that night he wasn't. Bremner was at the centre of everything and big Tam Hutchison tantalised the Czech defence. Joe Jordan, coming on as substitute for Kenny Dalglish, managed to break a few spirits and bodies and Jim Holton came of age and stamped a lot of authority on the game. Me? Well, I think I was forgiven for my absences. I believe I defended quite well and was able to execute some forward passes without making a monkey of myself. Just as they had done during that Celtic game against Leeds, the vast crowd became as good as another player on the park.

Willie Ormond had this knack of being able to put good teams together. At the end of that match, Bremner came over to him, pulled him on to the pitch and saw to it that he was hoisted on to the players' shoulders to receive the recognition he deserved.

A few days later, I met a wee guy in a hat who was writing for the *Sunday Express*. He actually did a big article on me and gave me twenty quid for it. As we sat in the foyer at the Park conducting our business together, he asked me if I thought I'd be playing in the return match against Czechoslovakia. Not wishing to be swollen-headed and take anything for granted, I said I didn't know if I would be picked or not.

He said, 'Listen, son, I'll eat my hat if you're not!'

In fact, I only earned one other cap and that was at home to West Germany in a friendly on 14 November 1973, when we drew 1–1. Prior to that, I had gone over to Czechoslovakia but my suspicions that I wouldn't be playing were confirmed. I think Ormond placed Tom Forsyth alongside John Blackley over there. Wee Willie could be a strange man at times and you never knew what he was thinking. He liked a nip but, in fairness to him, he did pick the best players for each position. I was disappointed that time but only slightly.

The next time I saw that wee guy from the *Sunday Express*, I said to him, 'Did you enjoy your hat?'

If I saw the funny side of that, there wasn't much else to amuse me at that time. In November of 1973, I had fallen out with Celtic, who were seeking their ninth consecutive title. I was on £65 a week plus bonuses. Compared to the ordinary working man, it might have been a lot for that time but we were playing in front of huge crowds and we thought we deserved a better share of that action. Davie Hay had gone out on strike over his wages and I came out in sympathy with him. I thought they might agree that I deserved more money but it didn't work like that. You had to fight tooth and nail for anything that you got and, even then, they made you feel they were doing you a favour. The strike could scarcely be said to have been organised by Arthur Scargill and it was soon over as far as I was concerned.

After the strike, there had been no improvement in my wages and, not only that, now I couldn't win my place in the team back at first. So I asked to be put on the transfer list. Although they agreed to my request, there were no takers and, ironically, I was brought back to the first team. Around this time, things are a bit of a blur but I know I had started putting on a bit of weight. I was carrying too much for my physique and this eventually led to me losing my place altogether. I wasn't happy and had begun to turn to drink. It wasn't anything crazy or over the top but it really wasn't what a professional footballer should have been doing. When times are bad and you rely on food or drink for comfort, you rarely knuckle down and pursue a sensible line. I had just moved house from Kincardine to Blantyre in Lanarkshire and had begun doing daft things like drinking after training. I can also remember going to the St Columbus Club in Blantyre after games, sometimes by myself and sometimes with one or two of the guys. The trouble was that there were no angels at Parkhead – Jinky wasn't one and neither was Davie. They didn't say, 'Aw, you're going drinking? Well, we're going home!'

I could usually find myself a drinking buddy but it didn't really matter if I couldn't. Between my home life – my marriage was heading for the rocks at an impressive rate of knots – and my wages, there was a lot to bring me down. Anyway, I had a ready-made bar companion in my brother Dan who was working through in the Lanarkshire area at the time. I know he took some of the responsibility for my drinking but I couldn't blame him. He wasn't pouring it down my neck – I was able to do that all on my own.

This is **Davie Hay**'s take on what went on at that time.

My discontent with the club really began to surface when my three-year contract ended. There was a two-year option which meant I was tied to the club – but, even without the option, they still held a player's registration in those days. First of all, I went to talk to Big Jock and put my case for a higher basic wage. I was negotiating as much for George as for myself. Then George and I had to deal with the chairman, Desmond White. We had won quite a number of games so we earned a lot in bonuses and, compared to the average man, we were bringing in a substantial income. However, in the previous season, I'd been injured and missed out on a lot of the rewards. I was looking for a basic £100 a week but the club argued that they weren't going to break the wage structure just for me. Desmond said, if he gave me a hundred, then he would have to give it to the rest of the players as well. I can remember saying, 'Well, I think they deserve it and you can afford it.' In simple terms of cold financial analysis, we merited a higher basic wage.

It was then that I was almost transferred to Tottenham, following a meeting with their manager, Bill Nicholson. Celtic had agreed a fee of over 200 grand with Tottenham so, when I got back from London, I wanted to find out what percentage of that would be coming my way. Then I learned that Manchester United were interested in me. Celtic said to me that, if I went to Spurs, they would give me part of the transfer fee but, if I went to Manchester, I'd get nothing. It was so unfair and I was absolutely raging about it. 'How dare you?' I asked them.

This happened in the October of 1973 and that, together with the low basic wage, was the reason I went on strike. George joined me as a mark of sympathy, which goes to show how close we were, and together we faced the might of Celtic. While the strike went on, I mainly stayed at home although some days George and I played squash at East Kilbride. We were pals and, if we drank together, we were going to negotiate together – I'll admit that we were a pair of nutters, though. But, after two weeks, I got a phone call from the football journalist Jim Rodger. Jim was working as a conduit between the parties and he suggested that I should go back as Celtic were about to play Rangers in a cup semi-final. I did what Jim advised and I also agreed that we would scrub all talk of transfers. I was going to concentrate on playing for the club and for Scotland in the 1974 World Cup. I needed to put everything else to the back of my mind so I decided we'd deal with the money side of things at the end of the season. But I never signed another contract. I explained my position privately to Big Jock, never in public. I just concentrated on playing and George did the same.

The strike was over but I can't remember exactly how Stein reacted to our action. He probably wished it hadn't happened although he certainly didn't hold it against us in his subsequent team selections. The only time he brought it up was when I eventually went to Chelsea. 'Maybe you're better going because you created unrest,' he said. I took it that, by this, he was referring to George. But probably in the back of Jock's mind was the fact that he was also dictated to by the policy of the club. You weren't exactly encouraged to challenge the authority of Celtic. Initially, I felt aggrieved by Big Jock's lack of support but, on reflection, I don't suppose he had any choice.

Soon, Kenny Dalglish, Danny McGrain, George and I were playing against Czechoslovakia and we qualified for the World Cup with a 2–1 victory at Hampden Park. George would have been part of the squad that went to West Germany but then he injured his ankle in a European Cup quarter-final against Basle and was taken to the Glasgow Victoria. There they put a plaster cast on him and any chance of him going to the World Cup evaporated.

Then, one day, totally out of the blue, George told me that he'd signed a new contract. I was very surprised. My exact words were, 'What did you sign for?' He kind of stammered a reply – something about how he was injured and that left him vulnerable. I reckon, in one of the quieter moments at Celtic Park, Jock would have caught him at a weak moment and pulled him in. Of course, George should just have said, 'I'll leave it now.' But I suppose it's easy saying that after the event.

I eventually left for Chelsea later that year and I think that had a big bearing on what eventually happened to George. He felt he had not been dealt with in the way he should have been and, once his best pal had gone, he must have felt very isolated. I'm sure that, together, George and I could have taken Celtic to another level – if I hadn't left the club, I'm convinced that George would have gone on to play a major part in the history of the club instead of becoming the lost legend that he is today.

Anyone who knows him recognises that he's got plenty of guts – enough to keep the ball up for ten minutes in front of a packed Celtic Park and enough to come out on strike with me in the first place – so you couldn't be angry with him. But I think that had a big bearing on what happened in the years ahead. I maintain that, if he'd been offered a better contract and I'd been similarly treated and not sold to Chelsea, this would be a different book to the one I'm contributing to – altogether different.

Somewhat inevitably, George slid towards the rocks. When he left Celtic, I remember saying to him, 'Look, George, you're that good, why don't you move down south to a different environment?'

He looked at me in that sheepish fashion of his and said, 'Ach, no, Davie, it wouldnae work.'

So, where did he go to play his football? At junior clubs like Tulliallan and Sauchie – at a level that was far below him. I'm not wanting to be disrespectful to those people but I would put it down as one of the biggest tragedies of the Scottish game that George Connelly finished his career in junior football.

I broke my ankle playing against Basle and the injury couldn't have come at a worse time. There was nobody near me when I slipped on the mud and broke it – exit your man in hoops. It really was unfortunate timing – Scotland were going to the World Cup and Celtic had their hot breath on the nine-in-a-row. There was just too much to take in so I signed a new contract and this at least relieved the pressure of career uncertainty.

I tried my hardest to get fit for that World Cup. I went on a diet of scrambled eggs and tomatoes and the weight came tumbling off – it dropped from 14st to under 13st in a very short time. I can remember paddling in the sea to try to heal the ankle. With the motivation of playing in West Germany and helping the team to another league title, I stopped drinking, worked really hard and became fitter than I'd ever been. However, it all proved to be in vain because, apart from the ankle break, the surgeon said I had also displaced a tendon. It was going to be a slow healing process and the medical people said they didn't think there wasn't enough time. But, despite this, I worked like the devil. I had Bob Rooney, the Celtic physiotherapist, put a harness around me and I was pulling him up and down the Park trying to get myself fit.

If joining Scotland for their World Cup campaign in West Germany came too soon, at least I would be fit for domestic football. Celtic won the league title in 1974 and now it was ten-in-a-row time. Mr Stein seemed to be pleased with the result of all my efforts. I remember he told reporters, 'George is not brooding over what might have been. If you sympathise with him, he grins and says, "There's always 1978!" That's the kind of spirit I like to see from a Celtic player.'

How I wish I could have justified his confidence in me. My once buoyant spirit was beginning to flag faster than he could have imagined and, in spite of my upbeat prediction about there always being 1978, I just knew it was never going to happen for me as far as Scotland or Celtic, for that matter, were concerned.

My professional life still held some pleasure, of course. In December 1974, we faced Benfica in a UNICEF benefit for children, for instance, and drew 3–3 with them. When Celtic were playing Benfica not so long ago, a newspaper man, Martin Hannan, pushed a letter under my door asking for an interview. The note said I'd been brilliant in that game. Had I really been brilliant? I couldn't tell. I remember only two things about that match: the first was Eusebio running out of the faraway dressing room and blessing himself before he ran out onto the park; and the second a sixty-yard pass which proved there was some kind of telepathy working between me and Jimmy Johnstone. I had picked the ball up right on the edge of our penalty area, then I looked up and sent it swirling away to drop inches over the head of the Benfica defender, Arthur, and right into the path of Jinky, who raced away to score a memorable goal. I knew Jinky was going to run on and I knew I was going to fire over the guy's head. What's more, Jinky knew it too. Brilliant players, and I'm not talking about myself here, just make things look so easy. Some players in middle-of-the-road professional teams think they can do this, that and the next thing and then they start to get all big-headed about their abilities. The truly great players are the ones who make things look simple and, usually, they're the most humble.

Talking of the great players brings Jimmy Greaves to mind. The goal he scored against Tottenham when he was still at Chelsea is worth recollecting all on its own. On that occasion, he beat about five players and stroked the ball into the net. That goal had class stamped all over it and yet it was scored by a man who couldn't get a game for England in the World Cup final against West Germany. To coin Greavsie's own favoured catchphrase, it is indeed a funny old game.

I might have had mince for brains as far as my private life was concerned but the football part of it worked quite effectively. When I was in my late teens, I used to go home at night and think about my mistakes and work out how I could try to rectify them. I can remember thinking about a Rangers forward called Dennis Setterington. I was playing centre half at the time and, while I stood back because I wanted to keep my position, I watched as he ran for goal from around the halfway line and scored. I should have gone over and cut him out and then he wouldn't have had the success he did. I lay awake thinking of this one night, determined that I should not do that again. Images like that wouldn't go away until I had addressed them but it all paid off in a way. Thinking things through like that was what helped me to know instinctively where to go. I would get caught out sometimes with my fitness and my weight but it was just a matter of balance and knowing what to do.

What ultimately brought me down, I suppose, was laziness and lack of motivation, and Davie Hay's departure certainly did contribute to me becoming demotivated. Indeed, I walked out of Celtic, for a second (official) time, just before our 2–1 defeat by Rangers in September 1974, just after Davie had gone. Mr Stein told reporters after the match that I hadn't reported for training for five days. We finally met another five days after that announcement and I told him, in the politest of terms, that I had no intention of playing at the time.

I also gave a rare interview to the newspapers at that time. It wasn't the Gettysburg Address or anything like that but I certainly think I put my point across:

I'm sick fed up with football. It hasn't just happened – the whole thing has been building up for a couple of years. During this time, I've never been really happy and I think the time has come to get out. I wish I hadn't inherited my football ability. The club have been in touch with me but there's no way I'm going back. I've made my mind up. Maybe it's something to do with me being from a village in Fife but I just can't put up with the pressure and the publicity of football. I don't like to be noticed. I want to be an unknown again. This is not a personal action against Celtic. The club have been good to me but I'm finished with the game. I haven't the slightest idea what I'll do now. I'll have to think about that one.

My outburst produced this reaction from the top journalist, Alan Herron, who wrote: 'Having said he will never play again, for anyone, this is a remarkable decision by a brilliant footballer. His value must be close to £300,000.'

Ooh, ya devil! That was some valuation from Mr Herron and, indeed, some speech from me, the Quiet Fella, but at least it had come out in the open. Oh, there were times I'd gone away and nobody knew about it because the club just kept it quiet. And it wasn't just the odd occasion – it happened umpteen times. Mr Stein could be a compassionate man as far as I was concerned. I think, if he had come down hard on me, like he had with other people, then I just might have gone the other way and not come back at all. That idea was never far from my thoughts. The whole situation was bad enough without the manager putting his oar in and, although I'm sure he was tempted to have a right go at me, I reckon he must have thought better of it. Whatever his reasons were, he played that card right. Faced with somebody telling me what to do, I just had the temperament to go and do the opposite. So, if Mr Stein had played the authoritarian, I'd have immediately said cheerio to it all.

Apparently, I also revealed in that press interview that I had been on a course of pills to ease the pressure, although I was no longer taking them, and that I'd also had about six sessions with the psychiatrists, something I've mentioned earlier in this book. And, significantly, I added, 'The wife's fed up with me.'

To be fair, she was not the only one – the only difference was that the others were hiding their frustrations with me better than she did. How did my manager feel? While Herron was delivering his judgment, Stein told the press, 'I saw all the players in the World Cup in Germany and there was only one to compare with Franz Beckenbauer. His name was George Connelly!'

I returned to Parkhead after a while but, to be honest, while the heart might have been in the mix, the head was elsewhere. No, there was nothing Beckenbauer-like about the way I was thinking. And, although my appearances became more and more sporadic, Stein still never gave me laldy for the disappearing acts. I think he believed I could still, on occasion, do a turn for him on the park so he tolerated my excesses and eccentricities. But, as I said already, all the commitments – a big mortgage, cars to run and children to support – and a lame marriage had made me a difficult customer.

By 1975, I suppose the club had finally had enough of my party tricks and the chairman cancelled my contract. After that, there were no bonuses to fall back on – bonuses which paid for all the nice things in life. I was now on £65 a week (£59 after tax etc. had been deducted) and it was actually costing me to play football professionally. I was going up to Parkhead on a Saturday afternoon and playing for the reserves and there would be maybe a hundred people at the game. I got £3 for a win and £1.50 for a draw – it was peanuts. I was continually asking myself, 'What am I doing here?'

The clock was ticking furiously towards a time of reckoning and it came suddenly one morning. I was running around the park, getting hammered in training, with sweat pouring down my body. I felt that my world was about to explode and fragment in front of my eyes and, all of a sudden, I knew I just couldn't be bothered any more. I knew by then that my marriage was over and there was no going back. I also knew that my time with my beloved Celtic had juddered to a halt for the last time. I wanted out; I wanted an escape tunnel. There was no need to look for one, really – I had been digging it for a couple of years and it was there, waiting for me to enter it. What I was about to do was certifiable. I mean, how many players are out of the game when they are only twenty-six years of age? It was nuts – absolutely nuts from start to finish.

They say that, when you are dying, you see all the significant events in your life in flashback. I can confirm that the same thing happened to me when I was in the throes of quitting football. I considered the past; it came to me vividly. Oh, it could all have been different: if Davie hadn't gone to London; if I'd had a different kind of marriage; if I'd met someone who'd have been right for me and I'd been right for her; if I'd lived life more traditionally instead of back to front . . . I even decided I'd have been better going down the pits first and finding something out about the world and its ways before going in to football. And I thought about all those guys I'd never allowed myself to get close to. Jinky, Bobby and Billy – they were all city boys who knew the score whereas I had just been a village boy, trying to learn from them. Billy, my hero, was especially prominent in my thoughts – the best Celtic player there had ever been, as far as I was concerned. Do you know, my hair started going grey when I was in my twenties? I can mind Big Billy calling me Jeff Chandler but it didn't bother me. You can accept anything from your hero. So what if he said that I'd told him I wanted to be a long-distance lorry driver? Maybe I did actually say something like that to him at some point. I just don't know – I find talking about the past confusing sometimes. I remember watching The Everly Brothers on TV one time and Phil Everly said he didn't like talking about the past because of the confusion it brought him so maybe I'm not the only one.

But, as I stepped out of memory mode at the Park that morning, I knew I had learned good things on the pitch and some bad things off it. I knew that, somewhere along the way, I had taken a wrong turn. I looked round at my team-mates – the men I'd shared my life with for a number of years. I knew what I was going to do and, this time, there would be no turning back. There might have been a host of poignant memories in my mind but there was no suggestion of a tear in my eye. The words that came out of my mouth were not perhaps the most eloquent I ever used but they seemed appropriate at the time. 'Oh, f*** it!' I shouted. 'That's me – I'm off!'

I didn't look sideways – I just ran and ran until I was off the park and straight down the tunnel. I changed into my clothes and I hurried away before anyone could say anything – before anyone could attempt to change my mind. Apart from one secret visit to say goodbye to Mr Stein and pick up my jotters, that would be my last time at Parkhead for almost thirty years.

Right then, there was no real sentiment attached to the moment. I was quite happy to get out of it all. I was going to forget the pressures of marriage and being a footballer and start to enjoy myself a bit for a change, wasn't I?

8

DROPPING A CLANGER

DAVID HAY'S STORY

So, how good was George Connelly? Three decades on from
when he was playing, it's a question that still lingers on the
lips and in the minds of many Celtic fans – it's a question that
perhaps can be answered best by someone who played alongside him many times. If I tell you he was a genius, just trust
me and believe it. I don't think anyone could accuse me of
being guilty of overstatement or putting a subjective slant on
it. When you're playing right alongside someone, you can
quickly appraise their worth and, of course, assess their limi-
tations. The only thing George lacked was speed – Mick the
Miller he was not – but he had so much of everything else that
it made up for it. He was extremely proud of his ability to pass
the ball long – he could boot it fifty or sixty yards with pinpoint
accuracy.

Here's a tale to illustrate just how proud he was of this
particular talent. I'd left Celtic by this time but the story goes
that, one day, he sent a long ball up to Dixie Deans. Apparently,
it went slightly adrift, maybe a foot or so, or maybe Dixie had
not moved his body enough to receive it. Anyway, Wee Dixie
is supposed to have turned round and shouted, 'Get it to feet!'
On hearing this, it seems that George thundered up the field
and a mighty punch-up ensued.

It's always difficult to make direct comparisons between players but the best I can do is to say that, in terms of quality, he was to Celtic what Franz Beckenbauer was to Bayern Munich and that is no exaggeration – he was up there with the Kaiser, believe me. The tragedy, however, in making this comparison is that Beckenbauer had his career whereas George curtailed his own career at an embarrassingly young age and wrecked his genius in the process.

When we first met, George was on the ground-staff and I was part-time. We trained together and played in the reserves together along with a group of the other guys. I don't know where we got the Quality Street Gang tag from but what I do know is that we quickly developed a relationship on and off the park. Soon, we were enjoying playing in the same team and enjoying each other's company away from the ground. I wasn't very close to him initially because I studied accountancy until I was nineteen but then, when I went full-time, we became closer.

After that, we seemed to do things in parallel. He was about a year younger than me but we both got engaged quite young and married almost at the same time in 1969. It was then we started to go out together, with our respective wives, Katherine and Christine. When he moved to live in the west of Scotland, there were more nights out together. I stayed in Uddingston and he was in Blantyre so we were on each other's doorsteps. We'd have a right laugh sometimes but it was always gentle fun – nothing outrageous. We'd also go out and have a pint and enjoy one another's company – we just really got on well. My wife had a kid, his wife had a kid. We had another one, so had they. It seemed as if our lives were almost mirror images of each other.

Meanwhile, George's on-field image was blossoming. You'd have to be wearing a blindfold not to see the exceptional talent he had. The first bit of glory came when he played in the 1969 Scottish Cup final and scored that fantastic goal by dispossessing John Greig. I think Greigy tried to recover the situation but found it beyond him. Meanwhile, at the Celtic End, George was strolling round Rangers' goalkeeper Norrie Martin with consummate elegance and tapping it in. The whole thing smacked of class. We, his tight band of pals within the Quality Street Gang (I'm talking about John Gorman, Davie Cattenach, Jimmy Quinn and myself), were so pleased for him. Of course, we would have liked to be playing ourselves that day but we were just delighted that one of our buddies had done it.

After the game, celebrations were in the air and we went through to George's home territory of Kincardine that night. We probably enjoyed that night more than George did – he'd had the glory of playing in the match but we'd had the pleasure and the thrill of watching him. Perhaps the pressure of playing weighed him down a bit but there was nothing to weigh us down. This was the breakthrough for us – one of the gang had dazzled and we were high on it.

I then started playing a bit more regularly and Lou Macari, Kenny Dalglish and Danny McGrain were all in the Celtic first team by this time.

George and I roomed together at that time – we had become really close. The genius that was George was well to the fore by then, of course, but I'd had a close-up preview of it. Midfield, at the back, on the wing . . . he could play anywhere with distinction. I remember, in season 68–69, we played Rangers in the Glasgow Cup final and Big Jock fielded a lot of the Quality Street Gang for that game. He also acted the innovative manager by playing three at the back – this was new ground being broken – so that there was Davie Cattenach and me, with George as the free man. I can't remember whether Colin Stein was playing or not and nor can I remember who the Rangers strikers were but I do know that they fielded a very strong team against what was almost a Celtic reserve side. We beat them 3–1 that day and George was at his classiest. As I said, three at the back hadn't been used a lot but George was the catalyst for the way the whole thing worked.

The fact that Jock Stein had played him in a cup final when he was only twenty is testimony to Connelly's footballing ability, as is the fact that, even before he won that first medal, Stein had taken him to South America for the World Club championships – although he didn't play.

Like I said, he was a guy for all positions but, ultimately, he was to appear regularly at centre half beside Billy McNeill. However, sometimes he and I played together in the centre of defence. Our views on how the game should be played were the same but I believe he was a silkier player than I ever was. Although I didn't have the dominance in the air that Billy had, I reckon George and I could have been the start of the double centre halves, playing from the back. It's true George didn't like playing out-and-out centre half. That's why, later on, he formed the perfect combination with Billy who was, of course, as domineering as any centre half you've ever seen and he offered total security in the air. This is where George and I disagreed. I used to talk about Billy's dominance but George wanted a football-playing centre half, so maybe that was him admitting his own insecurity in the air. George also felt, I think, that Billy didn't fight the case of the individual over things like new contracts. He tended to be a bit insecure with some of the players who were business orientated. He probably didn't understand the business side of things – maybe that's the best way to put it. I don't really know. What I knew for sure was that Stein really loved Connelly as a player.

This brings me to the mystery of the 1970 European Cup final. Ask anyone to chronicle the mistakes of Jock Stein, football manager, and they will look at you as if you have been beaten by the daft brush. Stein just didn't make mistakes; he was a man who didn't tolerate inefficiency or ineptitude; he led by example and rarely, if ever, left his fingerprints on potential disaster; and, yet, to my way of thinking, he dropped a right old clanger the night he left Big George out of the Celtic side that faced Feyenoord in 1970. I think he underestimated the Dutchmen – in fact, I think we *all* underestimated them. If Big Jock had played Connelly in midfield instead of leaving him out, I firmly believe we might not have lost that game. And, if we had taken them to a replay – which was possible in those days because the penalty shoot-out hadn't been invented then – Celtic might well have had two European Cup victories under their belts instead of one. As it was, Jock changed the system from a 4–3–3, brought in an extra striker and dropped George from the midfield, where he had been so dominant against Leeds in the two semi-finals. The way he'd played in those games had made his axing even more difficult to believe.

Leeds were the dominant force in English football at the time and they had players from the very top drawer – the likes of Bremner, Giles, Lorimer, Gray, Charlton, Hunter, Madeley, Jones and Clark – and Celtic weren't expected to beat them. The night before the first leg, we stayed in Harrogate before what was to become part one of the true Battle of Britain. George appeared in both the Leeds games and played brilliantly, scoring in the first minute of the first one. You can get a juggler or a circus act to go out and do the kind of entertaining stuff George did before the Dynamo Kiev game but it takes a football player of genius to do what he did against Leeds. I can't think of too many young players, then or now, who could have played the way he did. What I saw from him over those two games backed up the impression I'd always had of him and, as well as skill, it took real mental strength to play like he did.

That's why it was such a huge pity that, ultimately, he didn't have the mental strength to live through in the west of Scotland. Yes, I think that's the best way to put it – you've got to have a strong mentality to live over here because life is more 'in yer face'. He seemed to be more comfortable living in the west of Scotland when he roomed with me. I'm not trying to fluff myself up – it's just a fact that he felt more at ease when I was with him although I didn't realise the extent of this until much later.

Ironically, I never guessed that there were any problems with the Connellys' marriage and it was only when I looked back that I really appreciated how uncomfortable he was living over in the west. Still, there are a couple of stories that indicate how wrong things were even if, at the time, I wasn't fully aware of how badly wrong.

Sometimes the four of us used to go to a sort of nightclub called Hastie's Farm in Blantyre and we were in there one night when suddenly George came up to me and said, 'That so-and-so's looking at us, Davie.' It was almost as if we should do something about it – as if he thought we should go and give the guy a kicking. I said to him, 'Calm down, George. He's just looking at us because we are who we are.' I think that reaction of his maybe backs up the idea of how uncomfortable he felt being in the public eye and I very much doubt if he'd have behaved the same way had it been on his own turf.

The other time I remember was when Christine phoned me and said George had gone AWOL to Kincardine. She asked me if I would go there and see if I could get hold of him. This was in the days when there were no mobile phones so I went through to Kincardine and finally tracked him down in some bar. He asked me if I wanted a pint and I said OK. Suddenly, he said, 'Why don't you stay through here tonight? It's a good night!'

I told him quite sharply, 'Listen, George, I'm here to rescue you. I don't need someone to rescue me!'

I think those two tales indicate how he was being drawn through to his own territory, the familiar landscapes where he felt safe. The more relevant of the two things, to my mind, was the Hastie's Farm incident. Falling out with the wife or just needing to get away and be by yourself can happen to anybody but George had perceptions of things that simply didn't exist. Now, whether, in George's case, that constituted a quirk of character or a psychological illness, I'm not sure but, when he was playing for Celtic's first team, most folk he came in contact with would never have dreamt he had a problem.

Nowadays, any player who has a mental health problem or an addiction can go for therapy at The Priory or some other upmarket rehabilitation place. In fact, it's getting to the stage where, if you haven't been admitted somewhere, you're not really a star – although maybe that's being a bit too harsh on some of the people who genuinely do need help.

When George played for Celtic's first team, he certainly wasn't a heavy drinker – definitely no heavier than me. There's no denying we enjoyed our pints together – other than that night when I had to perform the rescue act in Kincardine – but I think a lot of his drinking happened after he had left Celtic. Progressively, George's drinking became more frequent and on a grander scale whereas I was able to curtail it so that it was only a social thing. During the time we played together at Celtic, we wouldn't normally go out through the week. If there was a mid-week match, then, yes, we might have a wee swally and maybe a few when we went out on a Saturday night after the game because that was when we felt we could switch off. But I would honestly say that, at that time, neither of us were overindulging in the drink department.

However, in the years after I left Celtic, things changed. George seemed to be busy building a platform for himself – one that he was going to dive off and land in a deep hole. How many tragedies does a man need? George suffered the break-up of his marriage and the loss of a wonderful professional career. Then he landed up in junior football at a level that was away below him. Junior football and George Connelly should never have been twinned.

Of course, during this time, we drifted apart but, many years later, when I came back to Scotland to manage Motherwell, I would phone him and ask him to come through for the game but he just wouldn't come. I'm not really sure why – he always did have his enigmatic side. And, when I had a pub in Paisley, I said to him we should meet up regularly – not every week, maybe, but certainly every second week. He would be due to come through on the Friday, stay overnight and then come to the game on Saturday but, inevitably, I would get a phone call at about 4 p.m. on Friday to say he couldn't make it. I think that backs up my theory that he just wouldn't be comfortable in that environment even though, by this stage, he'd been out of football for quite some time. In my opinion, it's some kind of psychological problem that prevents him from seeing things as other folk see them and he probably still has it today. He's a highly emotional person and a soft, soft person but a really lovely person as well.

For all that, he's also got a sharp sense of humour. I can still see him one Saturday night when I came back up from Chelsea. I had gone through to Fife for a drink. George had a dog and, when I was ushered into the house, George was pretending to be asleep. The dog was getting set to growl at me and I suppose I flinched. George kind of woke up, laughing. 'Aye, Davie,' he said, 'you're feart of the dog, aren't you?'

When I close my eyes, I can still see the football genius that George once was standing next to me on a football park. I particularly remember a game against Hibs, who were a good team at the time. Big Billy McNeill got injured during the match and so I moved to the back to play alongside George. This suited him fine as he'd always had this theory about how good we'd be playing together at the back. At that time, you didn't overplay in that position – you tended to move the ball forward more quickly and the forward ball was always preferred to the square pass. Anyway, I remember getting the ball that afternoon and passing it to George in the penalty box. We were down 1–0 but, instead of going for goal, he sent it back to me and he was actually smiling as he did so. This was a guy who felt deeply uncomfortable in unfamiliar social environments yet here we were playing in front of 40,000 people and he was showboating his skills. Big Jock was out of the dugout and beginning to breath fire and the Jungle was getting distinctly restless. You did not mess around in those circumstances – not unless you were George Connelly.

In those days, central defenders didn't pass the ball to central defenders as they do now. We left playing passing football to the midfielders – to men like Bobby Murdoch and Bertie Auld, two of the greatest midfielders you could get. By the time I got the ball back from George, I had lost my bottle. I was thinking, 'I'm not going to pass it to you again – I'm going to clip it forward.' And, as I did so, I heard someone laughing. The smile had turned to laughter. He was some player and he's some man.

9

THIS WAY DOWN

I think it's probably time to round up the facts and attempt to put them in to some kind of perspective. In 1975, the marriage which had torn me into little pieces was about to become a statistic of the divorce courts. It may have been finished but it was not to be forgotten – believe me, you never lose the bitter after-taste of divorce. The career that had taken me to the highest professional altitudes had suddenly vanished into thin air and, even though it was all my own doing, I still regretted the fact that I was no longer in the job I loved. The club still held my registration but that was merely a technicality. My association with them was just another part of history – an unfulfilled, unfortunate history, perhaps, but history nonetheless.

So there I was – halfway out of a marriage and all the way out of employment. And, in the little purpose-built dream world that I occupied, I imagined myself to be happy. Underneath it all, I suppose I knew I had perpetrated one of the biggest blunders known to sporting man. Some people would sacrifice anything just to play for a club like Celtic. And what would they give to have the bonus of playing for Scotland? I mean, had things been different, I could have got my act together, lost the bit of weight I had put on, persuaded the club I was worth another contract and maybe gone back to something approaching normality. It wasn't as if I wasn't a good trainer. One day Jock Stein had taken me aside and told me I was the best trainer at Celtic Park. Yet I'd tossed that career into a dustbin as if it had no more value than an old sweetie paper. So, when you are presented with a set of circumstances like that, sometimes it's necessary to find oblivion – a place where it is easy to forget the mistakes and what might have been. I found the most practical solution in the world and I began to drink with the enthusiasm of a fish – a big, thirsty fish.

The house in Blantyre was duly sold and I saw to it that the kids were properly looked after. It's desperately embarrassing when I look back on it but, towards the end of my career, I had been getting subs from my mother just to make ends meet. By the time the sale of the house had been finalised, I owed her £300 and that debt was quickly paid out of the remaining funds and, if I remember rightly, after that, there was around three or four thousand pounds left over. I didn't waste too much time in spending them.

By this time I had returned to my natural habitat, although not my own home. I had been desperate to leave the big city and here was my opportunity. I'd been renting out my little house in Kincardine to a lassie for a while but had given her notice to quit. While I was waiting for her lease to run out, I stayed with my brother Dan for a wee while. This was my initiation to what you could call the real deal. I was practising – limbering up for my A (Alcoholic) Levels. It was drink, drink, drink. It was like a scene out of *The Student Prince* but, in this instance, there was no handsome figure of Edmund Purdom to brighten proceedings with a song – not that singing interested much us in those days.

Now, my brother Dan had been down the pits but he wasn't working a lot then – he was fully occupied looking after me. Even after a career with Celtic, I still wasn't street smart enough to escort myself safely through life. However, Dan had more than enough savvy for us both so we were ideally suited. He wasn't what I would call a real drinker although some people might contest that statement. I'd say he was more a bottle of beer man who would take the odd half now and again. But that was the perfect combination as he'd be at my side when I began to fall about. You would never see him drunk and thus he was able to steer me away from potential trouble spots and there were plenty of those to be negotiated.

Can you imagine the number of people who just wanted to walk up to me and tell me what a mug I had been? Complete strangers would sidle up to where I was sitting, squeeze my leg as if they'd known me all their lives and say, 'Talk about throwing your life away ... You're a stupid bastard and no mistake!' When accusations like that were hurled at me time and time again, I found myself biting my lip so hard that I'd sometimes draw blood. I suppose it was a bit like sitting in the stocks and having rotten eggs thrown in your face. Dan, however, was adept at handling embarrassing situations that had the potential for something far more sinister.

Those were the days without doubt. There was no hanging about then. At eleven o'clock in the morning, with my tongue flapping like a shirt on a clothesline on a windy day, we'd be waiting for the pub doors to open. In many ways, I had achieved my ideal dream. The manacles that had bound me were off and I was a free man. The opportunities were unlimited, just like the beverages that I was now about to throw down my neck at every chance. The drinks were mainly on me and, remember, you were getting three spirit measures for £1 at that time. I suppose my favourite beverage, back then, was a double vodka topped up with a Britvic orange juice. I'd have a couple of lagers or lager tops to limber up before getting going with the real stuff.

The disappointing thing was that the pub closed at half past two in those days and suddenly drinkers would find themselves out in the cold till five. The disappointment had no lifespan at all, though. The answer lay in the off-licence. There was a shop across the road in Kincardine where you could get a bottle of sherry for 50p. I developed a liking for sherry. We'd pick up a bottle, drink it in the house and then prepare ourselves for the five o'clock shift. There was no training and no pressure. Life was as sweet as the sherry or so I thought.

Right in the middle of this time, a chance to climb back on the football ladder came along – and this was no bottom-rung opportunity or anything like that. No, this offer came right from the top – Manchester United. This wee guy called Peter Shaw was a friend of mine who used to live in Uddingston. Maybe I had given up on myself but Peter hadn't. He was a trier – I'll give him that. He, like many others, thought it was a crime that I had turned my back on what was potentially a great career and he never stopped reminding me about it. But he did more than talk – he acted.

He knew the United manager, Tommy Docherty, and he wrote to him telling him about my circumstances. Now, I think, at that time, Docherty was looking for a replacement for Martin Buchan, who was injured, so I suppose there was a vacancy at Old Trafford. The Doc knew me from my brief associations with the Scotland squad and he wrote back saying that he would take me down to Old Trafford on trial for a month but he had stipulations. Docherty, aside from knowing that I was on the drink, must have thought I was a bit of a mental case. He made it clear that I had to live the way he wanted me to live. I had to agree to stay in a hotel and abide by his rules and, by that, he meant I had to report to him at nine o'clock every night. In other words, I had to get a halo rather than a life.

I suppose I understood why he was doing this – after all, he'd had some really bad experiences with George Best and he didn't want or need players following in those particular footsteps – but that didn't make it any easier for me. I felt insulted. For all my drinking, I wasn't close to being in Best's league at that time. In my own mind, I had been destined to be a football star, not a drinker, so the inferences in that letter annoyed me and I said thanks but no thanks to The Doc's kind offer.

There was never one moment when I thought I was doing something wrong. I was in Kincardine and happy and Kincardine was never going to be replaced by Manchester – that was my so-called rationale. Can you believe that I said no to one of the greatest football clubs in the world? But, right then, in my head at least, it was not the big deal it seems now. I had been pleased just to get out of football and I had achieved a rhythm in my drinking. I suppose I didn't want anything to knock me off that rhythm – not even the fast-talking Tommy Docherty!

Another offer was to come my way but this was not a football one. Through a guy I knew from Falkirk, I got in tow with a couple of Glasgow boys and they gave me a job lagging pipes in Grangemouth. Believe it or not, I was clearing £115 a week doing this – far more than I earned in my latter days at Paradise. How's that for irony? So now I had more money than ever to donate to my favourite liquid charity. There were several men in that Grangemouth gang who knew their way around a bar and I never missed an opportunity to throw refreshment down my throat.

And yet football still hadn't finished with me. There were still well-intentioned people in this world who thought they could suddenly produce a miracle and make me what I had always promised to be. Falkirk came calling and, in August 1976, much against my better judgement, I joined them on a three-month loan. I mean no disrespect to them but, after playing for Celtic, being a Falkirk player was a terrible comedown for me. I tried to recreate some of the golden days during my spell at Brockville but it was beyond me. Because of my drinking, I had put on enough weight to go up a couple of divisions to heavyweight and take on George Foreman. Never known for being fast out of the traps, I was now appreciably slower. On top of the extra weight I was carrying, I also had a bit of an injury. I really can't remember what the technical term for it was but it affected my groin and, although I played a few times, I couldn't train in earnest and get properly fit.

If I remember correctly, I played for Falkirk eight times but, if I'm honest, I couldn't blame the groin injury for my failure to make it at Brockville. The blame lay solely with me in that I did a bit of drinking and I had no real passion to play for the club. Stories began to circulate that I had turned up gassed for one game. The rumour was that I'd been put under a shower before going on the pitch and then I'd had to be taken off at half-time but not a word of that is true. I had never done anything like that in my life – I would stand up and swear to it on the Bible! Even in the juniors, where I spent the last years of my football life, I would never drink on match days.

I'll tell you what I did do one time, though. I gave this old guy from Kincardine a lift home. He had a miniature of whisky for me and I drank it in the car but that was all – tame stuff in comparison to what folk were saying I'd been up to.

No, my heart never belonged to Falkirk.

Now, maybe I couldn't bring myself to play for Celtic again but that didn't mean I had stopped loving the club. Mr Stein knew that and so he threw me another lifeline. Didn't people ever tire of trying to help me? Apparently not – not even the great man. One day, while I was still on trial with The Bairns, he suddenly appeared at my door and tried to work a miracle cure. That persuasive tongue of his was doing its best to chip away at the pig-headed obstinacy that had invaded my brain and was preventing me from playing the game I loved. He wanted me to make a Celtic return and his message was simple – I could still have the life of a professional footballer. In other words, I'd to stop the drinking, put some polish on my shoes and regain a bit of self-respect. He wanted me to forget the past and try to identify a future.

'There's no reason you cannot come back,' he said. 'Instead of going to places like Brechin and Cowdenbeath, you can go to places like Ibrox and Kilmarnock.'

I can't say it wasn't a tempting offer but I just knew that the condition I was in at the time meant it was out of the question. I'd piled on so many pounds that I literally found it difficult to see my shoes for my belly. How long would it take to get that amount of weight off? Did I want to go through all the physical torture that Stein would have in mind for me? Did I need to go back into the pressure cooker of life that came with being a Celtic player? I hadn't been playing it fair as far as Falkirk were concerned and, deep down, I knew that there was no chance of playing fair with Celtic again. So, as much as it grieved me to do it, I said no to the Big Man once again.

Not that long afterwards, Geordie Miller, the Falkirk manager, came to me and said my three months with the club were up and they wouldn't be offering me a contract. That was me finished with professional football. I went back and entered the Park for the first and only time since I'd left Celtic. I'd just gone to get final clearance from the club and Mr Stein decided to free me there and then.

But he was a man with more surprises up his sleeve than a member of the Magic Circle and he wasn't finished with me yet. 'Do you want a reference from me?' he asked. 'I can write one for you here and now.'

I suppose, at the time, I didn't know where to look with the embarrassment that gave me. I couldn't cope with his

114

kindness and nor could I wait to get out of the door. I declined his offer as politely as I could and hurried out of the Park before any of my former colleagues could see me, as they were out training when I was in his office. What I'd done was certifiable – I'd just refused the offer of a reference from the biggest name in football! I cringe when I think about it now. What a prize that would have been! How much could it have advanced my cause in later life? What, for that matter, would it have been worth on the open market now that such things have become extremely valuable? And, if nothing else, I could have framed it and hung in on my lounge wall. Certain words always come into my mind when I think of that day and, in no particular order, they are 'sad', 'bonkers' and 'madness'.

I don't wish to seem big-headed or anything like that but, if a top player in Italy, France, Spain or Germany had gone so badly off the rails as I had done, I think he would have been offered better support than I got. If I'd played in any of those countries, I reckon something would have been done to help me with the problems I had. I do think Celtic could have done more to help me but they were always thinking about the money side of things in those days. It seems to me that, in football, once you're no good to a club, they put a big boot up your backside. However, maybe I'm being unfair in thinking this about Celtic as they probably realised that I didn't want any help – and I didn't. I wanted away to another place.

Tommy Docherty, who would have managed me if I'd turned up for a World Cup qualifier against Denmark, got it right when he was boss of Chelsea. I met him once and he spoke to me about a player who was on £120 a week. He was playing great stuff so Docherty told him he was putting another thirty quid his way so that he'd be earning £150 a week and, in my opinion, that's what should happen. However, maybe The Doc had the power to do that. Perhaps, unlike Stein, he could just go to his board, tell them he needed something badly and they'd just sign it off.

At Celtic, it wasn't like that. You had to chap on their door – maybe go to the lengths of breaking it down – before you'd be able to talk to them. And, even if you got to speak to them, they'd put up a fight. They played a hard game and not just with me. However, apart from that one time when I came out in sympathy with Davie Hay, I never really tried to take them on. I didn't ask for more money because I knew there would have been no point. Anyway, considering the state of my marriage, it wouldn't matter if they'd given me a thousand pounds a week – the money wouldn't have been any good to me.

After I finished at Falkirk, I went into junior football, first with Tulliallan (my first ever club) and then with Sauchie Juniors, where I stayed for the next five years. I loved some of it and hated some of it but that didn't matter because now it was time to cash in the reality cheque and look in the mirror to see what was staring back. And when I did, the ghost of the so-called great George Connelly seemed to be mocking me. So that was it – I was finished with football for good. The professional boots were hung up or, far more likely, thrown into some corner to gather dust.

I may have been finished with football but I'm sorry to say that drinking had not finished with me. However, I was to discover that there were benefits to be had from visiting a pub on a regular basis. One evening, when I'd been out of the professional game for some months, I was standing as usual at the bar in the Auld Hoose in Kincardine when the woman who would change my life walked in. Helen Blackadder was her name. We started blethering and that was it. Bingo! Yeah,

I was shy but I had known her a few years back when I was married and she was a beautiful-looking woman. I didn't find it difficult to go and speak to her because I had a couple of drinks inside me and that always gave me a wee buzz of confidence.

That night, Helen asked me if I'd give her and her pal Roseina a run to Falkirk but there was no way I could do it as, at the time, I was banned from driving. So I walked them up the road to my house and gave them a cup of tea. I think they later had to call a taxi because it was too far to walk and Roseina didn't keep very well.

Not long after that, we started seeing each other. Then someone told her I was going out with another woman. I may have been a footballer but I never was a ladies' man and I really wasn't seeing anyone else. It caused us to fall out and she went off to Australia for a year. However, soon we were writing to each other and things seemed to be back on track. Because of matters that are better kept private, she used to be embarrassed by our association and, when she was in Australia, she didn't want anyone to know that we were still in touch so she used to call me Ralph Puddock. What a name to choose! Anyway, she came back and that was it – we were bound together.

I had never thought about my life in any depth. It had consisted of being at school and then being a football player. I was never the type to plan anything out – I just went with the flow. Soon the flow was telling me that I should get married for a second time. I was never going to argue against that but I should have given Helen far more consideration, of course, because thoughts were running through my head – mad thoughts about how good life was when I had a glass in my hand.

I suppose, at that time, I was drinking on a semi-professional basis. I was quite good at it but a long way from being the finished article. Had I only known what going down the drink road would really entail, I doubt if I would have taken a few smalls steps on it, never mind follow it for miles.

10

MY FALLEN HERO

HELEN'S STORY

If you managed to capture a team of wild stallions, stuck a few harnesses on them, pointed them in the direction of Glasgow and tied George Connelly to them, I doubt if they would have been able to drag him more than a hundred yards in the direction of No Mean City. You can just imagine him digging his heels in so hard that would leave you thinking that a mechanical digger had been at work. The fact is that George and Glasgow are not the ideal mix. He has always told me that, every time he goes through there, the well-meaning fans of Celtic want to kill him with kindness by pouring so much drink down his throat that he feels he could drown at any minute.

He went to Glasgow to attend Jimmy Johnstone's funeral, of course, but that was always going to be an acceptable exception. But, prominent in my mind is the memory of another occasion where he broke his own rule and went through to the big city. We were separated at the time. It's just as well – I had reached the end of what was to be an extremely long tether with his behaviour. Separated? Well, that was the theory but, after I've revealed what our relationship is like, you'll understand that George has never been very far away from me or my home.

There are two sides to my man. One is the very acceptable

119

– he can be very gentle, generous and caring. Everybody likes that side of him and I just love it and wish it would never go away. There are times when I'm so proud of that side of him that I find it hard to express it in words. But then there's the other side – the one that emerges when he's had enough drink to float an ocean-going liner – and you don't want to become over familiar with this side or even acknowledge its existence. It's not that he's foul-mouthed – I've have never heard a bad word come out of him. And it's not that he becomes critical of folk – I've hardly ever heard him be abusive or badmouth anyone. Unlike so many drunks, he doesn't get nasty, aggressive or anything like that – it's just that, when he's drinking, he gets just so stupid I want to shake the life out of him. When he's like that, I feel like I can't stand him and I don't want him near me.

Anyway, let's get back to that day when he broke his own rule about steering clear of Glasgow. It was Christmas and someone had organised a taxi to take him there for some sort of special celebration. When he got back he was scarcely able to stand and he thought he'd just turn up at my place and I'd be happy to see him. He thought wrong! I soon put him on the right track. 'You're not on, George!' I said – or words to that effect. The way I saw it, at the time, the drinking had got worse. It now had him in its own private headlock and I was powerless to do anything about it.

Our son David was very young then so, that night when George got back from Glasgow in such a state, I took David up to my mum's house because I couldn't bear letting him see his dad like that. I left David with Mum so that I could concentrate on dealing with the rag doll that was George. Thinking that I would hand over the responsibility to someone else, I drove him to his niece's house. It was impossible. He might have been three sheets to the wind but he still had a mind of his own. I told him he had to stay at his niece's and I was going back up the road for David.

'You're no' going anywhere!' was the reply.

'Sorry, George, but I'll have to go.'

'Well, I'm coming with you.'

Somehow, we got back into the car again but there was to be mental torture ahead of me. I drove down to the pub, thinking that might be a more attractive proposition than his niece's place. If I could get him out of the car quickly, I could make my getaway. One thing was certain – he wasn't coming back up to my door like that. David was too young and not mentally equipped to deal with seeing him in that state. George did get out of the car but he wasn't going anywhere – not even into the pub – and, as I made to drive away, he suddenly threw himself across the bonnet of the car with his face almost glued to the windscreen. That face, bloated by alcohol, was not pin-up material and it was not the one I had fallen for, the one that I adored.

I remember that, while this was happening, the car radio was playing one of my favourite songs – Bette Midler's 'Wind beneath my Wings'. I don't think there's ever been a more poignant moment in my life.

Did you ever know that you're my hero . . .

Those words had the effect of putting a chainsaw to work on my emotions. I broke down and sobbed uncontrollably. Here was a man who had been the hero of tens of thousands of people; he had reached the top of his profession; he was, as they say, a legend; but now this legend, this hero, was in danger of drowning in an ocean of alcohol. And the lyrics continued to punch home the pain:

and everything I would like to be?
I can fly higher than a eagle,
'cause you are the wind beneath my wings . . .

At that moment, my wings wouldn't have taken me off my feet, let alone into the skies above and, for the first time in my marriage, I knew that I was beaten – I couldn't handle it any more. This was a job for someone else, someone far stronger than little old me. Alcohol, that crazy potion which poisons the brain, was bringing our marriage down. I had tried to bear the load but now the load was simply too heavy.

As well as the song lyrics, there were words coming from George's lips. They were just about coherent – 'I love you, Helen!' – and they only made me cry even harder. He loved me? Well, I loved him back. I always had, ever since the first time I had met him, and probably always would – no danger about that – but I had to find a solution for a problem that was very real at that moment. I had to take a drastic course of action. Eventually, I knew what I had to do and I drove down to the police station and prepared myself to report my helpless husband. I told George to stay in the car and, for once, he did as he was told.

I went in and the words came spewing out. 'I'm married to George Connelly – you'll maybe know him? He's had too much to drink and he'll no' let me get up the road.'

The policeman I saw was very understanding. If I remember correctly, his father or somebody close to him had a drink problem so he had first-hand experience in this kind of thing. He came out to the car and whatever it was that he said worked. George went into the police station without a murmur. The transformation was incredible. Suddenly, the helpless drunk had gone and we had a wee lamb in our hands. The policeman told George to go into a back room and he turned to me and said, 'Right, away you go, hen.'

Did it help? Well, it certainly helped me that day but I don't suppose it really did anything for George. As I remember it, he went into a back room and had a long chat with the policeman before being released without any charge, of course. Then he walked into the village and bought some more drink! Funnily enough though, the next Christmas, when George was temporarily off the booze, he was out jogging and bumped into that same policeman. He stopped George and they had a chinwag. The guy was surprised not only because George was sober but also because he looked so well.

It would be nice to end on that note and say everything else in my garden was rosy but that would be the Hollywood way and this is reality. Still, you learn a lot from situations like that. A lot of people are touched by alcoholism – it doesn't just affect the alcoholic but all those around the person too. Being an alcoholic doesn't make you a bad person but it's so difficult to live with and there have been times, like the occasion when George came back from Glasgow, when I've found it difficult – sometimes impossible – to cope with it.

But, when I look back on my life with George, it isn't always painted black. There's the other side of George that I described earlier. When George was sober, he could be the most caring person in my world. He adores Sharon and Susan, his children from his first marriage, and I know that adoration would have been repeated if our first child had survived.

In 1981, at a time when his drinking was on the right side of the line (well, just about), we had a beautiful, full-term daughter. She weighed 7lb 1oz and she had strawberry blonde hair, similar to George's first daughter, Sharon, from his first marriage, but sadly she was stillborn. It was a horrendous experience and I was very lucky to survive. Even today, I don't like discussing the subject. It was a rare condition – only one in 3,000 suffer from it – called vasa previa and it is potentially disastrous. The baby shares the womb with a time bomb which goes off at birth as the contractions can cause severe blood loss for the baby and the mother.

How did the loss of our daughter affect us? If I say that we never discussed it until recently, you can almost weigh its effect. George, in particular, had always refused to speak about it and, when he and I sat down to talk about it, we had a bit of a cry and then we quickly had to change the subject because it was so upsetting – and that's a quarter of a century later. However, I still have photographs of our wee girl.

Funnily enough, at the hospital, I had told the nurse I didn't want my husband coming in for the birth. She said she thought I'd got my man all wrong and that he was really kind and caring – a nice guy, she insisted. When the tragedy happened, I found out for myself just how right the nurse had been. This was when I really got to know my husband. His attentiveness meant that we grew closer and all that caring helped me immensely. He'd try to cheer me up by promising me this and that – a big house, a better car – but all I wanted was for us to be happy and generally we were in those days, especially when David George Connelly was born on 30 September 1983. He weighed in at a gorgeous 8lb 10oz and, not long after he was born, the hospital radio played 'Isn't She Lovely?' – it had been dedicated to me by a doting father.

On the whole, those were wonderful days but wonderful days have a nasty habit of ending sooner that you would have wished. George was haunted by the past and what had happened to him. I'd tell him there were people who had been through much worse than he had but you could tell he was embarrassed when, for instance, Davie Hay and his wife came here in a big car to visit us one time. I can remember it fine because everybody in the street was talking about their big, flash car.

We went over to the local and had a good night. I can always mind coming back to the house and Davie and George were in the kitchen, helping themselves to a hotpot that I had cooked. They were sitting at a wee, old-fashioned table that my mother had given us. We hadn't been married for long and we didn't have the spare room sorted properly. I think Davie and his wife slept in a three-quarter bed and I'm sure Davie's feet were hanging out of the end of it. This didn't bother me one little bit but it bothered George. We were just living in that wee house on the main street. We didn't have money but we were surviving.

Later, when the drinking got worse, George would come back from his sprees with some kind of present or other. This was a peace offering – his way of saying sorry in the only way he knew how. One day, he arrived back with a microwave oven tucked under his arm. If I hadn't felt so angry, I would have laughed because it did look quite comical. But my focus of attention was on him rather than the microwave. I simply didn't have the patience in those days. 'Look at the state you're in!' I snapped.

It's amazing how unrepentant and thick a drunk can be. 'That's a good microwave I've got you, Helen,' was his response.

I thought of other times I had received these presents of the conscience. Once he said, 'Look, Helen, that's a nice, wee patio I've built for you.' He was as proud as if he'd built me a house. Yes, sure, it was nice to have that wee patio in the garden but I'd rather have had a sober husband any day.

If we saw George the drunk coming about the home back then, David and I would just lock the doors because we didn't want him in the house in that state. It wasn't just as if it was a one-off. It was destined to go on and on for years. At first we'd take him back but then he would go out and start all over again the next morning. So, after I left him, I told him that, if he was drinking, he would have to go to his own place.

125

My reply regarding the microwave came in the form of a scream. 'Look, you take that thing with you and get out!' With the microwave still under his arm, he crossed the road and went away to the pub. What happened to the microwave? We never saw it again. I think someone in the pub offered him a pie to put into it. But, in this house, we've got a few microwaves and kettles and other stuff that we've acquired courtesy of the drinker in George.

At that time, as I say, we were back and forth in our marriage. George was telling me that, if I couldn't help him, then nobody would be able to. He was always apologetic – sorry for this, sorry for that – but he said he couldn't change without me. He promised he would try his best to give up the drink. It's difficult to shut the door on people when they're in trouble. I wouldn't have treated a dog like that so, when his promises came to nothing, I found myself relenting and allowing him to stay in our lives.

It was all so different when we met. It was March 1977 and my friend Roseina and I were going through to Falkirk but we had an hour to wait in Kincardine for our connecting bus. We never did catch that bus – what I did catch was George Connelly's eye in the Auld Hoose Bar. We'd gone in there to pass some time instead of standing out in the cold. George was standing at the bar and the first thing I noticed about him was his lovely eyes. They were like deep pools and you could imagine yourself diving into them. But there was something else in them that was very attractive – sadness. It was a sadness that tempted you to explore it. I felt sorry for him because he was standing there, all alone.

He sent us over a couple of drinks, we got chatting and, from there on in, I only ever wanted to be with him. I didn't know anything of his past at that time. I didn't know he had been a famous footballer. I was totally unaware that he was probably quite disturbed at this stage of his life and was blotting out the pressures with alcohol.

It was a funny relationship because he didn't want to go anywhere where people would notice him. Later on, he would get invites every year to go to functions – player-of-the-year awards, supporters' dances, that kind of thing – and I would be quite excited, thinking I could get a new dress to wear. But we never did go. Instead, we'd be sitting down on those old bus seats in the Auld House, where someone was playing a squeezebox and you couldn't see a yard ahead of you for cigarette smoke. But at least he was getting peace for most of the time – he just wanted to live a quiet life.

What I learned quickly that first evening was that he was a very complex person and he was forever occupied with his thoughts. But, whatever those thoughts were, he didn't seem to want to share them with anyone.

To begin with, I think he did like me but I got the impression that he wasn't really ready to start a relationship so it started off as nothing too serious. But try telling a young lady that when she's keen on a guy. I went away on a girls' holiday and found I was thinking about him all the time. When I got back, I went up to his house in Hawkhill Road, knocked on the door and discovered that he didn't expect to see me. He was entertaining someone – another lady friend – and I fell apart on the spot. What is it they say about hell having no fury like a woman scorned? I was so upset that I phoned a male pal and tearfully blurted out my suspicions. This guy was a bit of a hothead and he came flying round to the house to remonstrate with George. He stood outside the house, threatening all sorts of retribution. How did it calm down? Well, he never saw anything of George because he, quite rightly, kept his head down. My friend took me home and, on the way, he told me that I was never to see the so-and-so again.

My pal's intervention must have left an imprint on George's brain because he used to sleep at the front of the house but quickly changed to the back bedroom after that incident. He must have thought this guy was going to shoot him or something daft like that.

I was due to leave for Australia on a working holiday not long after that happened. One of my brothers, David, was out there with his new wife, Linda, and they had sent me a ticket. I had a fabulous time and tried my best to forget about George. I met a lovely big Frenchman and a couple of Aussies also took my eye but I was forever wondering what Mr Connelly was doing back at home.

Then a friend of mine sent me a newspaper cutting which said that tragically George's brother, Dan, had been killed on the roads. That cutting gave me a real shock. Next, I received a letter from George. He had gone to the bother of finding my address in Queensland. It was clear from the letter that he was shattered by his brother's death – they had been very close. I wrote back and then we spoke on the phone. We carried on writing to each other and, by Christmas, I was home.

There were no mobiles then and I didn't have a phone in the house. However, my neighbour had a telephone and soon George and I were using it to keep in touch. We had arranged to meet one evening but, when we did, the weather was atrocious so we just went to his place. Temperatures were well below freezing and there was more snow than you see on Christmas cards. Soon, all transport was cancelled and weather warnings were being repeatedly broadcast. 'The best advice is to stay where you are. Unless it is essential, don't go out – don't travel.'

How happy was I? Listen, just like the song, I was walking in a winter wonderland. Dean Martin might have been singing it. Who cared? I knew I had found my soulmate in life. We were stranded at his house in Kincardine together but this wasn't the kind of confinement that caused discontent. I was so happy being with him and I knew that I only wanted to make him happy. I never thought of him as a footballer – we never mentioned the fact or even spoke about the game for that matter. By this time, I knew that he'd walked away from it all and was happier talking about other things so I just left him with all his thoughts and enjoyed being in his company.

He had all the qualities I appreciated in a man – he was respectful, kind, considerate and quiet – and there was an innocence about him and a strength at the same time. He didn't speak badly of anyone and adopted the attitude that what had happened to him was so much water off a duck's back. But there was no doubting that he was sensitive and coped with things far better after he had sunk a few drinks.

Well, in the beginning he did. Sometimes he had a lot to put up with. If we were out for a drink, for instance, remarks would be made – cheeky remarks. Someone would come up and tell him how much of a stupid bastard he had been. I'd ask, 'Who was that?' and George would reply, 'I haven't got a clue!'

Things like that were said quite a lot but good comments would sometimes be made too. One of his goals for Celtic used to be shown before a certain TV football programme. We went into a Fife club one evening and it came on television. You could almost see George's head tuck into his shirt collar. If anyone remembers Smiffy in *The Beano*, that was George. He was as uncomfortable with praise as he was with criticism.

Socialising at this time still wasn't a problem. We got engaged and planned our wedding for 27 October 1979 – a happy day, indeed. All the players of Tulliallan FC attended the evening celebrations and then we spent the night in the Dunmar House Hotel. That night, the professional footballer in him emerged – it might have been our wedding night but he asked for a television to be put in the room so that he could watch *Scotsport*! I didn't mind that. We continued our honeymoon in Aberfoyle at one of the seven farms owned by one of my friends, John Cameron. A nice man and a good friend, John was a former president of the National Farmers' Union in Scotland and he was credited with being the European Union's biggest sheep farmer.

At that point, George was still training. I can still see him running up and down the farm roads, with three jumpers and a bin bag on. Things were all still good then. We just loved each other's company and, even at that time, I still didn't knew the full story about why he'd left football.

George would sometimes jokingly say, 'Your dad must have said I was a catch!' and I'd reply, 'No and I never even thought of it in those terms.' And I didn't. George once bought me a gold chain and he put one of his medals on it. I never ever wore it. I just thought it was too flash. But they were the good times.

I always thought I could make George happy, give him happiness. Sometimes I wonder if I got that right. Sometimes I was actually a bit too frightened to explore the sadness in those lovely eyes. Sometimes I don't even know if he's told us the right story about things. I remember only once he wanted to open up. He was awfully upset and wanted to tell me something. But I didn't really feel able to cope with what he was going to tell me. Although he spoke to me about happy times at Celtic, he spoke about some terrible things that used to happen in his life. What were they? I don't know. They are buried somewhere inside him. I still don't know – they'll probably never be exhumed. But, right back in the early days of our marriage, I wasn't to know then that the next twenty-eight years would be an uphill struggle for both of us.

He was always so shy. For instance, when we went shopping, you knew something was wrong because George would prefer to sit in the car rather than come into the supermarket. Maybe it was because it wasn't long after he had played for Celtic and he couldn't cope with the attention. Then I started to notice that he would have a wee drink before going out and then a wee bit more than other people while we were out. But it still wasn't really a problem – or, if it was, I wasn't aware of it. I wasn't conscious that it was interfering with our lives but he was probably doing a lot of drinking when he began playing and training for Tulliallan.

When David was born, George was a brilliant dad – he did all the feeds and all the caring. He did loads of things with David as a baby. But he became friendly with one of the Tulliallan players, an Andrew McGuinness, and I got friendly with Agnes, his wife, and that's probably when the real trouble started. Agnes and I would sit in with the kids because that's what we liked doing and those two would be away to all the clubs. I can remember we were quite happy to let the two of them go out. Sometimes, on a Sunday morning, he'd be getting his shoes ready and I'd say, 'You're no' going to go oot again, are you?' But he was and he did.

As things got progressively worse, I gradually started to make a life for myself elsewhere. Things I should have been doing with my own family I started doing with my mum – going on picnics and things like that. George, by now, had a licence to do what he liked. He was still keeping fit and we'd have nice meals together but we should have been doing things together instead of him going out drinking. But, there again, lots of women are married to men who work away and they seldom see each other. But the way we organised our lives allowed him to get into a rhythm with the alcohol. When David was older, he asked me if his dad and I had ever gone on a holiday together and I had to say that, apart from our honeymoon, we hadn't.

I was drinking less and less in those days because I was getting to detest the sight of alcohol, let alone the taste of it. Eventually, I stopped going out socially with George. His drinking began to make me ill. I can't say it didn't affect me because it did. I went to the doctor and he said he would try to help me. I also read extracts from an Al-Anon book and it told me how much this kind of thing would get to me. Until drinkers like George wise up, those close to them begin to plan their funerals every time they go out on a bender. I'd constantly be asking myself if this was the time he was going to end up killing himself with drink. Love was a solid citizen, though. I might have been down but I was always fighting his corner. Some of the doctors I saw during this time were good – they'd be very sympathetic – but others were less so. I remember one of them said, 'You could tie him to that table over there but he's not going to stop drinking until he wants to do so himself.'

I was naive in those days and I kept wondering why was he not getting help. To my way of thinking, he needed somewhere to dry out, someone to offer him a comfort blanket. When his drinking got really bad, I even hoped that it would deteriorate even more, so that they could take him into hospital and cure him completely. But now I know that doctor was right – George is the only one who can really do that.

I left George for the first time around 1986. He was working at Torness at the time and he was starting to lose work. The van used to come for him but sometimes he was a wee bit ill with the drink and couldn't go. I was going out to work myself and, on those days when he hadn't gone to work, I would come home to find that the bird had flown. So it had got to the stage where I was really beginning to get a bit peed off with the situation. I had friends telling me that I had to do something about it but still I'd tell myself if only I could keep the house a bit tidier, make myself look a bit nicer, keep things calm, he wouldn't want go out. Who was I kidding? Only myself! He was obviously missing that buzz – the buzz that came with playing football in front of thousands of passionate people.

So, I moved in with my mum and George got a house of his own. David would only have been about four then. When I left him, George was lying in his bed – yet another morning after the night before. The doctor had told me that, if an alcoholic loses his home, the shock of it can sometimes be enough to make him want to get himself sorted out. We'd see.

Then I went back to Australia to try and make a new life for David and myself. Oh, I tried so hard to make a wee life for myself but, once again, the pull of love was stronger than everything. I thought I might meet someone to make me forget George but the truth was I never met anyone who remotely came close. So I went back.

This schizophrenic side of George's nature remained in place. When we wasn't drinking, he was another person – caring, considerate, concerned about his family – but the drinking man was something else – carefree, disappearing for days or even weeks, so inconsiderate. Now I was back on the roller coaster that was life with George – the roller coaster that took you high but that also took you to depths you could not imagine.

One day, I was doing the ironing and listening to the radio. The show's presenter was Scotty McClue, one of those cheeky guys who invites people to phone up his show. A woman was on the line and she said her husband had been drinking since eleven o'clock in the morning. The radio guy exclaimed, 'That's terrible!' but I all I could think was 'I wish!' At that time, I hadn't seen George for four days and I thought to myself, 'Why am I accepting the unacceptable?' I felt as if I was beaten again – just like the time I'd witnessed him draped across the windscreen of my car. I had tried everything I could think of – getting doctors involved and whatever – to help him but none of it had worked. I put the iron down, leaned over the board and began roaring and greeting.

What could I do? I looked up the number of the Samaritans and they, in turn, gave me the number of Al-Anon, the organisation whose book I had read. They're there to help families affected by alcohol. It was a wonderful find and a wonderful friend. You quickly learn from them that the only person you can change is yourself and how important it is to look after number one. Now, I'm not going to begin preaching their mantra but they encouraged me to detach myself. It wouldn't help George, of course, but it was the only way I could help myself. I had to place more importance on myself and to help David. I could have ended up in a psychiatric hospital if there hadn't been some assistance. Yes, the only person you can look after is yourself and it helps your partner because you're not nagging or hiding bottles. I've managed to teach my son some of what I learned and I suppose it must have rubbed off on him.

Al-Anon also taught me that you take one day at a time. Let's suppose today, for instance, is a good day, you are grateful for that. You don't project any further than this. I asked an Al-Anon representative if someone from AA could come out and speak to George and an Irish guy called Matt came over. After that, George started seeing Matt regularly and, at first, he seemed to take to it OK. But then they wanted him to go to meetings further afield and he just didn't want to do it. He said he didn't feel anonymous. Recently, he's gone back to seeing Matt quite regularly again, so that's good, but it's early days.

The bad memories are a fearsome force and they will not go away. I remember telling George that, any time he was thinking about coming to the house carrying a cargo, he would definitely not get in. If the barmaid in Clackmannan phoned to tell me that they had Geordie in, I would say to David, 'Right, batten down the hatches! Get the doors locked!'

This was still happening only two or three years ago. But that was the insanity of it all – I didn't want him going out drinking but, at the same time, I didn't want him in the house. One time, I remember he tried to open the door two nights in a row and couldn't get in, so he spent both nights in the shed. There's a comfy chair in there and, on the second night, although I was furious with him, I couldn't help flinging a cover in for him.

Another night was particularly terrible. I saw the white hair coming and I just sensed we were going to have trouble. When he got to the house and realised I was serious about not letting him in, he started banging on the back door and then on the front door. They're really strong doors yet he was trying to kick them in. I phoned the police and told them they'd have to come out. OK, George was my husband but he didn't stay with me any more. Just as suddenly as he had arrived, George scampered off. His sixth sense that the police were on their way must have kicked in.

When the policeman arrived, he asked, 'What does he look like?'

I replied, 'He's over six foot and he's got pure white hair!'

The cop said, 'If we see him, he'll have a night in the cells!'

And that's when I crumbled. I was overcome by guilt. 'What happens if they get him?' I asked myself. I needn't have worried because they never did.

Strangely, George and I have never had terrible arguments – in fact, we've never spoken to each other unkindly. I decided the harsh words were best left to the doctors to deliver. One of the doctors really didn't approve of George and he asked him where he got the money to drink from.

George said, 'People just give me it.'

The doctor was incredulous. 'People just give you it?' he asked in disbelief before going on to give him a right rollicking.

But none of it made any difference, really. It would get to the stage where I'd just have to go and get some tablets from the doctor to calm him down. By then, my nerves would be shattered. George would sometimes stay at his daughters' for a day or two but then they would phone me and ask if he could come back. They want their dad when he's sober but they don't want him when he's drunk – and quite rightly so.

'We've got Dad here,' they'd say. 'What are we going to dae?'

I'd say to them, 'Well, I'm no' going to help him again.'

But, of course, I'd end up going to his daughters' and then heading for the doctor's again. Sometimes, when the folk at the surgery weren't helpful, I used to lose my temper with them but I'm a lot calmer nowadays. I think I've just matured enough to be able to cope with this disease. George's drinking started slowly and then it began to speed up but, in fairness to him, I think he did need to blot things out. Maybe it was his only way of insulating himself against the memories. I used to think that he needed to get things out of his system. I wondered if he felt he'd let people down when he walked out on Celtic and how it really made him feel when people were coming up to him and telling him he was an effing idiot. These may seem like small excuses for such overindulgence but we all cope with difficult things in different ways.

To begin with, he would go on the drink for long spells but, back then, he wasn't drinking the same quantities as he does now. No, now it's progressed – it's got to the stage where he's totally anaesthetising himself. He wakens up and, although he knows he shouldn't be drinking, he just goes at it again. Within a week, he's in a sorry state. How long does it last? For as long as it takes me to relent and go and help him. If I finally shut that door for good and say that's it, I'm not going to assist him any more, I don't know if he'd ever get off it himself.

However, when he comes off it, the sorrow is such that it is only a small improvement on a sob story. 'I'm going to beat this thing, Helen,' he'll say. I'm no' going to drink. I don't want to drink. I never did.'

But the fact is that I'm getting too old for this kind of thing. I've heard it all before. I need more deeds, less words. You know, David and I never saw a lot of his drinking because he just went back to his own place. And when he didn't, I used to like the dark nights because I didn't want anyone seeing him in a state like that. The summer nights were not so clever. Maybe it's being big-headed but, when I go to Al-Anon, I'm with women who've all got husbands who are drinkers but I always felt that their husbands wouldn't be getting spoken about the day after their next drinking binge. Mine would. Folk would be saying, 'Did you see that George Connelly who used to play for Celtic? What a state he was in!'

And yet I know the score now. This is a man who used to play for Celtic and was hero-worshipped for it. He has medals to prove it (although he plans to sell them in the near future) and yet he is so modest and so grounded. You know, I think he has about half a dozen medals left plus his Player of the Year award and they were lying in a sorry state in a wee box. It was me who salvaged them. George didn't even know where they were. David and I told him they were in a bank in case he thought about giving them away. The only thing that seems to mean anything to him is a Sekonda watch that lights up. He thinks it's a great thing and still wears it but, apart from that, he's not interested in the flash things of life. He adopts the attitude that, when you come from nothing, you can go back there very easily.

Right now, as I write this and touch whatever I can for luck, George is on the Antabuse tablets. Do I think they will work?

Well, they didn't before but these are new ones and they're supposed to be an improvement on the last kind. They might just work. Certainly, things have been better lately. He's trying hard, that's for sure. The writing of this book has helped him in so many ways because, to some extent, he's at last had to open up and let out some of those demons that have haunted him for decades. It's fascinating. Sometimes, David and I just sit back and listen to the stories that he comes away with – some he had even forgotten existed. He would never have contemplated that a few months ago. Sometimes, I know he could just murder a drink. He tries to fight it by training more excessively but David and I know the signs. David will say, 'I don't think it'll be long before he's back on it again.'

It was like a train – we would be able to see it coming from quite a distance. As this book goes to press, there's no train in sight but he can't have a drink until he's been off the Antabuse tablets for four or five days. I can only hope that, when the desire to drink comes on him, it will pass quickly and everything will be OK.

There are times when I feel a bit easier in my mind and I allow myself to think that my life is not too bad compared to what it was before. I've had a lot of family problems lately – in particular, my mum is suffering from dementia – but, in some ways, for George and me, it's getting better as he gets older. We've become used to each other's ways and perhaps we've reached a compromise. Now, I can see clearly just why I love him so much. For example, he's great with Mum. When she was living in her own house, he would go up there every day and put a note through the door to tell her what day it was. Now that she's in a home, he's more supportive than ever. I think he realises what the drinking has done to us and he wants to make up for all that if he can.

He might be George the alcoholic but he's got huge reservoirs of compassion and tolerance. If a friend needs help with a flitting or something heavy lifted, he's right there. He'll walk neighbours' dogs and he didn't flinch when an old neighbour was diagnosed with macular degeneration of the eyes. She had almost given up and yet he prepared breakfasts and suppers for her in an attempt to keep her strength up. He's great with anyone who comes into this house – he leaps up and makes cups of tea. Really, he's ever such a nice person.

You know, for all his drinking and people calling him an idiot, he'd walk away from trouble rather than get involved. Sure, it's been hard with all the alcohol but he's tried to bring David up to be a considerate and caring person too. Even when George was away from the house, if I had any problems with David, I just picked up the phone and it was sorted. You know what young lads growing up can like – they need a father figure.

The ironic but wonderful thing is that David has turned into a smashing young man. Perhaps he's done it against all the odds. If anything, he used to say to me that, because he was George Connelly's son, he would do things properly. He didn't want to bring shame on the family and he wanted to make his father proud of him.

In my opinion, the taxiing, even part-time, is not a good job for George because, even if he gets himself straightened out, he's never far away from pubs. Often, when he's out in the taxi, he has to go into pubs and shout for his clients. And you know what it's like when you go through a pub's door – the first thing that happens is the smell of drink hits you.

If George finally beats his problem, you can rest assured that David and I will be more than proud of him. We both love him dearly. Staying sober would make him the perfect man.

11

DEATH IN THE FAMILY

After Celtic, life for me was never going to be the same again. How could it be? If you forget the money aspect, ignore the fractured marriage that ultimately sent me running away from the game like an Olympic sprinter and just consider what it was like to be a professional footballer, even back in the 70s, you'll appreciate that being out of the game was going to bring huge changes for me. Instead of being in the ultimate comfort zone, where footballers are almost treated like royalty and you feel as though you are wrapped up in the middle of a ball of cotton wool, safe from any hard, sharp edges that could inflict injury, I was going to have to start fending for myself. I suppose I should have cherished my time in football more than I did because it just didn't get any better than that. Well, actually, it did improve – as is obvious when we turn on our televisions and watch teams of millionaires playing football. But, back then, we didn't know that would happen – we just felt privileged to be pulling on the jersey of a famous club. Sure, as a footballer, people either loved you or hated you but you could live with that – at least you were a source of some attention. And, remember this, whatever drawbacks there might have been, it did beat working for a living, right enough. But, as you know, not only did I not cherish it enough, I didn't even want to have anything to do with it. But, at the time, I had no regrets – they only arrived some time later when the reality of what I'd had and lost struck home.

Of course, the day after I'd taken the decision to quit, I suddenly had to face the meltdown of my identity. Once I'd been George Connelly, medal-winning footballer and former Player of the Year. Now, I was plain old Joseph Soap and no one really cared a damn for this Joseph. And why should they? In front of thousands and thousands of fans, I'd played football for the club I'd avidly supported since I was a wee boy but now I was back where it had all started, not so very long ago, and turning out for the juniors.

For the next few years, I would be appearing for the likes of Tulliallan Thistle, Sauchie Juniors (Sauchie actually gave me three or four hundred pounds to sign on), Oakley United and latterly Tulliallan again. The rewards were scarcely worth mentioning but at least it gave me some exercise to get the heart pumping and keep the beer belly at bay for a wee while longer. To some extent, it also made sure my spirits didn't disappear out the window altogether. But junior football didn't pay my living expenses. It didn't keep the new lady who soon was to become my wife in the style I wanted her to become accustomed to. And it certainly didn't pay for all the drink that I was throwing down my throat – for that, you would have needed a money machine and one that worked perfectly day and night.

My brother Dan and I saw to it that the proceeds from the sale of the house following the marriage break-up soon disappeared. I've already pointed out that, as a thirsty pair, we went hard at the booze for a whole year. Suddenly, there was nothing left in the kitty and there was no alternative but to get my hands dirty – work beckoned, hard, manual graft. Was I intimidated by the thought? Not at all. I had come from a family of miners, so it really was no problem.

The jobs came thick and fast. I was never going to run away from them. Pipe lagging in Grangemouth, as I have mentioned previously, was one of the first in a long, unending line of tasks demanding manual labour and plenty of sweat on the brow. Longannet power station followed, hotly pursued by Torness, near Dunbar, and a few bits and bobs before I got down to the rather more mundane life of part-time taxiing. Maybe, deep down, I was kidding myself on and putting on a show for the benefit of others but, early on in those days of manual toil, it seemed as if I was really enjoying myself. I convinced myself of it. I had at last found a bit of peace on this earth. One thing is virtually assured in this life, though – once you have carved out some peace and contentment for yourself, along comes something to blow you out of that bubble of complacency.

Dan's death did just that. He certainly didn't deserve to die. Who does? But, for Christ's sake, he was only forty-one and there was so much to come for him. In a way, however, his ending was typical of the man – Dan always had to be one step ahead of everyone else. This particular night, he had been in the pub until late and suddenly decided he wanted to go home. He'd arranged for someone to give him a lift, only he wanted that lift instantly. He couldn't wait a few minutes until the man who was going to give him a hurl had finished his drink so he set off walking and tried to thumb a lift. Somewhere along that road he got knocked over. That was the end of my beloved brother – the man who had shared my life almost constantly for that last year. The driver of the car said that Dan just ran out in front of him. Guess who was first on the scene? The guy who originally had offered him a lift! But the episode was pure Dan. He was one of life's chance-takers and this time the chance he'd taken backfired spectacularly.

I remember, when Longannet power station was being built, a few of us would be in the Bridge Bar in Kincardine. My other brother Tommy would be there with a guy called Pat McLaren. They would all be going through to a midweek match at Parkhead. Tommy and Pat would get a lift from a guy from Longannet but Dan would catch a ride with someone with a faster car. They'd all meet in a pub near Parkhead but Dan would get their first. It was the same when they were going to Hampden, maybe for an international. They would always choose different queues and, when the other two got through the turnstiles, Dan would already be standing there, reading a programme, as cool as you like. He always had to be first – that's just the way he was. But, ultimately, going places quickly cost him his life. What a waste!

Believe it or not, I wasn't drinking on the night he died. It was, at a rough estimate, about the only day in the previous 365 that I hadn't been drinking! I was at home when he took that fateful walk. The police came to my house and told me. I could see car lights through the curtains. And the next thing I knew was they were chapping at the door. I didn't go down to identify the body. Oor Tommy did that. I feel guilty about it now and then – I really do. Dan was having a problem with his own marriage at the time and maybe that problem had something to do with me. I mean, he had four kids and yet here was me getting him to go drinking every day. Maybe I escalated his drinking and maybe that caused ructions in his house. Remember, if you're not working and getting free drink, wouldn't you be tempted?

Whatever, his death shattered me. It was a helluva shock. I was alone as Helen had gone to Australia after we'd had a bit of a disagreement and I couldn't handle things by myself. I remember writing to her and pouring my insides out to her but even that was not enough – I needed her beside me. The morning after Dan's death, I went drinking with a vengeance and drank for long spells after that. I was, in fact, conspicuous by my absence if I wasn't in the pub in the weeks that followed the bereavement. But the fact was there was nothing I could do.

When a person's dead, they're dead. What else is there? Aye, you can grieve and you can disappear into terrible depression. I don't do that but I have my wee thoughts all the same. It was he who took me into civilian life again after being through at the Park. He took the blows for me, if you get my meaning. I can still hear him offering soothing words of advice when I began panicking about something or other. I'd be worrying about this one talking about me and looking at me while I was having a drink. Dan would stress, 'Dinnae worry about people. Put them right out of your mind!'

Dan's style was such that nothing got to him and he wanted me to be the same. But the real truth is that he wasn't the biggest, most important person in my life. In the end, I suppose I did more for him than he did for me – well, just as much. OK, he maybe wasn't a huge drinker but, there again, with me around, he was never stuck for one. There were times when it seemed as if he wanted to take me to the cleaners in a sense. For instance, I'd give him tickets for a game and then I'd get on the phone and ask him where the money was. He'd tell me it was in the post but there would be no money in the post. As far as he was concerned, I was the one with the money. But I was too busy enjoying myself at the nappy to really bother about it. It's only now, when I reflect, that I can see things. But, really, they were little things when you consider the big picture of life.

What's more to the point is had I been doing him any good buying his drink? Sometimes, in my quiet moments, I keep thinking he could and should have been alive today. He had a lovely family. Winnie, Dan's widow, has always been fantastic with me. She often looked after my daughters when my first marriage broke up. She's been a great friend and, what's more, she never blamed me for Dan's death. But she had to live through tragedy all over again when her own son, young Daniel, was killed by a car. Can you believe that? Knocked over – just like his dad. He just walked out into the road and fell in front of a car. Same bolt of lightning! Tragic.

Family. It's scarcely a big, complicated word, is it? Yet it can bring you so many complications. Families can be the strength of your existence and also the scourge of it. Now, if you try assessing these complications through a sea of alcohol, it becomes really difficult, believe me, because you may not always come to the right conclusions. A drinker, of course, is one of the most selfish people on earth. He doesn't know or understand the concept of giving and sharing. But ask me about my life, when I'm sober and haven't had a sniff of the barman's apron for weeks, and I'll tell you that the answer is simple. It revolves really around five people and five people only – Helen, my son, David, my lovely daughters, Susan and Sharon, and my teenage granddaughter, Rochelle. My immediate family, in other words. I have nothing but good to say about them. I've been so lucky. Helen's my saviour and my soulmate. As for David, he's a great guy – a better human being that I will ever be. He doesn't waste money on drink and so, when he goes out and buys designer gear for himself, I say good luck to him. Now he's planning to go to Australia in search of a better life. He deserves every good thing that comes his way. He'd get blood from me if he needed it. Susan and Sharon belong in that very same category. I dote on them all.

They're great kids – sometimes I think they're far better than I deserve. I think they love me. I hope they do because I'm not a bad man – or at least I don't think I am. I know they do love me when I haven't had a drink. That's an easy time for loving, though. I'm not so sure when I'm full of it. I know that I embarrass them when I'm hammered – just like I embarrass Helen. I know, when that happens, they probably can't wait to see the back of me. I only ask them to consider that perhaps the good in me outweighs the bad and they can forgive me for all the times I've indulged myself. Maybe now they realise why it's had to be this way. I have to say here that there's great love, also, for Rochelle. I don't see her often but that's teenagers for you. Anyway, she's in my thoughts and that's important.

But what of my wider family? There are times when I think that maybe I should spend more time with my sisters and brothers who are still living but I never go near their homes. Like most families, there are occasions when we are at war. They're all very different characters but I suppose they're quiet and reserved – they've certainly never been exposed to life as I have been.

There's our Jane, for instance. She's got a big house up in Oakley. She's the oldest in the family and she helped me out recently when I was having some financial problems. I greatly appreciated it and I paid her back. Oor Joe is, shall we say, a wee bit careful and it is doubtful whether he would give you a slide if he owned the Alps! That's just the way he is. But he's a brave man, a hero. He got hurt in the pit while he was in the process of saving a guy's life. A bogey filled with metal went out of control and it would have struck this guy and killed him if Joe hadn't stepped in. By God, I admire him for that. Joe has no time for my drinking – in fact, he despises me for it.

I often get the feeling that maybe they harbour a wee trace of bitterness towards me. Do you know what they did when my mother died in the late 80s? I was on the usual treadmill of drink and a family meeting had been arranged to discuss my mother's finances. However, I was not invited to join the rest of them at that meeting – that was their mentality. They all sat round in the house and decided to give me a hundred quid. Mum had no real money to speak of but she was a saver and had a few small insurance policies. But the fact is that I never knew how much she left. Their collective decision to only give me a hundred pounds was based on them thinking, 'Oh, he'll just drink it anyway.' Does that distress me? In a way it doesn't really bother me. No, any hostile feelings I have towards them had nothing to do with the amount of money – what upset me was the way they did it. At times, I actually feel sorry for them because I think they've got midget minds! Parochial, small minds! But there are many other times, of course, when I wipe such thoughts and feelings from my mind and take a forgive-and-forget attitude towards what's happened in the past – life's too short for anything else.

Death comes to us all. That's something that no one can dispute. My father died in his bed in 1978 and my mother woke up right next to him – he'd had a heart attack. I had a wee weep but, if I'm perfectly honest, it was just a bit of show. I don't know how else to analyse it. My mother died in Bo'ness and I was at a wedding at the time. When the news reached us – I'm not trying to be hard and I'm sorry about this – Oor Tommy cried out loud. 'Oh, no!' he almost shouted. I felt deep sorrow too but I just couldn't express it like him.

My view is that, if people go, that's it – story over. I did give my mother a wee kiss when she was in her coffin but that was all – I just didn't need to make anything more of it. Don't get me wrong – I liked my mother and father. I remember, when I was playing football, I'd sometimes take Dad to Dunfermline or give him a couple of bob in the bar and I loved being able to do things like that because it made him happy. But, for me, there was never any desire to put on public displays of emotion. I hear boys proudly saying they're away to see their mothers – for the Glasgow boys, of course, it's their 'mammies' – but I was never that type. Maybe it sounds as if I'm being hard-hearted but it has to be remembered that I was practically out of the house at the age of fifteen and, after that, parental care and control virtually switched to Jock Stein and others.

Maybe what happened in my working life also toughened me up, made me a harder person all round. It certainly wasn't easy. I remember my first venture into pipe lagging, for instance. You had to wear heavy masks. Sometimes I'd take the mask off because it could feel as if you were suffocating. But, mask or not, the fumes would go into your gullet – you would feel them go all the way down.

There were some funny times, though. When I went to work at Torness, I invited Helen and the girls down for the weekend. We stayed in this hotel and Helen told me she'd never seen another like it in her life – she said that you could smell the workers' socks as soon as you walked in the bloody door. We were told that we had the best room in that hotel but still Helen was not impressed. Sharon and Susan were thinking they were going to have a nice weekend but Sharon took a really bad migraine – it must have been induced by the smell of those socks! It was so bad that they (the girls, I mean, not the socks) just went up the road after one night and never came back.

It was mainly Irish boys and Glasgow boys I was working with and they'd all ask me questions about football. Sometimes I found it difficult knowing what to say – especially when it came to giving my reasons for leaving Celtic. I remember, one day, I just ran out of things to tell this guy and I was just looking at him, not knowing what to do next.

However, the important thing for me was that I was back in a working-class arena where I felt comfortable. This is when I learned to become at least a bit street smart. The guys I was working with were wise to the world and I began to realise I

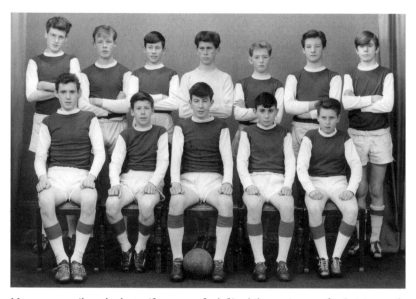

Not even a smile – that's me (front row, far left) while turning out for St Margaret's RC School, Dunfermline, in 1963

Player of the Year – I was so proud to receive this award

Happiness in Bermuda – (from the left) yours truly, Kenny Dalglish, Vic Davidson, Lou Macari, Davie Hay and Davie Cattenach

All for Gorrie's wedding – (from the left) Jimmy Quinn, Alex Smith, Myra Gorman, Davie Hay, John Gorman, George Connelly and Davie Cattenach

Familiar faces in 1967 – a few of the Quality Street Gang pictured in a youth tournament, in Casale Monferrato, Italy

By the left – the left was never my best side but it had to do this time in that same Italian tournament

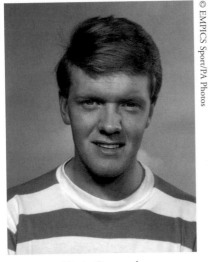

Davie Cattanach

Kenny Dalglish

SOME MEMBERS OF THE

Vic Davidson

John Gorman

Davie Hay

Lou Macari

QUALITY STREET GANG

Danny McGrain

Jimmy Quinn

Life among the Lions – that's me fifth from the left of the back row and I've been
promoted to the first team in August of 1968

Wearing that coveted first-team jersey –
I look like I'm just loving it

On my marks – the training that just
had to be done

It doesn't get any better – I'm twenty and I'm in heaven, having scored against
Rangers in the 1969 Scottish Cup final

But you can't win them all – Davie Robb and I go in for a fifty-fifty ball during
Aberdeen's 3–1 Scottish Cup victory in 1970

A real legend – Jimmy McGrory, the man who signed me for Celtic, arrives in style

A rare picture of dejection – my mentor Jock Stein goes through the Milan mill after losing to Feyenoord in 1970

Singing for a supper that never came for me as Scotland record a World Cup song – (from the left) yours truly, Erich Schaedler, Jim Holton, Donald Ford, songwriter Bill Martin (obscured), Willie Morgan, Denis Law, Sandy Jardine, Danny McGrain and, at the back, Kenny Dalglish and Tom Forsyth

That's my boy! – me with my son, David

wasn't so clever as I'd maybe thought I was. After having been in a shell for so much of my life, I started learning how to talk to people and soon nothing fazed me.

I became pally with a couple of English scaffolders while I was still in the smelly-sock territory of Dunbar. Scaffolding? I was scared of heights. I always remember, when I was training with Falkirk, watching some steeplejacks at work as they prepared to knock down a chimney. My heart jumped into my mouth and I was shaking. 'Oh, God, look at them climbing up all those wee steps,' I said to myself, feeling panic on their behalf. I had great respect for those steeplejacks and scaffolders, plus they were great folk to be around. Balancing on a wee rod eighty feet up in the air . . . really, it doesn't bear thinking about. But guess what? I even began to do a bit of climbing on those scaffolds myself. But I'd only go to heights where I felt safe and that would be it – there were to be no heroics from me.

In those days, I did all sorts of jobs from cleaning the ovens that made naan bread to plastering, to working for the council. The worst work of all was down the mineshafts, pumping cement. I had to climb maybe about fifty feet down a ladder, into the bowels of the earth. You had to wear oilskins and there was always water there. I remember one old guy saying to me, 'This is no job for a man.' And he was right because fear was in you all the time. Underneath those oilskins, you'd be soaking with sweat. There was constant noise and you were continually trying to catch your breath.

In the end, I was glad to settle on the taxiing. I needed to get a badge and that presented problems all of its own in that I had to learn all the streets and the quickest routes. Taxiing brings its own collection of stresses and pressures. It can be heavy going sometimes and it makes me wonder if the stress of driving all kinds of people about makes me drink even harder when I go on one of my sessions. I do get stressed out by the job. No matter what I say to some passengers, it often feels like I'm saying the wrong thing to them. I occasionally get drug addicts in the car and they're very irrational people. But, in general they're not too bad in this area. I'm sure I couldn't hack it in the likes of Glasgow or Edinburgh. That must be a nightmare for drivers.

On the violence front, I can't really complain. I have experienced very little of it but I do remember taking a couple of English guys to the airport. I don't really know what it was about them – I just felt they were a bit dodgy and they made me feel a wee bit unsettled. One of them said, 'Excuse me, driver, could you put the wireless off?' It was just the way he said it that put me on a wee bit of an edge. I've never wanted to get into fights with the passengers but there have been some who have wanted to mix it with me. I had this guy one night giving me a bit of hassle. I'm not sure what I did wrong but he was dishing out abuse like nobody's business because his taxi turned up late and he was fuming. He was battering my window. I was told by one guy in the taxis that I should carry something, maybe a sock with a couple of snooker balls in it, just for my own protection but, so far, I haven't had to act on that recommendation. Generally, I don't have too many problems as ninety-five per cent of my passengers are great and it's just the five per cent you want to worry about.

Mind you, it's all computerised now so, if you get a bad one, you won't get them again because folk who are known to have been troublemakers before just don't get picked up again. And, if there is any nonsense, the operator just calls the police. There can be a lot of wasted hours what with people being sick or peeing in the car. You wouldn't believe what some of them get up to. But, there again, it's often because they're drunk and don't know what they're doing. Well, I know all about that, don't I?

The main thing, however, is that I'm content with my lot and, in many ways, I'm well off. Helen would never see me stuck. Even supposing I was dying of alcoholism, she would nurse me – she's just that type of person. I sometimes wonder if I should have been like Muhammad Ali and never had a drink in my life. I bet I'd have been as fit as a fiddle. But then I think, 'Could I really have stuck to that kind of regime?' It would have been a pretty boring life, eh?

One day, my old friend Davie Cattenach, known to me as Catt, was talking about his late brother, Edward. He had had a huge drink problem – he was a terrible binger – and I said to Catt that I believed that people in general have a set lifespan. Some have a long lifespan and others have a short one – there's often nothing you can do about it. I was also talking to Helen about it the other day. I seem to be right bang in the middle of things. I'm thinking about guys dying, like my brother, my nephew and Davie Cattenach's brother who all went young – and they're not the only ones I know who passed away at an early age – it just appears to me that they've had their allotted time. And here am I, away past that age – it makes you wonder. I sometimes say to Helen, 'Maybe the hook will be out for me soon.'

I don't know. Now, I'm not going by my current health, by my lifestyle or my fitness. I'm going by the fact that most of my brothers and sisters, with the exception of Annie and Dan, are having long lives because they have looked after themselves. It's in the family. So here's me thinking to myself that maybe I'll have a long life because they've got long lives. But then, what confuses the issue even more is the Scotland thing, of course. Remember the half-back line against Czechoslovakia? Bremner, Holton, Connelly. Billy and Jim are both dead, away before their time – it haunts me. Will it be my turn soon?

151

12

TEARS FOR A LEGEND

It's almost impossible to believe that more than two decades
have elapsed since the death of Jock Stein. Even today, I am
still aware of his presence. It's just as if he's sitting in the next
room. When I close my eyes, I can see him standing there,
assured, authoritative and often even argumentative, yet never
in the slightest way arrogant. I'll never forget the huge waves
of darkness that swept over me when I heard the terrible news
that he had collapsed at Ninian Park, Cardiff, after Scotland
had qualified for the 1986 World Cup finals in Mexico

I do not consider myself an emotional man where death is
concerned but, when Jock Stein died, I changed. The curtains
weren't drawn in my house but it was difficult to see daylight
for days. His passing introduced me to endless night. I could
and should have gone to his funeral and yet I couldn't bring
myself to do so. I knew that in my fragile emotional state, I
would collapse altogether if I went through to Glasgow to watch
the final chapter of his life and times. That man was like a
second father to me. He was kind, considerate and tolerant of
my country ways. Yeah, I should have been there but, just as
so often in my life before, I couldn't bring myself to do what
would come naturally to most people. As you will have gathered by now, I am essentially a private person who does not
welcome the probing, far less the findings, of life's microscopes.
My emotions didn't fancy being exposed in public. There again,

of course, the other thing holding me back was my weakness for strong drink. With everything that would have been going on in Glasgow after the funeral, I would, no doubt, have surrendered to its temptation that day and very probably the next few days into the bargain, finishing up God knows where.

As it was, I stayed away and fell apart privately. I was in thousands of little bits and only a creative genius could have put me back together again. Without a drink in my hands, I sat in the house and cried my eyes out while watching the funeral on television. Helen had to throw me a tea towel to help me try to mop up my tears – and I can tell you there were plenty to mop! I don't know if you will understand my reasoning but, on the day of the funeral, my sadness was coupled with a lot of anger. I was very much aggrieved that this so-called wonderful game of football had taken the Big Man away so prematurely. He was strong and vibrant, he loved his fitba and, yet, look at the way it had repaid him. Death visited him less than a month before his sixty-third birthday. It came calling far too early.

I thought that perhaps he should have retired after the Celtic thing. I thought of how shamefully the club had treated him after his magnificent service to them when it was suggested that he should head up the pools department. There again, I wondered if he hadn't put too much pressure on himself by taking on the Scotland post. Did he really need all the aggravation that international management involved? On the other hand, was my own conscience clear? With my record of walk-outs, had I always done right by Mr Stein? Hadn't I run out on him too often for my own comfort? Was part of me feeling guilty for all the stress my behaviour must have caused him?

Ultimately, of course, everything else was secondary to the pain of his death. I remembered the good times and I wept again. He had so much influence on my life. I was what you could call his blue-eyed boy. I had known him for over twenty years and, during that time, he'd done so much for me. He pushed me so much, in fact, that I'm sure the other players wondered which George he was referring to – me or his own son. He just managed to extract all the good things out of me and put them into my game. He was a fantastic manager and a fantastic person, I would say. Oh, I know he had a fearsome reputation and he could go berserk with the best of them – I saw a good few instances of this side of him – but, for whatever reason, they were rarely directed at me, thank goodness. I'll always remember the generosity of his spirit which came my way, in spite of the provocation that I might have given him. It is often said that there are players who have a sensitive side and need an arm putting around them. I suppose I was one of them and Stein would have recognised that.

Of course, I was never privileged enough to work under any of the other greats of that era – Bill Shankly, Brian Clough or Bob Paisley – but, in anyone's money, Stein would have been hard to beat. During Celtic's nine-in-a-row extravaganza, he surely was the best manager ever – to me, he was a football god. There was no point really in talking to him about things like tactics. He was so far ahead of the game that he'd arrived half-an-hour before you got there so you were forever in a catch-up situation. The dugout became his personal Mecca. I mean, how much can any ordinary person learn from sitting in a football dugout? Precious little, I would have said. It is situated so low down that reading a game becomes very difficult and yet Stein had mastered its art better than anyone else. The Hibs and former Aberdeen manager Eddie Turnbull, for whom I had the greatest respect, would sit in the stand to get an elevated view of things and make his moves at half-time; but not Stein. He didn't need heights to tell him what was wrong. He would come into the dressing room at the interval and tell players like Bobby Lennox and Jimmy Johnstone they were playing too wide, too far up or too far infield. He would tell me to hang back a bit. Reading the game from that position might not have been easy but Jock was always spot on. He was unbelievable.

I was, I suppose, more than a bit scared of him – well, not of him as a person but of his knowledge. He was so firm and, football-wise, everything seemed to go right when he was there. Was describing myself as his blue-eyed boy taking things too far? Not really. I believe there was a special place in his heart for me. He just seemed to push me all the time. I don't know if it was because I came from Blantyre mining stock (my mother hailed from the same area as my manager, Burnbank) but I think the proximity of the locations went in my favour. I certainly remember being in the dressing room one day and asking if I was playing. One of my colleagues – I forget who it was – quipped, 'Of course you're playing – the boss's big boy always gets a game!'

Serious? Said in jest? I had no way of knowing but remember we're talking about the era of the Quality Street Gang and maybe there was more than a little jealousy as some people said I was the top man in that little firm. But, whatever it was, it didn't bother me too much. You know what football is like – you're never allowed to get big-headed so you just take all that's thrown at you and try not to blink an eyelid. It's only when you're alone in your bed and with your thoughts that you're even allowed to punch the air, or perhaps the pillow, in triumph!

Considering all the circumstances, however, it was a wonder Mr Stein had so much time for me. Let's go back to 1963 when he was managing Dunfermline. My mother's uncle, Ned Greenhorn, was friendly with him and they came over to our house in Valleyfield so that I could sign schoolboy forms for the Pars. I was playing for both St Margaret's RC School in Dunfermline and Tulliallan Thistle at the time. My Dad told Stein that we had already been contacted by Celtic, who were managed by Jimmy McGrory, with a view to signing.

Right away, Stein played the psychological card. He told me I should go through to the Park and see how many were players were training. This seemed a very considerate move by him but I'm sure it was calculated to put me off signing for the team of my boyhood dreams. To his astute way of thinking, I would travel up to Glasgow, have a fit of the vapours when I saw the opposition – the players I would be competing with for a place in the Celtic teams – and run all the way back to East End Park! The move backfired spectacularly.

With me coming from mining stock, you can imagine what a trip to Parkhead meant. In Fife, as in other mining communities, pit stoor was everywhere – even your hair and clothes were contaminated by that awful stuff. Football was the escape. I'd grab a couple of slices of bread, put on my torn jeans – there was never any money for new ones – and go away to play, to lose myself in my dreams. So, for me, walking into Parkhead was incredible. My dad and I went up one Tuesday night and there were about thirty or forty part-timers out training, including, if I remember correctly, Jim Brogan and Jim Craig. But if I was meant to be intimidated, I wasn't. There was not a shred of fear in me. If I was going to be a player, I wanted to be a player at the shrine. My dad wanted me to sign for the Celtic and I did without any hesitation.

I had defied Jock Stein for the first time in my life but not, sadly, for the last time. A few days later, his big, familiar form appeared at the door seeking an answer to his initial question. 'Now that you've seen the competition, son, are you going to get sensible and sign for Dunfermline?' Well, I'm sure that's what he would have said but I was never to hear those words. When I saw him coming, I almost had heart failure – I admit I was frightened of him even then – and shot the craw – immediately. I think I went out the back door and left my poor father to do the explaining. Cowardly? Yeah, it sure was, but who would fancy telling Mr Stein something that was not part of his agenda? Of course, it wasn't long before Stein himself came to Celtic Park, having enjoyed a short but successful stopover with Hibs at Easter Road.

As for me, when I joined the ground-staff a few months later, it was all worthwhile. Had he borne a grudge? Not a bit of it. I remember I was standing on a chair fixing a light bulb when he came into the room. He acknowledged my presence with a smile. He was whistling 'Mr Tambourine Man', the tune that was a hit for The Byrds. And you can bet that I felt like whistling on the day I signed professional forms when I was seventeen. Other clubs were in for me at the time but Stein's psychology won the day this time. 'Listen, son, if you sign for a Kilmarnock or a Dunfermline, no one will ever remember you. On the other hand, if you sign for us, everybody will remember you.' No more persuasion was needed. I was delighted to sign my life away.

Apart from Stein, I had the men who would go on to be the Lions of Lisbon all around me. After a few wobbles early on, which I've already explained, I began to settle down. I can remember Bucky (Billy McNeill) coming through and having a cup of tea while we sat on a hamper in the boot room. He had broken his leg at the time. This was amazing stuff for me. I was in clover and drinking in all the action. I developed a powerful thirst for that. There were so many sights, your eyes needed to be everywhere to take them all in. Jimmy Johnstone was full of advice – he told me that I should keep my feet rooted to the ground, no matter how much was written about me. I never forgot that advice.

By this time, I had made friendships that were to last a life-time. I used to travel through to Glasgow with Bertie Miller, who went on to join Rangers and then Aberdeen. He was from Lochgelly. He used to get on the bus at Dunfermline at 7 a.m. and I joined it twenty minutes later at Valleyfield. Getting up so early in those mornings presented no problems for us – we were just glad to be alive and playing football for a living. We'd get to Alexandra Parade in Glasgow at about ten to nine and then we either walked to the Park or took the bus. A real circle of friends began to shape in the form of David Hay, David Cattenach, John Gorman, the late Jimmy Quinn and me. We ran about together, managed to involve ourselves in many scrapes, as you have already discovered, and were almost insep-arable.

Being big for my age, I began playing junior football for Tulliallan Thistle where I was a boy among men. But there was no deterrent for me in those days. I appeared in a Scottish Junior cup tie against Aberdeen's Sunnybank, who were big noises back then. I took up the old position of inside left and scored from the penalty spot to help my team to a 4–1 win.

Now, I can't remember the crowd against Sunnybank but I can assure you it was nothing compared to the one that turned up when Celtic went into their European Cup quarter-final against Dynamo Kiev in January 1966. They say there were 65,000 fans in the stadium that night but that just added to the spice of the occasion. Mr Stein asked me if I would go out to entertain the fans with a show of keepie-uppie. There was a reward, of course. He threw me a sugar cube in the shape of a fiver and a fiver was a lot in those days. I must admit I was scared at the thought of it, especially when I was standing in the tunnel waiting to go on to the park. Indeed, the sound of 65,000 voices was so intimidating that I almost decided to call it off. But, then, after taking a series of deep breaths, I went out there and proceeded to go through the routine that I had practised so often in the back garden of my home with my four brothers. I suppose it was familiar territory for me. My nervousness disappeared into the evening air. There again, once I started I suppose I was too stupid to be nervous. I'm one of those people who normally stands back when others go forward. If someone asked me to do a display of keepie-uppie now, I would be so paralysed with fear that I wouldn't even be able to start. Anything like that scares the hell out of me. A television appearance? Don't be daft! A radio interview? Behave yourself! But, when you're young and silly, it's diffi-cult to appreciate the real value of fear. Take David Marshall for example – he could do anything when he was younger and, remember, he played against Barcelona with some distinc-tion, but ask him to do it now and I'll bet he'd lose about five goals! Maybe that's being a bit unkind to him but you get my drift, don't you?

The night of the Kiev match, Celtic wanted to introduce their new signing, goalkeeper Bent Martin, to the crowd. John Divers, Charlie Gallagher and Stevie Chalmers were going to have some shots on goal for him to try to save. Mr Stein asked me if I would put on my display before this happened. There were all sorts of estimates as to how many times I kept the ball up – some said I managed it approximately 2,000 times. I wasn't counting but I don't think it was anything like that. In fact, I don't imagine my tally reached a thousand. I think it was nearer the five or six hundred mark but maybe I'm guilty of underestimation. Still, that was the night Celtic supporters became aware that there was a George Connelly around. I suppose it was quite an achievement in front of all those people. Making it even more difficult was the fact that I was doing it on the move. I walked on to the park and into the centre circle. From there, I visited both ends, returned to the middle, went over to what was then the Jungle and went back to the stands. Frank Cairney, one of the Celtic backroom staff, told me that I should have walked right off at the main stand – at which point I would have got a standing ovation – but I didn't do that. People started laughing when I turned back again and walked around the centre circle. I didn't know what to do but then Bent Martin came out of the tunnel so I just stopped and went over to join the others shooting at him. It's funny, you know, but there wasn't even a tremor in me when I came off. I had survived the test of strong testicles. Mr Stein must have thought a lot of me to place so much confidence in me – I mean, it could all have gone horribly wrong.

I also realise that, if I had been a little bit older and therefore stronger, I would have been a Lisbon Lion. But, never mind, the breakthrough was not that far away. Stein was able to pitch me into the 1969 Scottish Cup final at the age of nineteen. He knew I would have the courage for the situation. Anyway, I went home after the Dynamo Kiev game with cash I never knew had been coming my way. I was well pleased and I suppose I was walking on a cushion of air.

As I said before, Stein always seemed to know best. I particularly remember picking up a few tips from Peter Lorimer, the man who packed a donkey kick in his right foot. I watched on television as the Leeds player went wide and got all the space in the world. At the time, I was playing on the right wing and I remember thinking to myself, 'I'll have a bit of that' and trying it out in a game. But Stein came in the dressing room at halftime and got a hold of me. The difference between Lorimer and me was that I had no pace. Stein just thought I was posing for the crowd and said as much. He suggested firmly that I started coming more infield from the right, looking for the ball. You knew with Stein you were not encouraged to join a debating society so you simply obeyed orders. I played as he'd told me

I should and, in one match against Rangers, I hit the ball from about thirty yards out and it flew into the net. It not only helped us beat Rangers but it demonstrated that Stein was right – there would be no more posing in far-out areas from me!

So, yes, I suppose I was a bit of a favoured son although I did get one rollicking from him that I was never to forget. In this professional game of ours, everyone wants to play and, at that time, plenty of players were chapping on the manager's door presenting their credentials. Jim Brogan, Yogi Hughes and Co. were all singing from the same hymn sheet, the one that said, 'Why am I no' getting a game?'

I was no different but normally I didn't have the courage for a face-to-face confrontation with the man who saw to it that my wages were paid. However, one day the village boy in me was determined to assert himself and steal a march on my city-slicker colleagues. I summoned up every bit of nerve I possessed and went into the manager's office to say my piece. I wanted a game. It wasn't the world's longest interview but two things occurred to me at the time: firstly, I emerged from his office with my head still sitting on top of my shoulders; and, secondly, from this, I believed that Mr Stein must have taken my message on board.

My optimism wasn't misplaced. We played Partick Thistle at Firhill and I was in the team. Well, let's be more accurate and say that my name was down on the team sheet but guess what? I was rubbish. When we came off at full-time, Stein got me in front of everybody in the dressing room. It was time for me to put my head down as his words echoed across the dressing room. 'So you've been wondering why you're no' in the team, have you? Well, my granny could have done better out there the night!' My case was dismissed. I was dismissed. I did not even consider answering back. I was speechless! Cruel humour, yes, and I was the butt of it but there was no point in arguing with him. If there's a gale outside your front door, you don't try and walk into it, do you? Not, of course, unless you're terminally stupid. And I wasn't quite that bad.

But Stein didn't just have cruel humour in his repertoire – there was a caring side to him as well. Just before the '69 final that made my name, we were down at our base at Seamill. Mr Stein had named me in the side and I became a bit nervous of what lay ahead. I remember Billy McNeill, the boss and I walking up the stairs to our rooms, and Jock talking to Billy in particular. 'Players are entitled to feel nervous the night before a cup final,' he said. That statement was made to Billy but directed at me. I can tell you I felt a whole lot better when he said it.

Another time, however, one of his remarks reduced me to tears. This came when the full Scotland team had arranged to play Celtic Reserves at Lesser Hampden. I was in the boot room, changing my studs – old habits die hard when you're a former boot boy – when Mr Stein came in and told me he was making me captain for the game. 'It's for the future,' he explained, meaning that, some time in the future, I would captain the famous Glasgow Celtic. Now, my life had been immersed in Celtic culture so, when I was told that I would be the leader of the pack one day, I'm afraid that was a bit too much for me to contemplate. After Mr Stein had left the room, I closed the door and had a wee greet to myself. I knew he thought a lot of me but I didn't know it amounted to quite as much as that. Captain of Celtic . . . what an honour! But, also, what pressure! Just trying to accommodate that thought in my mind blew me away!

All these memories and more were jostling for position in my mind as I watched Mr Stein's funeral on television. I also remembered the training at Parkhead. Good days, indeed. In spite of all the desertions, when I was at my work and really concentrating on football and not all the other things that would clog up my brains, I really put some sweat in. I was considered to be quite good in that respect. But listen, training for the most part was easy, really, because the programmes the Celtic coaching staff had in place were unbelievably good. Jinky once said that he thought Jock sat up all night thinking up new training routines. His variations were fantastic and there was something different every day. They contained everything but boredom. You didn't know what you were doing from one day to the next and, remember, he was there for nine years. It was brilliant.

Yeah, I miss the man they called Big Jock. He was great for football and good for me even though occasionally I failed to acknowledge it at the time. You know, sometimes I think about all these agents coming up to the Park nowadays, asking for loads of money and conditions for their players. They are gallus chaps and no mistake – so pumped full of their own self-importance that you might think someone had blown them up. You can hear them asking for so many clauses in their players' contracts, stipulating this, stipulating that. And it's then that I immediately think of Big Jock. Can you imagine it, eh? Imagine them coming up and chapping on the door if he was in residence. 'Excuse me, Jock, but could I have a quick word about my client's wish list? He would like a villa over in Majorca so that he could go over there and get away from it all for a few days every now and then – just to escape the pressures, you understand. Oh and can we insert a clause whereby my man can leave after the first year, if there is an offer of £1 million in for him? We think that's very fair. Oh, by the way, his wife would like to go down to London shopping six times a year – a bit of retail therapy keeps the good ladies happy, eh?'

As I sit here thinking about it, there are no tears this time –

I'm roaring with laughter. I can picture the Big Man's face if he was confronted by the likes of that – it would be guaranteed a place on the wall of Kelvingrove Art Gallery.

13

THE VOICE OF DOOM

When the celebrated actor and writer Peter Mullen was interviewed in depth in the May 2004 issue of *The Alternative View*, he revealed that none other than yours truly, George Connelly, was one of his all-time Celtic heroes and that he would love to play me if a film of my life was ever to be made. He also said he'd heard stories that I was hearing voices in my head, even on the football park.

I suppose it's not surprising that such rumours began circulating – when somebody has succeeded in sticking two fingers up to logic and done something as daft as walking out on his career, it isn't long before a series of urban myths start springing up. If a believable explanation for irresponsible behaviour is not forthcoming, people will use their imaginations and draw their own conclusions. Now, allowing for the fact that, over the last thirty-odd years, I've been about as available to the media as the Abominable Snowman, it's hardly surprising that a mountain of theories about me has developed. I don't mean any disrespect to Peter Mullen – he only repeated an urban myth – but the explanation that bugs me most of all is the one that says I started hearing voices during my time with Celtic, voices that told me I was in the wrong game and I should end my time with the club. If this had been true, the obvious conclusion to draw would be that I was barking mad. Well, I might have been a lot of things then

– a bit stupid, probably very naive and, yes, rather fragile of temperament – but I can assure you I wasn't crackers. So I would like to trample on that one once and for all Yes, I did hear voices once but it was when I was suffering from *delirium tremens* – usually shorten to the DTs – during a self-imposed detoxifying process. It was awful and I can only hope to God that it never happens again.

I've got to tell you that simply mentioning this incident makes me frightened but, if it's time to place the cards on the table, it had better be the full deck – so here goes. I had been out on a bender and I was staying in Kincardine because I'd been bin-bagged by Helen at the time. Oh, I suppose Helen has told me to get out fifty maybe a hundred times since we've been together. It became such a common occurrence that it was treated like one. Some guy would walk up to me in the pub and say, 'How's tricks, George?' and I'd just reply out of the corner of my mouth, 'Bin-bagged!' There was no need for further explanation – he'd know the score. It got to the stage where it didn't even register a note of surprise. It was almost like someone saying hello in the morning. Bin-bagged – the embarrassing situation where a wife has thrown her man out on his lughole. So after a while, when that was the call, nobody flicked an eyelash plus I suppose some of them were glad. The hard-drinking crew feel better when they see someone else bevvying – it makes them feel more comfortable about what they're doing.

Anyway, this time, after one of my many benders and having offered Helen a bucket load of apologies and promises, I was back home again. I'd begun the process of restoring myself to the normal world and was all right for two days. Then, on the Saturday, I was watching snooker on the television and John Higgins was on, I think. I'd normally have been fine by then but something wasn't right. I felt irritated and restless – as if

I needed to make myself more comfortable – so I shouted to Helen, 'I'm away up to bed to watch the snooker.'

But I wasn't to find any comfort up there in that bedroom – only horror. I was there only a few minutes when I heard a harsh, rasping voice in my head. 'George, are you there?' This was a voice unlike any other I'd ever heard before and it was enough to make me want to greet. It sounded like the voice of the Devil.

'Are you there?' it insistently asked.

There was no place to run, no place to hide. When you hear something as vivid as that, you're almost tempted to respond. Does that sound crazy? You're even contemplating talking to a voice that does not have a body. Through it all, I was beginning to think someone had spiked my last drink and put something in so they could talk to my brain in some kind of delayed reaction. It was classic DTs although, at the time it was happening, I didn't know it as I had never experienced them before.

It started to get worse. I can't remember the exact wording but it was close to this: 'You want money? Are you f****** talking to me? Are you wanting f****** money?' By now, I had started panicking and I was frightened. But my fear offered no protection – it couldn't stop that voice from splintering my brain. Sometimes it would swear, other times it wouldn't. I was shaking. I jumped out of bed and raced through to the bathroom, ran the water and jumped into the bath. I shouted to Helen and asked her to bring up a carton of orange juice from the fridge. I was as frightened as hell because there was simply no escape from this weird voice. Helen brought me up two full cartons of orange which, through the fog of fear, I thought was odd because we were skint at the time.

She said, 'That's David's orange!'

I didn't care whose orange it was. If it had belonged to King

Kong, I'd have fought him for it. I drank the two cartons, one after another. For some reason, I thought they would help. They didn't. The fear was coming at me in waves. And these waves were so huge that a fit man could have surfed on them.

God knows what Helen was thinking. I was trying to hold on to my sanity so I fired some questions at her. I asked things like: 'What's my mum's name?' 'What's Dad's name?' 'Is David all right?' and all the time I was throwing water over my head as if that would make the demons go away. Helen was trying to soothe me by telling me that I was all right but inside, where it counted, I knew it wasn't all right. I was an animal on the run from the hunters.

I managed to towel myself dry and went down the stairs. I lay on the couch. The late frames of snooker were on. I had no concerns about who was playing, or who was winning: I was fighting my own battle and it was being held on far more dangerous territory than the green baize. Although I had changed rooms, there was no escaping the voice. It was still there and it was even more sinister than it had been before. 'George, you kill your wife! Do you want f****** money? You'll get the money – don't worry, you'll get it.'

The voice just wouldn't give up and now it was bawling at me to kill Helen – ordering me to do so. And I was lying there, panicking like f***, so I turned to Helen and yelled, 'Get oot of the hoose! Get oot of the hoose and phone the doctor!'

I could scarcely believe the horror of it all. This was a Saturday afternoon and I should have been enjoying a safe, relaxed period with dear old *Grandstand* but instead I was standing on the cliff edge of terror, frightened I was going to kill Helen – kill the woman I had loved more than anyone else on this earth, the woman who had borne me my wonderful son, David. Can you imagine that? Have you any idea what that was like?

Helen did as I asked and went next door to phone the doctor.

How long do nightmares last? I have no idea. Some say it feels as if they go on forever when, in actual fact, they only last minutes. I found out later that this one lasted an hour.

Helen's pal came over from Falkirk but the voice was made of stern stuff – it wasn't going to be put off by an audience – and it kept screaming at me. Eventually, the doctor came. He said he wanted to take me inside and, by that, he meant to a secure unit. Helen thought it would be for the best because she was so frightened – she suggested that I should go in, even if it was just for the night. At the time, I was being treated by a detox guy from Larbert. He came on the phone and talked to me but he also said, 'Maybe you'd be better going in for the night.'

But I didn't want to go near one of those places. The realisation that I was close to being in a mental hospital was starting to come into my head and take up residence. You can imagine what that would have been like. There would be people saying, 'There's George Connelly in a mental hospital!' and, after that it would be time to roll the final credits.

I was scared – that's what stopped me giving in. Eventually, the doctor gave me some heavy-duty tablets to take and they calmed me down enough so that I could get some sleep. The feeling was still slightly there the next day but, as long as I kept taking the tablets, I knew I would be OK. Helen phoned up the detox guy the next day and asked him what it had been and he said it was a classic case of the DTs. That was about ten years ago. I was hammering the drink at the time – hammering it so hard I almost had my own workshop. It had never happened before and, touch wood, I hope and pray it will never happen again.

So I more or less know all about alcohol now – I certainly know how bad it can get. A lot of drinkers are scared to give up drinking in case they get the DTs. It's very bad to just stop drinking at the snap of a finger – you've got to reduce your intake gradually. If you're drinking two bottles of whisky a day, you shouldn't just go suddenly to six cans of beer. You should go from two bottles to one bottle, to half a bottle and then go on to the beer or wine. At the time when the DTs struck me so horribly, I was on sherry and whisky – not at the same time but I would take both on the same day.

When some folk come off the drink, they feel suicidal – in actual fact, it's possible to kid yourself on that you could easily top yourself, but it's not easy. What I do know is that this was the most frightening moment of my life. I thought I was going off my rocker, completely and comprehensively off my rocker! You know I've done things in my life that have made me afraid – I've gathered a host of Scottish Cup and League medals and that required some bottle but, I tell you, that one incident was more scary and intimidating than all the others put together.

You'd think that this might have put me off the drink. I suppose it would have been enough to turn a lot of people off forever but not me! Alcoholics are fearless and it wasn't long before I was back drinking again just as heavily as before. I suppose I'm just lucky that I haven't had the DTs again. Having mentioned that alcoholics can be fearless, there are a lot of contradictions about people who drink. Although I was back on the sauce again not long after the DTs, it doesn't mean that the terror isn't still with me – I can assure you it is. I believe that, if you take alcohol when you've got the DTs, it can kill you – it's to do with the wrong message being sent to your brain and causing a stroke. But, even though I know how dangerous it could be, I'm sure I would have been daft enough to do it if Helen hadn't been there that time. Oh, yes, I'm daft enough for anything where drink's concerned. So how, in God's name, did I ever get to be like that? Maybe part of the answer to this is to be found in the past – back in the days when a man with the curious name of Joe Doctor came up to Scotland to live with my sister, Annie.

I was in the second phase of my adult life by then in that I had met and married Helen and we'd had David. My first marriage was long gone and my football career had dropped off the edge of the world. There was happiness amidst all the rubble but sometimes happiness in the home just isn't enough – you think you want something more. I had long since begun my education in drinking and it seemed like only common sense that I should complete that education. I'd experienced hellish pain and pressure – far too much of both for my liking – and now I was looking for the joy of release. I told myself I would find such a release in the bottom of a glass. Drinking is like an anaesthetic – it allows you to forget about all the bad times and dream about the good ones. But how does a man learn to drink? I mean, really drink?

I'm not just talking about throwing a few pints and halves down your neck and still being OK the next day. No, I'm talking about the real deal – I'm talking about throwing gallons of the stuff down your neck for days on end until you smell like a skunk. How do you learn to find the true oblivion? How do you learn to arrive in places and situations which would scare the hell out of normal human beings? Does it come naturally or do you pursue the time-honoured tradition of trial and error? There are other ways, of course. You can seek an education in it by calling in an expert tutor – someone who has been around the block so many times he'd find his way there in the dark. That's the option I chose and the man who would be my mentor and help me confront all my demons was my brother-in-law, Joe. Somewhere, in my fevered imagination, I imagined he would be the one to fill in the gaps of an unfinished education.

Joe was from Liverpool and I swear that he came with a special licence to drink any man or woman under the table.

Now I've stood and drunk alongside real hardened specialists but he was the worst – or should that be the best? – I'd ever seen. Some men hero-worship others for their ability to play football, for the way they can paint a picture or for the way they can send a golf ball around a corner; but just imagine virtually hero-worshipping a man for the amount of strong liquor he can put away. Well, I'm sorry to admit it but, for one short, significant period, I began to think of Joe like that. At his expert tutorials, I wasn't content with learning how to leave the railway tracks – I signed up for the honours degree course where you tumbled down the embankment and exploded into flames. I was having a great time to myself – or so I imagined in that blinkered, blind little world of mine. If I remember correctly – not that I remember too much of those crazy days – no one else liked it. My beloved Helen, my mother and the rest of my family must have hated it but, to be truthful, it is hard to remember what their exact sentiments were and here's another admission – I wasn't caring what they thought.

I was in a vice and happy to be caught in it. Strange things happen to a man when he's locked into this vice – he loses all sense of reasoning and all sense of shame. I wasn't caring who thought what in those days. The way I was, I was just thinking of little old me and that's the way things usually are for alcoholics. I had built a mental barrier around myself and it was made of powerful stuff. No one was allowed or entitled to trespass on my immediate space. Anyone who said anything I considered to be negative about my way of life was about as welcome as a squad of gypsies in the grounds of Buckingham Palace.

My sister Annie would join Joe and me in our drinking sessions and we had several venues for the important business in hand. At first the three of us would often convene in the little house that Jock Stein had helped me to buy at the time of my first marriage. Then Annie and Joe got a house of their own and events moved to their place. I was the only one to go into that house. Tommy never went there and nor did Josie or Jimmy. And no invitations went out to any of my sisters either. Quite recently, I spoke to Jane about it on the phone but she really didn't want to discuss the subject. Annie wasn't a well woman. She and Jane had been close and Jane really didn't like what was going on as Annie shouldn't have been touching alcohol. But me? I have to admit that I didn't give a toss at the time. As long as I was getting my quota of drink, I didn't bother about anything else. As I said, drinkers are a selfish bunch whose last consideration is anyone else's feelings.

I used to stay at Joe and Annie's house in Valleyfield for a few days at a time. As I said, Annie wasn't in great health – she'd suffered an aneurysm. She couldn't get about much and she shuffled rather than walked. Joe used to try to motivate her to get some exercise which included sending her over to the Asian shop to get a packet of fags and a bottle of QC (Queen's Counsel) sherry.

Theirs was a house where day and night had no point of separation – they just merged into each other without a seam in sight – and things had become really heavy. We would grab a few hours' sleep here and there but, for the most part, we'd just get on with the far more serious aspect of life – drinking. A new day would dawn at approximately 6 a.m. and, from then on, it was a case of lubricating your throat until it tired of the lubricant. And some chance there was of that with Joe around! He could drink to a pipe band playing and yet he could sober up incredibly quickly. It was wholly impressive – or should I say I imagined it to be wholly impressive in those days? Looking back now, in this sober moment, the idea that I could think like that makes me feel sick.

At first, I had no place in Joe's league. I was strictly amateur class because it would take me days to come together after a particularly heavy session. At times like those, I would stagger back up to the marital home, throw myself on Helen's mercy and do a spot of foot kissing. However, it wouldn't be long before I returned to the house of no shame. Gradually, I was able to last the pace a whole lot better although I would never consider myself in Joe's division. For me, the main attraction of being in that house was having my memory banks wiped clean. While I was there, nothing about my previous existence could torment me. There, I wasn't George Connelly – I was just another sad drunk, poor but seemingly happy.

Annie had always been a spotless person and she was fiercely house-proud. She was very sharp witted and wouldn't let you away with anything. In the old days, she wouldn't have let anyone stay up in her house drinking or using it for dossing purposes. No, there would have been none of that kind of stuff going on. When she and Joe got together initially, she kept him right but I think it floored both of them when she had that aneurysm and things changed. Joe was drinking all the time and their flat was absolutely stinking of cigarette smoke. Soon the house was pretty dilapidated – it was liveable but only just. My brothers wanted Annie to go into the hospital but Joe wouldn't let them take her away because of the money he stood to lose. He was getting a fortune every week as he was entitled to twenty-four-hour care allowance money for her.

Annie had another aneurysm and this, together with a bout of pneumonia, eventually killed her. I don't really want to go into it any further because I know Annie's daughter, Carol, will be awfully upset – and rightly so. I think she hates Joe for taking her mother away from her when she was about fourteen. I don't believe Carol has ever got over the death of her mother. She visited recently. She's got a top-class job and a husband who does very well too but it seemed to me as if she is still hurting.

THE VOICE OF DOOM

This is what **Helen** remembers about that time.

When I was going steady with George, we'd go through to the Valleyfield club on a Sunday and visit his sister, Annie. She was well in those days and hadn't had those aneurysms that eventually killed her. She left her husband to set up home with Joe and her daughter Carol has never forgiven Joe for going off with her mum. Who could blame her for that? Anyway, Joe was progressing into alcoholism in those days and Joe and Annie's house was where George would often go when he was going to drink. The 70s were just about fine but things got worse when Annie got ill in the 80s. That's when George began to let himself go and I just hated seeing him going about looking so untidy. That was the worst thing for me. His standards had always been so high and by then they'd slipped and he started going about needing a shave and a change of clothes. I felt awful for David. He should have been full of pride for his father – the kind of pride that would allow him to say, 'My dad played for Celtic.' But, instead, he was seeing the raw end of life. The repercussions of those days with Joe Doctor still haunt us.

Joe's drinking was a night-and-day affair but George always had something in him that made him want to call a halt to it. Back then, I used to go out and get George and then sober him up – since discovering Al-Anon, I've taken their advice and stopped doing this. No one liked Joe and it was obvious that George's drinking really escalated when he became involved with Joe. But no one could get through to George at that time, not even his brothers. I tried to get him to stop for his own sake and I also told him that he shouldn't let his sister drink but the anaesthetic that was drink had sedated George's mind. He would only say that, as they were a married couple, they were going to do it anyway and this was their pattern in life. He was so deep into this illness that none of the family had any influence over him. With him and Joe drinking all the time, it meant that every day Annie was sent up the shop to buy the drink. The shop was only about fifty yards away but it was still wrong to make her go. Mind you, Annie was besotted with her man. She didn't want anyone else at the time. It was Joe this and Joe that.

Normally George doesn't show a lot of emotion and, even when Annie died, he just sort of got on with things but I know how hard the reality of her death hit him. One of the floral tributes came from Annie's first husband, who had been high up in the navy. The words on the wreath were extremely poignant: 'I'm sorry we got lost in life's jungle.'

After the funeral, we got into the car and drove away but soon we had to stop. The composure crumbled and both of us wept. George may make out that he doesn't care but that's only for show. There is warmth – it's just that usually he doesn't want people to see it.

Joe Doctor and his son attended the funeral together but later he went to live in Gloucester. I was delighted – we were all delighted – but, unfortunately, the legacy of that horrendous time lives on. During the period around George's fifty-eighth birthday, I felt I wasn't going to be able to get him off the drink and he wasn't going to be able to do it either – he said so himself. Normally, I would know how to wean him off it and he would want to do it, but not then. That was not such a good time. However, thinking I'd cracked it, I bought three bottles of wine for £10 to begin the weaning-off process. When I got up in the morning, the three bottles were away and the words I've heard all too often in the past were offered to me again. 'I'm sorry, Helen,' he said, 'I'm struggling!'

Sometimes, he's full of remorse and he asks himself why he can't drink normally like his brothers. George comes from a very private family. I don't know how they'll take these revelations. One of his brothers said recently, 'Don't put anything in the book about the drinking. I've read so-and-so's book and there's nothing bad in it.' But I say, 'Who's wanting a boring book like that?' It would be like telling the story of Cinderella and forgetting to mention the Ugly Sisters. Isn't an autobiography meant to tell folk the truth about a person? If you're not going to tell the truth, why write it in the first place? Oh, I think they're surprised that he wanted to do the book but I don't think they'll be surprised about some of the things that are revealed in it. They know what went on, anyway. I just hope they'll realise how sick their brother has been and how much help he needs.

I've strayed from my story, though. Surprise, surprise, he did clean himself up that time after his birthday. Maybe there was a fog in his mind but there was enough of a breeze to clear it. How he can go from one extreme to the other I'll never know – one minute he wants to be fit and healthy and the next he wants to be full of drink. It's like there's a wee monkey perched on his shoulder and it's there at all times, dictating what he should do. What can he do to rid himself of that monkey?

I'll come to my fifty-eighth birthday soon enough – it's a beauty, I promise – but, for now, let's just say the demon drink has ruined my life and no doubt. Without it, I'd have had a lot more money, I'd have an idyllic marriage and I wouldn't experience this horrible feeling of being the man caught in the middle in a tug of war. Sometimes the pull from the left is stronger and I succumb and sometimes the team on the right pulls me back from the brink. Here, in the year 2007, for example, I am still haunted by an incident that was sparked off by alcohol. Come to think of it, just playing it back in my mind causes me to want to go and hide in a corner or burst into tears. I let myself down so badly.

If someone says something out of order to me, I normally turn the other cheek. I walk away – sometimes I even run away. Remember that Kenny Rogers record, 'Coward of the County'? That's always been me. But this time was different. Helen and I had been at a wedding and we thought we'd round off the night by going to the pub in Clackmannan. I had fallen out with Helen over something and nothing – probably having had too much to drink – and, suddenly, this guy came up and said something cheeky to her. It was just some stupid little insult and I'd meant to throw my drink over him but the glass flew out of my hand and went straight into his face, propelled, of course, by anger. Dear, oh, dear! Why am I trying to put a gloss on it? It really hurt him – plain and simple. He had to have stitches in the wound. The disgrace of it all! The guy was drunk and so was I but that does not excuse my conduct for a second.

The court was lenient with me because it was my first offence and I was fined £600. I came home and sat in the middle of the floor and wept. Since the incident happened, it feels like I've spent the rest of my life apologising to the guy. We're like friends now but I can't forget the night I went right over the top.

I'm too ashamed to talk about this any more but this is what **Helen** remembers of what happened.

Violence had never been part of our marriage but that night it took off. We'd ended up in a pub in Clackmannan and George was awfully drunk. The guy was as drunk as George and had, apparently, been aggressive earlier on in the evening. When he said something about me, the balloon went up. It was time for a free-for-all – like something out of a Wild West film. Oh, my God, George had a great big black eye. They tried to knock him out but he was still standing when the police arrived to cart him away to the cells. That was on the Saturday and he was kept in the police station for two nights.

When I woke up the next morning, the nightmare hadn't gone anywhere. The whole incident had happened because of one guilty party – drink. I remember going up to my mother's and she gave me hell. She just wouldn't have it that he had stuck a glass in someone's face. 'That's just not like George!' she snapped. She adored George and wouldn't have a word spoken against him.

When details of the story came on the news that night – 'Ex-Scotland and Celtic star George Connelly . . .' – George was in a terrible state. He was almost suicidal and he only got worse when he read the court report.

Jimmy Miller, the guy who had looked after him at Sauchie Juniors, came down to see him because he had taken it so badly. 'Look, George, you must get a grip,' he told him. 'These things happen, unfortunately, and you've just got to learn from it. It could have been much worse, so get a grip. Sure, it's a terrible thing you've done but just put some kind of perspective on it.'

The guy he'd injured also came to see him and between them they sorted it out – both of them knew they had been in the wrong. That guy also started going to AA meetings and now, if you can you credit it, he and George are quite friendly!

14

FATHER, DEAR FATHER

DAVID'S STORY

It would not be any exaggeration to say that I love my father
to death but I'm going to start off my story by slaughtering
him. I wouldn't allow anyone else to do it – apart from my
mother and sisters, of course – but I feel that I'm entitled to,
that I have earned the right. So here goes. Now, birthday celebrations seem to be one of his specialities. I know he's going
to go into detail about his fifty-eighth towards the end of this
book – let me tell you, it was quite something and went on
forever or so it seemed – but, come to think of it, he didn't
deprive himself on his fifty-seventh, either. I remember it well.
How could I ever forget it?

That night in March 2006, I had my own bit of celebrating
to do. I went through to Glasgow for a friend's twenty-first.
To put you fully in the picture, I shall recall it in as graphic
detail as possible. The night out was far from being over when
we left Glasgow and headed for the home territory of Kincardine.
Our transport was a stretch limo, no less, and everyone was
suitably impressed and in high spirits. As we arrived and about
a dozen of us tumbled out of the limo, we were just heading
towards the house where a party was to be held when, suddenly,
one of my friends turned round and said, 'Hey, David, there's
your dad!'

I stopped in my tracks and looked. In those few seconds of realisation, I was having a crash course in consternation. My head was shaking. My tongue was making clicking noises. I looked over at the library steps and spotted this bundle of clothes lying there. The trouble was Dad was inside those clothes. He was lying fast asleep on the steps. I walked up to him and woke him up. He took some waking, I can tell you. But when he came to, he started talking rubbish, telling me how I had saved his life. Apparently, he couldn't get anywhere to stay in Kincardine. He'd tried to get home to his house in Alloa but, well, there were no taxis around at the time and so he'd just lain down and fallen asleep outside the library. He kept saying he needed something to eat. I asked the lads whether it was OK if we took him back to the party with us. They didn't mind although it must be said they were probably considering revising their opinions not long afterwards. Anyway, we took pity on him, got him up, took him inside, gave him a heat – he must have been freezing his whatsits off – and fed him. The trouble was he started having a drink there as well and then he began to get quite cheeky. If I remember correctly, I think I ended the night by booting him out! Imagine throwing your own dad out of a party. I hated seeing him like that.

Oh, I've lived with George Connelly, confirmed drinker, for many years but, when he's on one of his benders, my mother doesn't allow him near the house so I'm not accustomed to seeing it in action. I did that night – in not so glorious Technicolor. Some of my friends said they felt really sorry for me but I really didn't know how to feel. Can you believe that I was not embarrassed? I mean, a couple of my friends' relatives are alcoholics and it makes them embarrassed but not me. I don't know why. Perhaps all those years have conditioned me. I know my mum takes a red face about it and I think Dad feels the same way too, normally. But, right at that moment, he was not worrying his shirt about the incident. He was decidedly worse for wear and I had no option but to chuck him out. I gave a fiver to the taxi driver to take him up the road to Alloa. The trouble was he wouldn't go – he just refused to leave and kept saying he was going nowhere. I started shouting at him just to get out that door and I sent him on his way – by this time he was wearing only one shoe. It was quite sad, really. I felt bad about it afterwards because, believe me, as sober dads go, no one can beat mine. He's been wonderful to me in so many ways, teaching me all about life and how to approach it, giving me things and making sure I'm happy, even going out on rotten mornings and nights and doing my rounds for me when I was a newspaper delivery boy and, for some reason or other, I didn't fancy making the gig.

I look back on that night and weigh it all up and try to rationalise it a bit. Aye, I was angry with him then but that was the only time I've felt such anger. Sometimes I've gone up to the local pub and, if he's been sitting there, I just leave. I won't have a drink with him. I have never drunk with him. I never will drink with him. I wouldn't even consider buying him a drink. That would be seen as giving him encouragement. It would be like sitting next to a stranger, really. You must understand that he's not violent at all when he drinks but he just turns into a completely different person – daft and stupid. No aggression, no anger – just different. He starts talking about things he doesn't talk about when he's sober and would never dream of talking about when he's sober. They're weird things. But, as his son, I'm used to it.

You know, I was aware there was something wrong when I was only about four years of age. My dad was chapping on the door and demanding to be let in while Mum and I were hiding behind the couch! The sorry situation is locked into my memory. I can remember another time, not long afterwards, he was in the house and was away with the wee men. It was the same day Roy Aitken left Celtic so it was back in 1988–89. Dad came back that night drunk and I remember Mum shaking him, beating him on the chest and telling him to get out of the house. 'Don't let David see you like this,' she said. But the point is that I did see him. I saw, even then, what strong drink does to a human being. How it reduces them and leaves them as wreckage.

Since then, Mum has tried to keep him away from me when he's been in that state. At other times, she had no option but to allow me to see what was going on. There were occasions when I was young that she would drive us into Kincardine after he had gone missing for a couple of days. I'd have my Celtic top on and Mum would be going round the pubs asking if George Connelly was there. I suppose we made an odd couple. Sometimes he wasn't in the pub. Sometimes he was. When he was, Mum would drive him back up the road to try and get him off the drink.

It is a strange life, I agree, but I understand why he does it. Well, I think I do. I mean, a professional footballer leading an imperfect life in retirement sounds daft, doesn't it? Especially when playing the game is the dream of most young boys. It sounds like a great life, with a grand lifestyle, playing in front of big crowds. But how must he feel when people come up to him in pubs and tell him how daft he was and what a waster he is? There again, after playing in front of those really big audiences, he needs to have that buzz so he's obviously turned to drink as a substitute. The drink also helps to blot everything out. He's got regrets. Of course he has. He was at his peak when he quit. We all have regrets in our lives but that must have been really heavy gear for him. He probably reflects on all that stupidity now and seeks a bit of refuge from it.

Look, it all might have been different for him had he been

born twenty or thirty years later. Football's completely different nowadays. You're taught how to deal with the media. You have dieticians and someone to watch out for your every need. We're so different, me and Dad. If I'd had his talent, I wouldn't have lived it up like he did. But, like I said, he's a totally different person. Call him a one-off and you're not far wrong. I wouldn't have drunk alcohol – not while I was playing. No, if you take your profession seriously – and I would have done – I wouldn't have touched the stuff. Being a football player means your fitness should be everything. It's paramount.

Now, I like going out with my friends for a few bottles of beer but I could do without it. It is not of any great importance to me. I can't remember being drunk to the point where I've forgotten what I've done. Some of my friends can't remember what they did the night before but I've never been in that kind of state in my life. I don't drink spirits, which is a good start.

As it was, I was quite a good footballer but I suppose I preferred watching the game and, in any case, I was never really pushed. I don't think Dad liked the idea of grown men shouting at young boys from the touchlines. He just didn't agree that this was the way to encourage anyone to play football. Of course he went to the local park and played seven-a-side with me and my friends and practised ball work. He taught me how to trap a ball, how to pass correctly and how to perfect the solitary sport of keepie-uppie. Dad may be a special kind of drinker but he was always thinking about his fitness and his health and encouraging me to do likewise. He told me, if I didn't, it would catch up with me one day.

In many ways, I'm glad I never played the game for real. People were always going to say, 'OK, he's all right but he's not as good as his dad.'

No, give me a game to watch and I'm happy. But I'm sure, even if I had made it as a footballer, I'd still have been compared to him. I mean, I was OK, I wasn't bad. I was a centre-back who played long balls to feet . . . hopefully. Obviously, though, I didn't do it as well as Dad. What a player he was! I've got DVDs of him playing and I sometimes sit and watch them in awe. It's a weird feeling, sometimes, watching them with my friends. Maybe they expect me to jump up and shout but I don't. I don't really brag about it or anything like that. They say that, if it was their dad, they'd be really excited. I just can't describe the feeling I get.

To me, he's just my dad and I don't know what it's like not being his son. But now that I'm older and know what he did in football, I'm really proud of him. He was still playing junior football at forty years old, you know, and still turning out in the seven-a-sides until last year. Yeah, at fifty-seven, he was playing in his jacket and a hat. Then his knee went and it was over. He's still got his touch, though. You lose your fitness and your pace but you don't lose your touch. He can still hit balls forty or fifty yards. You've got to stand back and marvel at ability such as that.

But the applause in my head fades slightly when I look back and remember the early days of my life. For instance, I was given a new Celtic tracksuit for my fifth birthday. Kids want their dads there at times like that but my dad wasn't there to hand it to me. Mum and I drove down to the pub in Kincardine to look for him – another disappearance. She was furious he had gone AWOL.

There were times of despair. When I was fourteen, I wrote to Tommy Burns, who was Celtic manager at that time. I said I was the son of George Connelly and told him that my dad was an alcoholic. I don't know what I was thinking of at the time. Was it a cry for help? Who knows? But what I do know is that a letter from Mr Burns came back, inviting me up to Parkhead to meet the players and tour the stadium. I was delighted. I went up there with Mum and met Paul McStay, Paolo Di Canio, Jorge Cadete, Pierre van Hooijdonk and Andreas Thom. John Collins had just left but Tommy Burns and Davie Hay were both there. That was the first time I had met Davie but obviously Mum had met him before 'cos he's Dad's great pal. Both Mum and I were in awe of what was happening to us. I remember Burns and McStay standing talking to me and asking me if I played football. I just turned out for a wee local team in Alloa at the time.

'Are you any good?' they asked.

'Aye, I'm all right,' I replied. 'But the team are not all right. They're bottom of the league!'

I was pretty blown away talking to Tommy and Paul. I still have the photographs. I went back in 2000 – I can't remember who invited me that time – and met Henrik Larsson, Martin O'Neill and Chris Sutton.

Being the son of such a famous player has obviously opened many doors for me. I was on a night out at Celtic Park last Christmas when word spread around the room that my dad was George Connelly. One of my friend's girlfriends had put the word out – and, no, before you say it, I didn't pay her! I was approached by a few people – I think they were from Clydebank – but they didn't seem sure that I was on the level. 'We don't believe you,' they said.

So, jokingly, I said perhaps the only way they would believe me is if I phoned him. But I didn't need to as I had a photograph of him on my mobile and this convinced them. Then they started asking me to send the photograph to them. I did it through the Bluetooth technology, which I found quite ironic. These guys were in their mid forties so they had clear memories of Dad. One was kind enough to say he was the greatest-ever player to wear the Hoops. This started an argument with his mate, who said, 'Naw, it was Jinky.'

It was great hearing their discussion. I surely know by now the high esteem he's held in – even a lot of the Rangers fans say good things about him. Certainly, there's always a great sense of pride when I hear people talking of him, especially when I go to Celtic games. I changed seats from the family stand when I was sixteen and, as an adult, I've been in my new position for six or seven years. During that time, I've sat next to more or less the same people and, at first, I never told them who I was. But, last season I got talking to this guy beside me called Davie, who had been there for umpteen years. Anyway, I revealed my secret and the next thing he was getting the autograph books out for me to sign. Then he told the guy on his other side. He was very complimentary, too. 'You've sat next to me for seven years and you never told me you're the son of one of the greatest players to play on that park!'

I'm not a swell-headed guy but I love hearing things like that. Celtic, of course, is tattooed into my blood. I have been a season ticket holder for twelve years now and I've been happy to put my cash to the cause. However, I'll have to put buying next season's ticket on hold when I go to Australia in search of a new life. Until then, I'll continue to travel to the games with a local supporters' club and they're a good bunch of guys. At one point this year, I thought I might not renew it for the coming season. I mean, we'd won the league and the football was beginning to get boring. But, a couple of weeks in and I feel completely different about it now. Like so many Celtic supporters, I travel all over the place and spend a whole lot of money in the process. I've been to Liverpool, Manchester, Leicester, London, Rosenberg, Stuttgart, Milan and, of course, Seville. I also went to Bordeaux. That, mind, was only £100. I took the bus. I remember getting to Paris and thinking, 'Great, it can't be far now.' Really? When I asked someone how far it was to Bordeaux, they suggested it might be another twelve hours due to heavy traffic!

Around the time I went to Seville, I was working at a garden centre, selling plants. But, even there, you could not get clear of football. Kevin Keegan turned up with his wife one day. I managed to get his autograph. Now, I know it's crazy to spend all that money travelling to football matches but it's what Celtic fans do. It's frightening the number of fans who go to places like Old Trafford. Crazy! You can maybe say that Manchester United have the most fans around the world but, if you're talking about actual dedicated followers, then no club comes close to Celtic.

Dad, of course, instilled a love of the club in me by buying me that tracksuit, even if he wasn't on hand to deliver it personally. I attended my first game in August 1994 and it was against Kilmarnock. That's when the addiction took hold. I was always wanting to go to the football but Dad would never take me so it was left to our good friends Jim Doyle and his son, Scott. Dad probably didn't want to go in case he was recognised. I remember around the late 80s asking him to take me. He wasn't exactly enthusiastic about it but agreed, after some persuasion, to travel to a reserve match at Stark's Park, Kirkcaldy. It was highly comical, really. The crowd was scarcely sell-out material yet he was so paranoid about getting noticed that he went in disguise – he wore a hat and his driving glasses. Even that didn't satisfy him. We rushed out of the ground a good bit before full-time so that he couldn't be approached.

Until recently, I never tended to ask him about the past. I figured it was his business and that I should respect his privacy. But, one night not so long ago, the dam burst. He told me about everything – why he left Celtic, his drinking, the lot. I think it was a heavy weight to get off his chest and I think he felt a lot better for it. I've certainly seen a noticeable difference in him ever since. Our relationship's a lot better now than it's ever been. I can talk to him about things 'cos I see him as a good friend now, not just my dad. When things go wrong for him, it sometimes gets me down. I feel sorry for him but also angry that he should be this way – that he became afflicted by this disease. Luckily, I have a wonderfully caring mother who is always there for me. I hope, in turn, that I'm always there for her.

Is he going to beat the drink? I hope so – oh, God, I hope so – but it's just been part of our lives for so long that you begin to wonder if there is indeed any hope. I think, on occasions, that, even if you poured every drop of drink in the world away, he'd still find a way to get back on it. It's such a shame.

15

ANATOMY OF A GENIUS

In the mid 1960s, three men witnessed, with mounting excitement, the genesis of George Connelly, total footballer, and then, with increasing dismay, the gradual erosion of that genius. Now, former Celtic hero Billy McNeill, who captained him, assistant manager Sean Fallon, who signed him, and respected sports journalist Alan Herron, who watched him from a distance, each tell their highly individual stories.

BILLY McNEILL'S STORY

There's a golf course called Bonnyton which is situated just outside Eaglesham. It was a big favourite with Jock Stein and Sean Fallon, who I think was a member there. Anyway, this particular hole offered itself as more of an all-out assault on the respiratory system than a test of your sporting skills. Appropriately, they called it Cardiac Hill. To be quite honest, its contours were such that it could have been mistaken for the north face of the Eiger and it might have been more prudent to take crampons rather than golf clubs to tackle it. But we didn't go there for the golf – or mountaineering, for that matter – we were there to make ourselves fitter and faster than the next football team. Demands such as these tend to inflict pain on people. And, when you ran up that particular fairway, your lungs felt as if they were on fire and about to explode. If and when they didn't, you jogged back down the hill.

I'll never forget the day, in pre-season training, when George changed all the rules. He ran up the hill, which was all well and good, but then he just kept on going. Indeed, he ran all the way to the car park, clambered into his car and disappeared! That's the last we saw him for a good few days. It happened around the time when Celtic were impressively on course for the nine-in-a-row phenomenon and, on the surface, it seemed like things couldn't be better; but, as far as George was concerned, the danger signals were flying and the alarms bells were clanging.

There was another time while we were in the middle of training at the Park and he suddenly bolted up the tunnel. Everyone ran up the tunnel after him and we saw him go straight out the front door and jump in his car. Off he went again – it was almost like something from one of those Keystone Cops films. Now, the reaction of the boys in following him up the tunnel was just a lark. It was as if we were saying, well, if he can run so can we. We'd seen him do it before and I think this time the boys were actually ready for it.

By that time, things had started to become serious as far as George was concerned. I clearly remember Big Jock's reaction – he went absolutely mental. This was probably due to a combination of things – no doubt he was angered by the players' spontaneous reaction but more deep-rooted, I suppose, would have been the realisation that slowly, bit by bit, he was losing the genius of Connelly. And, believe me, we are talking about genuine genius here. He was so talented, it was terrifying!

There was not one player at Parkhead at the time who didn't respect George's ability. Along with Dalglish, Macari, Hay, McGrain, Davidson, Wilson and Cattenach, he was very much part of that team we called the Quality Street Gang. They were typical boys who just loved their football and who enjoyed having a carry-on too – all of them were enthusiastic and effervescent. There was always a lot of nonsense when they were around. I was one of the older ones and we'd be doing different things from them. At that time, the Lions were maybe a bit wary of them and what they might be getting up to so, more often than not, we'd stay out of their road. As captain, I might have been expected to wave the big stick and I'm not saying we didn't have any arguments but, really, there wasn't too much need for me to come down heavy on them.

They were a good crowd of blokes and we always had a laugh. Big Jock was clever enough to know when the laughing had to stop. But the younger element in the team was absolutely fabulous. They were really talented players and their nickname encapsulated their ability. Within the group, however, there were some very different personalities. Kenny wasn't someone who would get involved in anything too daft and neither was Danny McGrain but Davie Hay, Victor Davidson and Davie Cattenach ... well, they were always game for a laugh. Some of the things they would do at times made you wonder if they were off their heads. But there was never anything malicious about it – it was always friendly.

George was very much one of the quieter ones of the group. Davie Hay was his real pal, his amigo. They were as thick as thieves and Davie was great with him yet they had totally different personalities. There were enormous differences but by God they were close. Davie tended to look after him. Not on the park, though – George really needed no one there plus he could play anywhere. I remember the 4–0 Scottish Cup final win over Rangers. Big Jock left out Wee Jimmy and played George instead which was astonishing. Oh, sure, George could play anywhere but he'd never really focused with any intensity on the role of winger and yet he adapted amazingly that afternoon. He just went out there and performed as if he'd played there all his life. I've never understood to this day why Big Jock dropped Johnstone – I was dumbfounded then and I am still dumbfounded – but hats and caps come off to George. Anybody who could play centre half at one time, or beside the centre half, which was his best position, and then play as an outside-right, well . . . it was an incredible performance. Quite incredible!

Now, there are footballers of modest ability and achievement who tend to ram their personalities down your throat all the time. There are others of towering talent who are very much backward at coming forward – they withhold their personalities as if they are frightened someone is going to steal it. George Connelly belongs to the latter variety of footballer. We in Scotland don't produce too many world-class players but George had the ability to be world-class – he had that special thing that separates the great from the good. Unfortunately, he didn't allow himself to play long enough to achieve what he should have achieved in this sporting life. He had everything and more besides – skill, passing ability, shooting ability, strength and physique. The tragedy was the boy had everything except, maybe, the right mental toughness.

What is for certain is that his walkouts affected everybody. Everybody knew that Jock was dealing with a really nice lad. I mean, George was a lovely guy, quiet and unassuming, and there was no evidence of a ragamuffin in his make-up but nobody could understand why he was doing these kinds of things. And, as ever in football dressing rooms, it became a bit of a laugh. Players tend to treat these things in a light-hearted way. Yet this guy's talent was absolutely enormous, immense. He wasn't just your run-of-the-mill footballer – he was quality. He was so different it was frightening. There again, he was sitting on a knife-edge – that was the thing that worried us all.

However, none of us appreciated what was really going on there.

The trouble was that, in those days, there had been no precedents for things like this. None of us had ever seen anything like this happen. So what were we to do? George became quieter in the dressing room and he didn't take part in anything like the rest of the players. He'd just come in and just sit still, staring at the floor. He wouldn't take part in any of the banter going on around him, which was strange because dressing-room patter's great on occasions. So it got to the stage where it wasn't a great surprise when he used to disappear from time to time. It just became something that the players got used to.

To be fair, I wouldn't disagree with the conclusion made by some people that it was all over for him when Davie Hay left for Chelsea. It was after Davie's departure that he started disappearing in earnest. Big Jock was good in those situations – he knew it wouldn't help the situation if he was too hard on George. But it is my belief that Jock was always fighting a losing battle. Whatever George was suffering from, it was a very difficult thing to handle.

As I said, George was not one for conversation but, one day when Willie Wallace and I were sharing a room, he surprised both of us by coming in and asking us what we thought we'd get as a bonus for winning a certain game. I can remember he was pleased with our forecast. He said something like, 'Ooh, ya beauty! Now I'll maybe get a new bathroom suite!'

George was married to Christine then and had just moved to Blantyre. He was really made up over the bonus situation. At that time, there was no indication that he would begin to disappear from training. The only other time I remember him contradicting his own personality was when we were flying back from a trip to North America. He sat beside me on the flight and, for some reason – maybe it was fear of flying or something – he just never stopped talking. Mind you, quite a few of the boys were terrified of being airborne – it was nothing unusual at that that time – but it was highly unusual for him to be so talkative. I remember Big Jock coming up and saying, 'Come on, lads, you're making too much noise! Everyone else is trying to get some sleep!' Everyone else was trying to get some sleep? That was rich. I was trying to get some sleep! But my wishes did not have any obvious effect on George as he simply refused to shut up. He kept going on about getting a career in something else – I think lorry driving was mentioned – and I told him straight, 'Listen, George, as for you driving lorries, you'll have people driving them for you! You've got a career that anybody would give their right hand for. You have so much talent that it's unfair. It's been a long, hard season. Go home and get away on holiday, you and Christine. Away and relax yourselves and come back all set for the new season.'

When we arrived at Prestwick Airport, I told Christine about our conversation and she also mentioned the lorry-driving theme – she said that it had got into his head for some reason or another. That's when the problems started to show. With the benefit of hindsight, Christine had given a wee clue about her husband. I don't mean any disrespect to those who drive lorries but, with talent like George had at his disposal, his forte belonged elsewhere. He could have gone to any country in the world and been a real quality football player. The world was simply lying at his feet. All he needed to do was pick it up and embrace it. Give it a bit of love, if you like.

The first wee indications of instability were there, then, but it was a little bit later before it became really noticeable. To be fair to Celtic, there was a stage when he had to get the proper medical attention but I believe it just didn't work for him. It didn't work because, at that time, George was a very confused young man who had reached the top of the football ladder –

he was an international who was mixing with a whole lot of really quality young players. Playing for Celtic should have been an ideal opportunity for them and most of the others, such as Macari, Dalglish, Hay and McGrain, had their successes. But, in hindsight, with the things George was doing at training, God knows what he was like to live with. It would have been difficult for anyone, let alone a wife, to be associated with all that stuff. Dr John Fitzsimmons was the team doctor and he told me that Connelly had serious problems, ones that they had never encountered before. The tragedy was that everybody recognised George's ability – nobody was in any doubt about that – but, in the end, he just flushed it straight down the pan. Tragic.

Mind you, it was a tragedy all round. Just consider the club before Connelly's problems began. I mean, the boys who had won the European Cup were a class act but the Quality Street Gang weren't far behind us and initially there was no fear over the future of Celtic. If anything, these were boys with more natural ability and talent than the ones that had gone before them. Can I pay them a higher compliment than that? Aye, Jock had a few gems in the jewellery box. Even the lesser ones, the likes of Cattenach and Davidson, were really good players. But, all of a sudden, they started to demand the money they felt they were entitled to. To this day, I think that, if the Celtic board had done something about it then, the team would have been so powerful.

The old guard was beginning to break up quite dramatically and, before you knew it, only me, Jimmy Johnstone and Bobby Lennox remained. Then Jimmy and I left at the same time, me into retirement, Jimmy on a free, and suddenly there was one. If Hay, Dalglish, Connelly and Macari had still been still there, Celtic wouldn't have had any problems but, ultimately, they all left. Davie Hay just didn't think he had been treated properly and Dalglish and Macari felt the same. Consequently, in stepped Chelsea, in stepped Liverpool and in stepped Manchester United to offer them the type of contracts they thought they were entitled to. That broke up a really powerful young side. Dalglish obviously went on to lots of other European honours, Davie still had a good career but was unlucky with his injury and wee Lou did well at United. And, as for Celtic, the clearout had just been too great – no club could have survived that without showing any ill effects.

At times people have inquired whether I was asked by the team to go and see Jock about the money we were getting. Well, I wasn't. People really did their own things in those days. Big Jock had different ways of dealing with players. Youngsters maybe didn't get exactly what they wanted but it has to be remembered that they were all internationals and they were talking to other boys at other teams. They weren't daft and knew those boys were getting far more money than they were getting so it's understandable that they wanted their fair share of it. But, for whatever reason, Celtic decided not to take that route. The new generation, of course, was a bit more aggressive than the last when it came to these matters but, to be fair, the previous lot were entitled to it because they were really good players.

If someone said negotiating with Celtic in those days was like attempting to draw blood from a stone, they would not be far wrong. Macari just stayed away from training – he felt that was the best way of getting a move away. Kenny lasted longer than Lou but, when he did go, he was positive he was doing the right thing. Celtic should have sorted them out with better deals but they didn't. When you start to lose players like Macari and Dalglish, then things become more and more serious. Celtic, basically, became a selling club. As it turned out, of course, I don't think they came close to transferring George. They did threaten to on at least one occasion but they must have been desperate to cling on to that wonderful ability.

As it was, George was sometimes playing beside me at centre half but Jock always had the idea that he could play much further forward and I think, if all had been well, he might have played him right in the middle of the park, as a creative player. Personally speaking, it would have been wonderful for me to have George beside me. It would have been good for him too because I would have been on at him all the time. But something just wasn't right. When you hear him admitting that he wept on hearing that he might be captain one day, well, that's another indication that something was wrong. That's where the tragedy really kicks in because, apart from being an outstanding football player, he was a really nice boy. He wasn't nasty or troublesome generally but he just couldn't handle the life of being a professional footballer or the west of Scotland attitude, I suppose. That dressing-room attitude is hard. If you ever make a mistake, then they won't half jump on you with it. But that's part and parcel of life. You've just got to make the best of it.

In some ways, his disappearing acts made things worse because, by doing that, he drew attention to himself and the other players would say, 'Where did you get to yesterday, Geordie?' You must have the ability to survive in a dressing room. Compliments don't get handed out to you willy-nilly – not even when you are as multi-talented as George.

The Celtic fans, of course, still remember him and I've been asked loads of times why he left. I just tell them that the big fella had a problem that he couldn't figure out. And I suppose that's just what happened. But I don't tell them anything more than that because it's not a particularly nice thing to talk about, is it? But it was a real loss to football, I can tell you, and a massive loss to Celtic.

When I think of George nowadays, I prefer to think of the great days. I remember the time he played keepie-uppie at the game against Dynamo Kiev. That was a show that demanded nerves of steel. He kept it up for almost ten minutes but the reality was he could have kept the ball up for a week if he'd wanted to. And not only that, he could play the game too.

I said before that he was a really nice lad but I'll go further – he was the nicest boy you could wish to meet in your life. I'm really sorry for him because he didn't deserve to have problems. You can only think that, in normal circumstances, he would have got progressively better. What a colossal star he would have been had everything been right!

SEAN FALLON'S STORY

There was only one guaranteed way to escape the wrath of Jock Stein and that was to grab your passport and clamber up the steps of a plane as fast as your legs would carry you. Jock had a temper right enough, and he could lose it in the time it would take you to click your fingers. There were occasions I tried to hold him back but sometimes I wasn't successful. Well, it was man swimming against a strong tide, wasn't it? I've seen him throw players right across the room – some of them very prominent players.

I remember it happened once before an important European Cup tie. They'd been out of order, the players, and the man singled out for the rough stuff was responsible for leading them astray. We were preparing for a game on the Continent and the players had been told to be back by nine o'clock. Well, when they eventually came back, none of them were drunk or anything like that but they had broken the curfew and that was enough. Jock was very strong in that respect. He threw the culprit right across the room. Fortunately, there was a couch against the wall, so he had a soft landing but, put it this way, there was no comeback from the guy – no recriminations. He received the message loud and clear and it never happened again.

You might have thought that, considering all his disappearing acts, George Connelly would have been supplied with some of that powerful, strong-arm medicinal stuff but Jock was a good psychologist in that respect. He knew that, if he pushed George, then the disappearing acts would probably lead to something far more comprehensive. In other words, we would never have seen him again. Aye, there's a lot of psychology involved in football management. Every good boss will study every player, from goalkeeper right out to No. 11 with a view to how to get the best out of them and which way they should do it. You have to be wary – some you've got to be hard with while, with others, who you know to be sensitive, well, you have got to tread carefully and you can only do that by studying the man. The worst thing you can do is come down on hard on a sensitive soul, particularly in front of the other players. And, believe me, George was sensitive.

You know, I get the credit for signing nearly all the Quality Street Gang – Dalglish, McGrain, Hay, Macari and Connelly. They were supreme in their own positions although Connelly could play in most positions. McGrain, for instance, was probably the best right back in Scotland, if not in Britain. Dalglish was something else. A phenomenal player, Kenny could see things so quickly – any club in the country would have been delighted to have had him. Hay and Macari were also great, great players. Connelly? Now the word you're searching for is immense. What a player!

So, yeah, I signed all these boys but I'd been put on to them by perhaps a scout or a well-wisher, someone who would give me a ring to say, 'Sean, you should see this player. It will be worth your while.' I followed everything through. Some were positive, some negative. Not checking someone out is the biggest mistake you can make.

In George's case, he was with the junior club, Tulliallan Thistle. I ended up going to see him and wasn't disappointed – he had all the skill you could want to see. But there were times – and this is something that's been with me for years – that he gave the impression he had no interest in the game. Which is a strange thing to say, I suppose, particularly because he was so much better than the other guys on the pitch. But he just made it look easy – too easy. Anyway, I liked just about everything of what I saw and made arrangements to talk to him. But, when I went round to his house, he just disappeared out of the room. One minute he was there, the next he was gone. He said something about having caught a cold while he was over in Ireland. I soon learned that he just didn't like being in the company of people he didn't know. He probably knew of me but he was just shy and never spoke to me. People never realised just how shy he was. I've taken so many kicks in the head that I forget things now but I do remember there was talk of Leeds being interested in him. Then, of course, Dunfermline and Big Jock were keen. Let me put it this way – any club in Britain would have been glad to have had him.

Still, he came to Glasgow and we put him on the ground-staff. But then, for some reason, he didn't come in initially. I can't remember what was up with him. So we had to get him back again, which we did. Eventually, he started playing with the third team and he went on from there. Soon, I was counting my blessings that I hadn't given up on him. I remember the night against Dynamo Kiev. He was full of contradictions, was George. I mean, who would have thought that this shy young man would have been able to go out and entertain the masses like he did? Suddenly, his name was on everyone's lips – he had become a star in ten minutes. We thought it would be good for him to be on the ground-staff but he always trained with us. We didn't push him too much early on because he was just a youngster and he was still growing – and you had to be careful handling a boy in his teens. You could put him in a sick bed quite easily, you know. George didn't like the running over much but give him a ball and he was happy.

When he started coming through the ranks, you could see what a player he was going to become. I closed my eyes sometimes and saw shades of Beckenbauer or something very similar. It was the way he used to break with the ball. He was absolutely imperious, with great balance. That, of course, is very important and George had that all right. He also was the best passer of a ball I've ever seen. You see a lot of players failing because their final ball bounces away from their team-mates because it's just not accurate enough. But Connelly delivered these great running passes, with either foot, that were easy for the striker to run on to. In addition, he could read situations on the park and get himself into great positions. What more can you ask of a footballer?

Remember, he was only eighteen when we took him with us for the games against Racing Club in Buenos Aires and Montevideo, in order to sample the big occasion. In those matches, you saw some of the South Americans with their great skill on the ball but George would have been equal to any of them. That's perhaps the best compliment I can deliver his way. He was as good as any of them and yet he was only a teenager. The next year, he was destroying John Greig in a Scottish Cup final. If anyone asked John Greig who was the best player he had ever faced, I'd bet he'd probably say George Connelly.

Oh, sure, Jock and I spent a lot of time on him, a lot of time, but he was worth it. When he began to disappear, I admit there were times when I'd think, 'Ach, forget about it.' But he had so much to give to the public and the club that we'd try every-thing possible to get him back in as a player. Jock understood him – or understood him as well as anyone could. He was due a lot of credit. Yeah, he could fall out with people very easily but he was also very sensitive. People didn't realise that. He was a hard man but one with sensitivities. I've seen tears coming to him. He would never stand there, for instance, and see anyone being abused – never. Or, indeed, anyone being taken advan-tage of. He'd stand up for them immediately. So he was happy to put the work in with George. We'd just emphasise to him that, if he worked at it hard enough, the pot of gold was there was him. All he had to do was bend down and pick it up. But again, you had to watch that sensitive side. You had to be careful what words you used.

Aside from that, football can be such a wicked environment. Sometimes, players can be cruel to each other. That's all right if you're thick skinned but George wasn't. One or two players – I won't mention them by name – weren't very nice to him. One in particular was always making remarks about him – remarks about his drinking and whether or not he'd been up all night, saying different things about him. You shouldn't make those kinds of remarks about a person who was as vulnerable as George. Some of the players could have helped us with him but they chose not to. The trouble was that, when this happened, he'd go into a shell and you'd have a helluva job getting that shell to open again. Of course, you couldn't always be on hand and see what was going on. Sometimes, players would have a go at him and you didn't know about it until later. That's when I think he used to disappear and then you'd have to go and try and get him out of his house and back into the Park.

On those occasions, we'd tell him that some of the players were jealous of him. We'd attempt to heal the wounds by saying, 'Just you go out there and show them you're a better player than them 'cos that's what annoys them and you just keep on doing that. They can say what they like to you but they can't play any better than you.'

A lot of psychology was involved in dealing with George. There again, put him on the pitch and a magic wand was waved. The confidence he had on the ball was unbelievable. He was a different guy altogether when he was playing football. On the social side, he'd go into a wee corner, head in his hands but on the park he was the big picture.

But the Park wasn't the only place where George had problems. His brother, Dan, was a problem as well. He used to drink with George. I got to know the way to Fife very well. As you crossed the bridge down into Kincardine, there was a pub on the left and that's where they'd do a bit of drinking. I used to go down there to get him back to training and, once, I was actually amazed because he wasn't there and I actually found him walking along the road. Latterly, he disappeared for quite a while and I had to go and get him back. Sure, he came back in but his fitness was really done. He had put on some weight and had lost interest by then.

In the end, when his contract was cancelled and there were no bonuses on the go, George admitted that it was almost costing him money to play for the club. To my mind, Celtic had got away with murder. They just didn't like shelling out a lot of money. Neither Jock nor I were paid very much, either. You were just paid enough to survive and keep yourself properly dressed. Money was tight but there wasn't much you could do. The board was very strong and it wasn't given to many extravagances. Mind you, I remember when I was still playing, I went along to see Desmond White in his office in Bath Street. As true as I'm sitting here, he pulled out three fivers and said, 'You'll probably want to have a meal on your way home.' That was a lot of money then and that was the good side of him.

But, ultimately, what with money worries and marriage problems, I suppose George just wanted away. George didn't tell me about the marriage but I got word about it through the grapevine. As far as I know, a lot of people knew about it. Whether it was his fault or her fault, I don't know. I never tried to speak to him about it. It was his private business. But quite probably it spilt into his professional life. There are roads you take in management and roads you don't. But, I tell you, I was shattered when George left the club. I'd have given anything to get those skills back. Without the slightest hesitation, I'd say he was the most gifted player I'd even seen pull on a Celtic jersey. And, had he stayed on at Celtic Park, he would have proved one of the best, if not the best, to play there. What would he be worth in today's money? Oh, Jeez, the money they'd pay for his talent now would be colossal – millions upon millions. I don't know how many clubs would have the money to buy him.

George Connelly was simply that good.

ALAN HERRON'S STORY

It was September 1973 and, if Scotland didn't have a foot in the next World Cup, due to be played in West Germany the following year, they had at least a few toes. They had to beat Czechoslovakia at Hampden in a midweek qualifier. The Czechs were a formidable crew so it was going to be a close-run thing. I was working for the *Sunday Mail* at the time and so, as I was not writing a live report, I could sit back in the press box and savour what was on offer. In short, I could enjoy myself. Wrong. I took a phone call from Rod Stewart, a great pal of mine. 'Look,' he said, 'I'm out of the country right now – any chance of you giving me a commentary on the match?'

I asked him where he was and he told me he was in Canada! Now, I knew Rod. He was a bit tight. So I was thinking on my feet. 'Tell you what, Rod, you put a telephone in the press box at Hampden and I'll do it.' I gave him my seat number and that's what happened. He paid for a special line to be put in and I did an exclusive commentary for him, would you believe it? Scotland did the business, with big Joe Jordan coming on as substitute and scoring the winning goal. Rod's Cockney response? 'Magic! Bloody magic, mate!'

The trouble is that, when you are concentrating on names and numbers and just watching the ball, you're not really analysing the game as such. But, even then, I remember George Connelly on the night – the quality, the control, the class. He possibly had no entitlement to be there given that he had walked away from Scotland in an international match prior to the Czech game – the match against Switzerland in Berne – and Willie Ormond didn't even know he was away. Despite that, he came back to play in two internationals. He looked very comfortable that qualifying night but then he would, wouldn't he? I'd liken him to a mixture of Franz Beckenbauer and big Duncan Edwards, who was a very different type of player. But merge those two together and you get a composite genius. The big fella gave himself so much space. He was light-footed – a tap dancer. And his passing was superb. I don't think I ever heard him shouting during a game. He was so quiet I think the boys had to gee him up occasionally. He was a strange character. But to think that a player of such ability had only two caps . . . When you think of who's playing for Scotland now, there's a temptation to weep. Connelly should be in the Hall of Fame with fifty caps, no problem.

But, as I say, he was strange. I remember watching him playing against Clyde in the latter stages of his Celtic career. He must have been playing central defender, with maybe John Clark alongside him – I can't exactly remember – but I do remember he looked as if he was totally not interested in what was going on. I said to someone sitting beside me, 'He's going to walk off here. Someone should get a grip of him!'

I met Billy McNeill sometime afterwards and George's name cropped up. Billy said that George had indeed lost interest in the game and that the Celtic management and players were worried sick about him. They were having to say, 'Come on, George! Come on!' all the time. That was it, you know. They all loved Connelly, admired him and worried about him. Jinky said he was a terrific player, a genius. But he also said George couldn't cope with the gallus patter in the dressing room. The patter was good. Celtic were a team together and George had come into this team. His trouble was that he came in immediately after the Lions. He thought all those players, like wee Jinky, Bobby Murdoch, Bertie Auld, Tommy Gemmell and Billy McNeill, were superior to him. They were all legends. In doing so, he underestimated his own talent. He played nearly every game for two successive seasons and ended up Player of the Year yet he was still overawed. The other thing about him was that, although he played in all the major games, he never went to functions. You simply couldn't get him to go. And, if you tried to do an after-match interview with him, he was away, off-ski. He didn't want to speak to anybody. He didn't hang about. He'd get his gear and go. The Celtic doctor was baffled by him. Jock Stein was baffled by him. All the press were baffled by him. I never spoke to George Connelly in all the time I was a journalist.

And yet he was the kind of man you wanted to speak to and discuss this infinite talent. The first recollection I have is of him juggling the ball in the match against Kiev. I remember turning round and asking no one in particular, 'Who the hell is that?'

I was told that this was a young lad coming through. Well, he was going through my mind that night. I couldn't get him out of my head. He looked as if he could have done the ball-juggling all night. In the end, it was almost as if they had to drag him off the park. He was utterly brilliant. They talk about Ronaldinho and all that but Connelly was supreme that night. That was the first time I'd seen a player juggle a ball with such confidence and concentration.

Looking back, it's ironic but I never spoke to Stein directly about Connelly. I used to see the Big Man every Friday morning for years and years and the only time he mentioned him to me was before that Scottish Cup final against Rangers. The fact that Johnstone didn't play in that game has always been something of a mystery. But wee Jinky had a problem. He would often turn up late for training and Stein would have him. Jimmy's wife would deliberately let him sleep in because he had been bevvied and she knew that Stein would give him pelters. There was a hatch as you went into Celtic Park in those days and Stein could sit in his office and see everyone who came in. He would see the wee red hair coming and he'd shout, 'Sparra!' and that was it.

That particular Friday, Stein said he would play Connelly at outside right and Bertie Auld at outside left. In other words, those who were good on the ball were put on the wings and the runners, Bobby Lennox and Stevie Chalmers, would go through the middle. He predicted that his side would destroy Rangers because he thought their manager, Davie White, was technically naive. The funny thing was, after that, every paper was talking about Rangers being 'outmanoeuvred' and 'technically flawed'. Stein had got it right. He was so bloody confident of beating them.

Ultimately, that confidence drained away regarding Connelly. Stein knew what a great player he was and wondered just how to handle him. He brought him in and gave him chances, and brought him back again after he had walked out. Just imagine what kind of valuation he would achieve on today's transfer market. It would be colossal! Even today, everyone still talks very warmly of him. If you speak to players like Steve Chalmers and Bobby Lennox, they'll say, 'George, what a bloody player he was!'

In his last couple of years at Celtic, when he went missing, people inevitably went looking for him in the Kincardine area. When they asked about his specific whereabouts, they would be pointed to a bar. How is that for an epitaph?

16

QUALITY RESTORED

On 6 June 2007, a bright Wednesday morning, I turned a significant corner in my reclusive life by finally accepting an invitation from two of my closest friends to reunite and share recollections of our time together at Celtic. For a variety of reasons over the last few years, I've always ducked out of meeting David Hay and David Cattenach but now the closest trinity in the Quality Street Gang were going to be together again. The venue was the Three Kings, just outside Falkirk, and, appropriately, the host was the owner of that function room, Cattenach, for it was he who was the founder member of the Gang's inner circle. Given the sensitive nature of my ongoing relationship with alcohol, the refreshments were of the light variety and talk of that delicate subject was to be steadfastly avoided. Soon, two things were apparent: firstly, time spent apart has erected no barriers to our friendship; and, secondly, false modesty did not belong in that room.

Bryan Cooney was also present and, at some points, he helped to give our conversation some direction.

HAY: It started with you Catt, then it was Geordie and then me because I was part-time at first. Lou Macari appeared on the scene and then it was Danny McGrain, Kenny Dalglish, Paul Wilson, John Gorman, Jimmy Quinn and Victor Davidson. It was an exceptional group of young players. The three of us, plus Jimmy and John Gorman, were especially close. Remember those crazy parties through at Davie's house in Falkirk? That's probably where it was nurtured. The other thing was that we all got married quite young.

CONNELLY: I remember those days – the reserve team could have played in the first team. The talent was so great you could have reversed it and probably no one would have noticed.

CATTENACH: Remember we beat Rangers six nothing at Ibrox in the reserve cup final? And then took them back to Parkhead – I think it was 12–1 aggregate. Daft things like that. A good result for Rangers in those days was 3–0 against.

HAY: The reserve game I always remember was the one when we beat Partick Thistle 12–0 or 12–1. I think we were playing three at the back. Were you playing that day, Geordie?

CATTENACH: There's a funny thing – there was a sportsmen's dinner here about a month ago and Joe McBride was here. Do you know, that's the game he spoke about!

CONNELLY: See that day, Willie Wallace scored four goals.

HAY: It was our League Cup section; Rangers had played the night before. We had to win by six or seven nothing; Rangers, if I remember, had a party that night, celebrating; they didn't expect us to win by that margin. But we won. Bertie Auld played that day and McBride. There was just an abundance of talent. Real talent.

CONNELLY: We played the Lions against the Quality Street Gang in training; first-team dressing room against second-team dressing room. Our training games were better than some of the Premier games now. It was all two-touch stuff. Serious stuff.

HAY: I think that's what made us the players we became. Playing alongside the Lisbon Lions. Just imagine it. Training with the best manager, who had us as a group. And I think he actually enjoyed the fact that we could give them a game in training. It certainly kept the level of training high.

CONNELLY: I think I remember someone asking me what made us so good. I replied, 'Well, we were playing against the Lisbon Lions.'

COONEY: And what were the scores on these occasions?

HAY: An edict went out: the Lions must win! If Sean Fallon was refereeing, though, we were in with a shout.

CATTENACH: There were a lot of characters at the same time. The likes of Wee Jimmy. He was a one-off. The day I arrived at the club, I was shaking like a leaf. Billy McNeill walked past me, then John Hughes. I was seventeen and awestruck. There was a wee tap on my shoulder; it was Wee Jimmy. 'Your first day? Come with me,' he says. 'Everyone's got a nickname here. I'm just looking at you with your blond hair . . . you're Cattanoochie!'

The Wee Man took me training for five days. On the Friday, he shook my hand and said, 'All the best, son. This is Celtic!'

I was indoctrinated. Within the club there were a lot of characters so there were plenty of good laughs. Although you had your personal wee team, everybody got on.

HAY: As long as we showed them respect and didn't overstep the mark by saying anything wrong, you were OK. They could see there were some right good players coming through.

CONNELLY: You learned off them. I think the thing I most remember was the fantastic training.

HAY: You looked forward to it.

CATTENACH: Remember thon circuit on a Tuesday morning? Big Stein just made it up. There was nae SFA coaching manuals there. No Largs stuff. He just made it up. It was hard. You did the circuit on the grass park at Barrowfield. On the ash park, you played eight-a-side and you weren't allowed to walk. At the very least you had to jog. I think the biggest thing Jock brought was at the start of every season, saying, 'Look, that's your ball.'

HAY: I think at that time he was well ahead with his training. I know they talk about sports science and all those things nowadays but he had the fundamentals. Particularly the pre-season when you did the circuits and the ball. We used to train on the park; we used to go round in sand shoes, it wasn't trainers then. Wee things like you'd train with the sand shoes for the first week so that you wouldn't get blisters. The balls weren't even blown up hard to begin with. You got put in your own group, with your own ball – it almost depended on your size and weight.

CONNELLY: See what they do at that level, it determines your season. See if you've had a really good pre-season training, you can go and have a great season. Anybody who missed half the build-up was struggling to get back in the side again, you know.

CATTENACH: When did you sign, Davie, 1965, aye? What about you, George?

CONNELLY: I came to the Park in July 1965. I was on schoolboy forms from '63 to '65.

CATTENACH: I was '63. And I can compare the two pre-seasons. Under Jimmy McGrory and Sean Fallon, we got taken on a bus to about twelve miles from Seamill. And you had to run to the hotel. Then you got back on the bus and came home. He did that twice in a week, on a Wednesday and Friday. Everything in between was just running. You never saw a ball. Then it changed totally when Stein arrived. Until then, the method of getting fit was running.

HAY: There is a place for these things. You have to do the running in pre-season, which we did. But, as you said a moment ago, Davie, we actually got our own ball.

CATTENACH: That was clever as well.

HAY: We ran round the circle with the ball. We'd be jogging with it. Then he'd sometimes order us to sprint. Sometimes he'd co-ordinate it. You passed it back and you had to receive another ball. Now there was a couple of cock-ups. He used to make you run right round the circle, with someone chasing you. This was pre-water breaks. Unbelievable! We'd be training for over two hours without a drink. You used to come in and your mouth would be under that tap. I remember the first night after training, you could hardly go upstairs. You'd wonder, 'How am I going to manage tomorrow?' But we all did it.

CONNELLY: We used to order lemonade out of this shop. The guy used to put it in the fridge for us.

HAY: The only concession was that they would take us to the Beechwood Hotel for a bite to eat. That's actually where Kenny Dalglish met his wife, Marina. The hotel's over at Hampden.

CONNELLY: Davie, back to running around the circle. I can mind Jock standing there. He used to shout, 'Right, when I blaw the whistle, two balls. Next three balls; and the next four.' It used to knacker me.

CATTENACH: He used to go up on the eighteen-yard line and you'd play the ball up to him and he'd tee it up for you to shoot. If you gave him a bad ball, he'd whack it away and you'd have to go and get it. Let's say it concentrated the mind.

HAY: The funny story about Big Jock was, before he came, there used to be a snooker table at Parkhead. Then he changed it to table tennis. And he was no' bad at that game. Me and Geordie used to play doubles and that; being left-haunded, Stein would always stand this way and whack it. But if you could spin the ball into his body, he didnae have a backhand. Geordie was the one who could dae it. Stein would actually get annoyed. 'That's no' a right serve! Serve it right!' he would say. But Geordie was brave enough to try it.

COONEY: If Stein claimed sporting injustice, his employees felt they were hard done by in a financial context.

CATTENACH: Do you mind the day he brought that financial guy up? We couldnae stop laughing.

HAY: Nae wonder we were laughing. A guy from financial services coming up, considering the money we were on.

CATTENACH: My first wage was £14 a week.

CONNELLY: I started off at £12 and then went to £14. Then £25, took a spell at £35, then £45 and when you break into the first-team pool, it was £65. That was it; that was your whack.

HAY: The only thing they would dae when you signed a contract, you could negotiate for a signing-on fee. A couple of grand or something; whatever it might be. It didn't necessarily depend on how good you were, but how much you could argue to get it. It was a balancing act. But that led to the dispute and to me leaving. Geordie was maybe a bit quieter than me about the money but his belief was correct; he thought you shouldn't need to negotiate for your worth. No, you shouldn't but, unfortunately, you had to.

CONNELLY: That's no' a nice thing, I don't think. You shouldn't have to tell them you're a great player and that you should be getting this and that.

HAY: We were called rebels but we weren't really that. But I think they broke up a team too early.

CONNELLY: I was going to say that earlier on, Davie. They let Yogi Hughes go and then Willie Wallace go. There were so many great players at the time but, at the end of the day, there were no great players coming in.

HAY: As far as I remember, I don't think the Rangers players were earning any more than us. It wasn't like a Souness era, when the Butchers and Roberts etc. were earning superior money. I think it was compatible. I'm not sure.

CATTENACH: They were on about £100 a week.

HAY: If that's true, it was quite a disparity, considering we were the better team.

CONNELLY: That's about £35 a week less – an awful lot of money then.

COONEY: What kind of stance did Stein take in all this?

HAY: Initially, it was 'How dare you ask for more money?' There was a frightening aspect to it in that you didn't want to chap the door too loudly. But your sense of injustice built enough for you to say, 'I've got to do it.'

Then, what happened was that you talked more to Big Dessie White than you did to Big Jock. We got the chance to buy a lot of flats near the BBC Studios. They were to cost thirty grand – what they would be worth now you can only imagine. We went to Big Dessie and thought we'll sign for £65 a week, if we get the loan. A lot of players were getting loans at the time for pubs and that. That was their way of compensating players for the contracts issue. We decided we would go and ask Celtic for the money. But we got totally kicked into touch.

CONNELLY: My backside still hurts. Seriously, they told us it wasn't feasible.

HAY: Geordie thought Big Dessie bought the flats. We were young and that but they could have given us some of it and we could have got the rest from somewhere else and we could have been tied to Celtic for life. Then Celtic could have kept on paying us the wage we were on without giving us the increase we were looking for. We would have been supplementing our income by renting out those flats. What an asset they would have been. I wouldn't have thought of going to England. I think the mainstay of that team was Geordie and myself. The one thing I'd say in favour of Big Jock was that he wasn't paid that well, either. It's not until I became a manger myself that I realised that. So a bit of sympathy goes to Big Jock. In spite of it all, I liked Big Jock; I thought he was the greatest ever. We owe a lot to him. I have no qualms about him.

CATTENACH: Aye, dinnae get me wrong; he was years in front of himself; a million years in front of the rest of Scotland; and you only found that out when you got into that club. But you had so many players at Celtic Park who had pride in themselves. They were good trainers, they wanted to play; they could play for themselves. They had that pride. Put that in with Jock Stein and the combination was hard to beat. How many players have you seen, Davie, where you know they're just there for the money? It sticks out like a sair thumb.

HAY: Although I ended up fighting for a better contract, it wasn't because I was greedy – it was because of the unfairness of the whole thing. When negotiations stopped, that didn't hinder me – I wasn't saying, 'I'm no' going to try as much because they didn't give me that.'

CATTENACH: But even in the middle of negotiations, you and Geordie were still giving everything.

CONNELLY: I think they knew that, Davie – knew we would never give anything less than everything.

CATTENACH: It's unusual that you get so many good players together at the one time.

HAY: Aye, well we played under a great group of players. We were learning from them. But not only did we get on on the park but off the park as well. That would mix together. OK, we eventually went our different ways and that but, when you see them after all those years, it's just as if it was yesterday.

CATTENACH: I've already told you what Wee Jimmy done for me on the first day and you never forget that. That was instilled in me immediately and any young lads who came received the same treatment. You made them feel welcome. Mind Pat McMahon? He used to sit at the window and read a book.

HAY: Aye but eventually he came round.

CATTENACH: Do you not mind what happened? We played Morton in a testimonial on a Monday night. And everybody was at Seamill. There was a band sorted. Big Jock went away and Sean was in charge. Wee Louie was always up for it. Two in the morning and there was a chap on the door. Pat opened it and got a pail of water over him. Whack! Pat went and got the fire extinguisher and he was chasing us. He was all right after that.

CONNELLY: Back to the money thing. They knew we were playing for the jerseys and they were wanting us for as little as possible. That was the end of the story.

HAY: We had a good lifestyle compared to the average working man – I'm never disputing that. But we weren't paid what we were worth or what Celtic could afford. Do you remember going up to Big Dessie's office, Geordie? He was bringing out balance sheets with the names of Tottenham and Arsenal on them, and he would show you the salary of the top players down there. According to those sheets, it wasn't that different to our salaries. It was compatible to an extent, if you were winning every game, but my bone of contention was the basic wage.

CONNELLY: See that time of the walkouts, Davie? I can remember Jock Stein writing in the paper that we were getting an average of £200 a week. But that was with us winning everything. The other thing is you had a lifestyle geared to that kind of money. Then you got hit with a surtax at the end of the day.

HAY: Yeah, there was that aspect as well. It wasn't like the modern-day player who might be on a hundred grand a week. When that happens, the bonuses don't matter to such an extent. We had maybe set our lifestyle to maybe ten grand a year but, without playing and without the bonuses, you were on three and a half grand a year.

CATTENACH: What were the bonuses in the reserves – £3 for a win? I'll never forget when we drew 0–0 with Hearts at Tynecastle and we got £1.50 bonus. Crazy!

HAY: I know we're talking about money but it wasn't an issue when we trained or played. It was an issue when you thought about it – from the point of view of fairness, no' from the point of view of greed.

CATTENACH: The thing is you just wanted to play for Celtic.

HAY: You did. But, as you got older, you looked for fairness to be brought into the equation. I was out on strike for two weeks, Geordie might have been out a week. We invented Solidarity before Lech Walesa. But, never mind my departure, what about yours, Geordie? I'm not trying to be patronising but a talent was lost to Celtic and lost to the game. You can't get away from that, George.

CONNELLY: It's taken me a long time to look at it, Davie. I think I hid myself from it for a long time, too. But, just in recent times, I say to myself, 'Jesus Christ; I was oot of the game at twenty-six.' That's what inspired me to write this book.

CATTENACH: Gorry was the first of our little team to go – to Carlisle. Jimmy Quinn went to Sheffield in 1972; then there was us three. I went to Falkirk, Davie to Chelsea and Geordie out altogether. Did you feel, Geordie, when Davie went that the nucleus had gone?

CONNELLY: To be honest, Davie, I cannae mind a lot about that time. But I can mind walking out for the last time. But I think maybe that's what it was as well. Different players coming in and you weren't seeing familiar faces in the morning. Maybe that was in my heid. There again, it was costing me money to play. So that was it.

HAY: People used to say that George was complex; he wasn't. I knew him better than anybody. His philosophy was he shouldn't have to fight for money. I once said to him, 'Geordie, see if Pelé was here, he'd need to fight for money!'

I told him, through negotiation, there were players with far less ability than himself, without naming names, who could earn more than him. And it wasn't right. I told him to believe me and stand by me. I wasn't doing it to strengthen my case – it was to strengthen our case together. That, then, was going to be the nucleus of the team.

CATTENACH: Big Jock knew that.

HAY: Maybe he thought that there were so many good ones that it could just carry on and that it didn't matter that we left.

CONNELLY: That was the only thing I knew from school. The fitba was everything.

HAY: Geordie's philosophy was that the club would look after him well. And they didn't. They took advantage of the situation.

CONNELLY: When I finished with Celtic and went out into the world, I used to talk to the pipe laggers at Torness and they were earning more than us; of course they put the hours in.

HAY: And now you've got Bosman freedom of contract.

CONNELLY: It's phenomenal nowadays.

CATTENACH: It must have been hard for you as a manager to negotiate with players, Davie.

HAY: No' really. The difference is now that the manager doesn't deal with the players as far as salaries are concerned; that makes your job easier. Your relationship will never be soured as it was in the old days. I mean, Big Jock might have been soured by me knowing that he wasn't earning maybe as much as I thought he had been. Whereas, nowadays, they fall out with the chief executive, not the coach. The problem arises now where you get maybe a chief executive maybe wanting to pick the team.

CONNELLY: Aren't a lot of those players not on more than the manager, Davie? Isn't that a bad thing?

HAY: I think you could be right. There is the old bit that the manager should always be paid more. If you get the chief executive of a company, none of the subordinates will be paid higher than him. I think there was a disparity years ago with Alex Ferguson but I think that changed. It had to change. Will Jose Mourinho be getting paid more than say Joe Cole? There'll no' be much of a difference, George. There again, if you're a manager and earning £1 million a year and there are players at £2 million, £1m is not too bad. Will Frank Rijkaard get paid more than Ronaldinho? I'm not so sure.

CONNELLY: What I was getting at, Davie, would it not invite disrespect?

HAY: Where you might be right is it might be a case whereby, if a player is earning a certain amount of money, does that stop the drive of ambition? Now I would say someone like Steven Gerrard, whether he's earning ten or one hundred grand a week, would be the same player anyway. Maybe some players who are earning more than they're worth could switch off.

CONNELLY: When we were playing for the jersey, that's what it was. It meant something. Nowadays, it's kissing the jerseys. In my opinion, that's just for show!

HAY: We live in a world of showbiz and cameras. In our time, if you kissed the jersey, they'd think you had a sair chest or something. You can only ask the individual if it's genuine or if it's false. I would tend to think that a lot of it is done for effect. But the supporters actually look for it now, George. It becomes part of the show.

CONNELLY: It's just an add-on. They're getting all this money so they add the jersey-kissing on too.

HAY: In our time, we thought a good pass was a way of showing the fans what we were at.

CATTENACH: So much has changed. You just got told in the old days which supporters' club you were going to on Saturday or Sunday night. That was it, end of story. It doesn't happen now, I wouldn't think.

HAY: Tommy Burns, in his time, tried to make sure that players would attend functions.

CATTENACH: At Larbert, three or four years ago, they couldn't get a player to come to their function. Danny McGrain came through one year and Tommy Burns another but no player. And it was their Player of the Year function.

CONNELLY: It was claimed at Rangers that Dick Advocaat stopped the players going.

HAY: I always remember me and Geordie would go to a few and it wasn't big, plush hotels and all that. It was wee halls and ladies' choices. But you actually realised what the club meant to these people by going to these functions. And, once you got there and got a couple of bevvies down, you enjoyed yourself. Certainly, the supporters really appreciated the fact that you were there. It was a big highlight of their year. But those days are gone, I fear.

CONNELLY: It really wasn't until I stopped playing, Davie, that I realised what the club meant to the supporters. Twelve o'clock on a Saturday and their minds were set; they were away hame to change and get through to the Park.

CATTENACH: Can you remember wee John Dick, my cousin? Celtic was his life and I mean his life. See if the team got beat, he didn't come oot until Monday. You have no idea, really. There are a lot of people like that, you know.

HAY: It took over their lives. But see because of the coverage now, there's more spotlight on everything. Maybe, in a strange way, that's as close as the player gets to the fans now. Whereas, in our time, we were more intimate – you couldn't be aloof in that era. Also, our intimacy was actually in going to functions like that. Whereas this shirt kissing is their form of intimacy and the fans are expecting it now. It's how the whole thing works. The whole coverage is different. In the past, you played the game and then looked forward to the next one. Now, you've got e-mails and everything; everything's constant. I suppose life has changed as well. They still go and support in their numbers, still love their team, but it's scrutinised more now and analysed more now.

CONNELLY: See when you were through at the Park as manager, Davie, did the players have the same keenness for training and playing?

HAY: Aye, I would say so.

CONNELLY: I asked the question in light of all this money they're getting.

HAY: When I was manager, they probably weren't at the same level as they are now, George. Players were on about £300 a week then – it had increased but it wasn't as astronomical or obscene as it is now.

CONNELLY: But they still had that keenness for training?

HAY: You're talking about 83–87, George?

CONNELLY: You managed a right good team.

HAY: Aye, they were a decent team. Home-grown lads and some from other Scottish teams. Where we might be a bit critical of the boys – is it wrong that they're earning more money?

CONNELLY: No.

HAY: Does that make them less ambitious? Probably not.

CONNELLY: Do you think the present-day players are less enthusiastic?

HAY: I don't watch the training a lot. But I think the style of play has changed; there is more possession being kept. I think there's a kind of possession for possession's sake rather than possession for a purpose. Not just with Celtic but in general.

CATTENACH: Six passes across the park?

HAY: That never happened in our time. George's theory was you built from the back but at Celtic you weren't allowed to do that. You would sometimes play it to your wide men, up front, then back to your midfield. There was naebody better than Geordie to ping a sixty-yard accurate pass; is that no' better than taking ten passes to get there? When some people play a long ball, a long accurate ball is sometimes better than short passing. Not hopeful. George Connelly never gave you a hopeful kick.

CONNELLY: If Davie was playing at the back with me, I was never scared; it was my ace card. I still think today, if you're building from the back, you're instigating a good move.

HAY: Geordie would maybe break in there and ping a great ball up to the forwards, who would ping it back to the midfield. You've got to remember, George also played midfield. He started, of course, by playing wide right. Scored in that 1969 cup final. That goal took class to score. First of all, he dispossessed John Greig, who then tried to welly him – an almighty welly as it happened. He jumped out of the way. Then, it looked as if he was slow-strolling round Norrie Martin – no' a lot of players could do this but that's ability, class and confidence. They don't come much better than that.

CONNELLY: Back to the fitba we were playing – if you watched our games, you would never see much back passing. It was forward passing all the time. I can't be bothered watching them sometimes nowadays.

CATTENACH: I was at a game about six weeks ago and, honestly, I was fed up. I was bored – really bored.

HAY: That is the style of the game nowadays. Is it quicker? Probably. With the technology, athletes run quicker, swimmers swim faster, but, as far as fitness was concerned, we were as fit as the modern-day player. Big Jock was our sports scientist. Neil Mochan could throw in one or two bits of advice as well.

CATTENACH: Paul Scholes goes forward and takes it off everyone. Everybody gives him the ball. Meanwhile, there's Michael Carrick – £18 million?

CONNELLY: There's also that German guy who plays with Chelsea, Michael Ballack. He's on a hundred thousand pounds a week. It beats me. Mind you, he's no' going to say no to the money, is he?

HAY: I take it he didn't go out on strike?

CATTENACH: Do you think Chelsea would have given him money to buy those flats?

HAY: Talking about money, here's a great story – it happened after the second leg of the European Cup semi-final against Leeds. Obviously, we never knew what it would be before the game. You got what you got and it was decided afterwards. We used to get paid every Tuesday and it was cash. You didn't get paid through banks in those days. There was this guy who accompanied the man carrying the money; he was the bodyguard. He had a walking stick. I suppose that might have helped, you know. Anyway, the semi-final was over – we'd beaten Leeds. There had been a massive crowd at Hampden. We got £1,000.

CONNELLY: I think it was 1,200, Davie.

HAY: I cannae remember. Anyway, this one was paid by cheque, with whatever tax deductions, because they couldnae pay you that amount in cash. So we were having a meeting and deciding it wasn't enough. It was in the dressing rooms and you had the massage beds in the middle of the room. We received the envelopes. The talk was that we should give them back. I think we were comparing it to 1967. Big Jock comes in. He smells the discontent. 'Whit is it?' he asks. There are a couple of rumbles of discontent.

'Well,' he says, 'if that's what you think about it, it's up to yourselves. If you don't want them, the cleaning woman will be in shortly!'

And then he walked out. All you saw, slowly but surely, was all the players picking up their envelopes. Naebody missed!

COONEY: Did Stein have a sense of humour?

CATTENACH: I never saw too much of it.

HAY: I think it came across in training if someone did a trick or something. If Wee Jimmy pulled one off, there was a bit of humour there.

CATTENACH: He wisnae a morbid person, though.

HAY: As long as you let him beat you at table tennis, he would have a smile on his face. I think, if he could see a smile on our faces, that was OK. He could sense if there was anything untoward. We used to go away for trips, two and three days at a time. Look at the European games, we used to travel on a Monday, before the game on a Wednesday, and not fly back until the Thursday. Part of the trip was we would have a good time after the game. Now they go out maybe the day before and they fly straight back. I wonder if they should actually stay there and have a little recreation. The argument against that might be that a bit of a swally defeats the purpose. If we came back early, we probably would have gone out in Glasgow, I don't know. Back to Jock's humour – he could see we were all happy together. Jim Steele was the club's jester. That was Jock's way; he would get humour out of Steely giving up humour. Steely played a big part.

CATTENACH: They'd put him on the microphone on the plane. 'There are some very famous personalities on this aircraft,' he'd say. 'There's Lulu at the back. Hello, Lulu! Haw, haw, haw.' The place would be in uproar.

HAY: Big Jock could see the humorous side of that. Steely was the catalyst of the humour, particularly when we went away trips.

CATTENACH: There was nae humour when getting beat by Rangers was involved. Stein just detested it. I remember the first team got beat 1–0 by them at Celtic Park. The reserves had won easy at Ibrox. Everybody was in on the Monday. We were going up the terracing with a medicine ball. We were just being hammered. We'd won and yet were getting absolutely slaughtered along with the first team. Nae mention about nothing. That was him saying, 'You got beat on Saturday, you'll run this morning!'

HAY: The other thing is we used to go to Bonnington golf course and run there.

CONNELLY: That was a hammering session as well, Davie. I used to get butterflies in my stomach. I kent what was coming. 'Here we go again . . .'

He would just keep us on our toes. Sometimes you weren't allowed your cars up to Barrowfield; you were either walking or running. And, at Barrowfield, you were playing two-touch fitba – kept you on the go again. When I played for the juniors, I made them all play two-touch, Davie.

HAY: Did two-touch in training stop Jimmy Johnstone dribbling on a Saturday? No. If there hadn't been two-touch in training with Jimmy, nane of us would have got the ball. It was the pace, the intensity and the quality of training.

CATTENACH: Do you mind playing a pre-season game at Blackpool? What a game it was – we got beat 4–3. But it was all Celtic supporters there 'cos it was in the middle of the Glasgow holidays. We were standing in the dressing rooms before the game. Wee Sean was in charge but Big Jock came in, right? Mohair grey suit, white shirt and a tie – he was immaculate. That Irish comedian, Frank Carson, followed him in.

'Ah, Jock, do you think that style will come back?' he asked.

'Ooh, ya, f*****!' We all went like that.

HAY: Aye, with Stein, it was a case of, 'Who's first?'

CATTENACH: Well, I've never seen twelve players going to the toilet at the same time. Oh, he was raging!

CONNELLY: I can mind that game, Catt. I can remember being told that this scout was here and that scout was here. They were all watching from the stands because we were up and coming. And I made a bloomer in the first minute, giving Blackpool a goal, eh? I never had a good game after that.

CATTENACH: Do you no' mind we went with Sean down to Rotherham? They started all that stuff. We all looked at each other and acknowledged what was going to happen. Well, we just about booted them off the park. Do you no' mind what Tommy Docherty [Rotherham's manager] said after the game?

'That was great,' he said, 'sticking it to those English bastards!'

HAY: We used to play a lot of England Second Division sides which were decent at the time. It was experience for us. I see Celtic are talking about playing in other leagues now.

CATTENACH: Stein wanted to put the second team through to Stenhousemuir and play us in the old Second Division.

HAY: That was mooted way back. There was an edge to the game then; we played on a Friday night and you could have five, ten or fifteen thousand, depending on who you played. You were playing on the first-team park. Now they're playing in front of a handful of people at small grounds; it's not the same level of intensity; that's why Peter Lawwell is talking about playing in another league.

CATTENACH: We played Rangers in one Glasgow Cup final; beat them 3–1, at Hampden. Must have been about 80,000 there that night.

HAY: This is about 1968. Stein almost played the reserve team; Jim Craig and Tommy Gemmell played, Bobby Murdoch, too; the rest was all us. We played three at the back; this system had never been heard of before. This was Rangers' first team. They scored right at the death – John Greig or someone like that. Geordie was just pinging the ball from here to there, while Catt and I were the markers. George was the catalyst for the system – that's why Big Jock was a genius.

CATTENACH: What about Feyenoord? Wasn't that game totally different to Lisbon? I'm talking about the atmospheres.

HAY: Aye, the Feyenoord fans were noisier so we were taken aback by that. Would you believe Feyenoord were 4–1 to win the game?

CATTENACH: Even the build-ups were different. The second one was away up in mountains, twenty miles away from Milan, in a sort of monastery, whereas, with Lisbon, we were right in the middle of everything. It was a Holy Obligation the day of the game. Stein got Sean and the players to walk to Mass in the middle of the supporters. And walked back.

And the place was packed. And the atmosphere was electric.

When I announced that I had power-walked for ten miles the previous day and that I'd taken cramp for the first time in my life, humour was back in the room.

CATTENACH: I mind when you were in danger of suffering something much worse than cramp! Remember? On that trip to Bermuda?

CONNELLY: I'm sorry but I cannae remember it.

CATTENACH: Well, I can. We'd just played Feyenoord and had gone out to the States and then Bermuda on tour. We were on a night out – we went to a club and were well bevvied. We're all sitting watching this act whereby the man in the middle had to dance between flailing sticks. The timing had to be spot on, otherwise there was a good chance he would have broken his ankles. Suddenly, our Geordie decides he can do this. We cannot believe it. He's shy, isn't he? No' this night he's no'. He gets up on to the stage and dances like he'd been doing it all his life; he never missed a beat!

HAY: There was supposed to be something about Geordie and a hypnotist that night; I think Celtic thought he's probably never come out of the trance since. Was he hypnotised? Naw. The boy just whispered in his ear.

COONEY: What about the other two members of the inner circle?

HAY: Have you seen Wee Gorry recently?

CATTENACH: I spoke to him about a month ago. He was in Spain.

HAY: He's got a place there?

CATTENACH: Aye, he was just over for a week. I see he's

chief scout at Southampton now.

CONNELLY: Superb.

HAY: There was a closeness between us that will never be broken.

CONNELLY: When Jimmy died, it was so emotional for us. Terrible.

HAY: Geordie and Catt knew Jimmy better than I did. But having said that, we all knew one another and, when you go to a funeral, it brings back the memories and that. I remember Jimmy's wife wanted to see George. Away back, though, the first hoose we had was that one in Uddingston – a room and kitchen, with an outside toilet. So we had a party. I remember Jimmy leaving, must have been Pat Wheldon he was with. I could see he had something underneath his jacket.

'What are you daen?' I asked. He'd been trying to nick one of my LPs. See if he'd asked me it would have been OK.

'Gie's that back!' I said to him. There was always a bit of devilment in him.

CATTENACH: I ran a pub just down at the bottom of the hill there. My mother used to come up to clean. It was a Saturday morning. This would be about ten and we opened at eleven. I was stocking the bar through the back. I just heard this big, crazy laugh. I says, 'That sounds like Jimmy Quinn.' He just appeared with this boy – it was his young cousin. And he had a good drink in him. You ken what he was like when he started thon laugh. 'Was I quick or was I quick?' he'd ask.

HAY: Jimmy Quinn was the quickest player ever.

CATTENACH: Did I tell you what happened when he was on the building site? They were sitting there having their lunch, talking about Jimmy's speed. This boy, about twenty year old, has got the trainers on and that. He says, 'I'll race you!'

231

Jimmy's around forty by this time and he's wearing a pair of workman's boots. They marched out and started to race. Whoof! Jimmy just left him behind.

HAY: What age was he when he died? Fifty-four, fifty-three? How long ago was that?

CONNELLY: The funeral was on a Friday. It was a Rangers–Celtic game on the Saturday. Rangers won 3–2, that Lovenkrands scored the goal that beat us. Four years ago, Davie. The thing I discovered about Jimmy and you're talking about his pace – see the faster a player was, the faster Jimmy could go. He could beat George McNeill likely, you know. Whoever it was, he was faster.

CATTENACH: Wee Macari had it all organised for Jimmy to run at Powderhall on New Year's Day. He was off ten yards. Lou was getting the money on. Mind, Jimmy pulled out at the last minute. Off ten yards, naebody in the world would have beat him – I'm no' caring who it was.

HAY: Jimmy won the pools or something, didn't he?

CONNELLY: He did. He won a few thousand on the pools. 'Cos I phoned him a couple of days after. I had to tap money to get to the pub and I phoned him. He'd told me to phone him but he couldn't remember. He must have been drunk. I never saw him again.

HAY: We used to go up to an Italian restaurant in Parkhead. We either went to Joe's Kitchen or the Italian. We must have been flush or something so we went up for a bowl of pasta and maybe a glass of wine. Jimmy had the big Zephyr car at the time. There was always wee bits of fun in those days.

CATTENACH: We were down at Seamill. It was the first hotel with the therapeutic waters so all the old women were going down there. Willie O'Neill used to sleep on the floor because of his bad back. For some unknown reason, he stripped naked and went out to lie down in the corridor. But soon he was battering on the door. The old ladies had spotted him.

'Let me in, Catt! Let me in, they're going to attack me; they fancy me!'

Willie and Gorry both went to Carlisle and stayed in club houses next to one another. Willie used to get up at six on Sunday mornings and steal Gorry's newspapers. Crazy!

HAY: Lou was never far from the fun. He didn't take a drink but that didn't stop him mixing in the company. To sum him up, he was good company. I'm sure he actually took a book on the *Wacky Races* – the cartoon characters. Now I'm sure he did it for a laugh. But, I've got to say, somebody actually bet on Dick Dastardly! Everyone knows he never won a race.

CONNELLY: Stein told me that Brian McLaughlin could have been better than any of us if it hadn't been for his injury. I think he'd been playing too long, Davie. I noticed that. He was only seventeen or eighteen and he'd had one game too many for his age. He got that bad injury against Clyde. He was never the same player again.

HAY: For Jock to play him so young, he must have thought a helluva lot of him. Brian played for me at Motherwell. Nowadays, see if you get any kind of injury, medical science is such that the chances are you will recover.

CONNELLY: Keyhole surgery is the thing nowadays.

HAY: Aye, that's the whole thing. They have the specialists in Colorado who did it for Ian Durrant. Brian got back playing but maybe he was never just as sharp as he'd been before. He'd have been sensational.

CONNELLY: Even in the games he played, you could see he was absolutely brilliant. He had two natural feet, he could go past people, he had pace and he could ping the ball about.

HAY: Big Jock played him wide right to begin with.

CATTENACH: His older brother, Hughie, played with Stirling Albion when I was there. He was a fair player, too – played in the middle of the park. It was obviously in the family.

CONNELLY: He came round to see me a couple of years ago when I was on the bevvy, eh? I think Brian likes a drink, tae.

HAY: Aye, he likes a pint of lager. But it's never come across to me that he's in any way bitter. Maybe in his quieter moments. And he got back, maybe not at the level he could have done. He went to Sligo Rovers for a wee while, then Ayr United, before Motherwell.

Once that sombre moment was over, another character from the past was remembered.

CATTENACH: We had some laughs with Dixie Deans. Remember at the Albany and the 1988 Centenary? It was four in the morning. He disappeared, then reappeared about half an hour later. He'd a chef's uniform on and he was carrying a big tray of sandwiches.

HAY: What about Jersey? We were playing Southampton. Jersey had laws that permitted all-day drinking. We were waiting for the bell to ring at 2.30 but of course it never did. Great. There was a beer delivery in progress. Dixie, for a laugh, got a hold of the guy's overalls and came in hefting a beer barrel.

CONNELLY: Wasn't Jim Steele playing in that game? I've still got the mark on my leg to prove it.

HAY: He was naughty. Ron Davies and Mick Channon were playing. They were all bevvied.

CONNELLY: Steele just missed me with his studs. The hairs on my leg will still not grow to this day.

CATTENACH: By the way, Dixie signed for Celtic on a Saturday night and we left for Malta on the Sunday. Remember that trip?

HAY: Aye, when we were coming back, we all used to get stuck up the front. Nae drinks and that but, of course, we used to manoeuvre a couple our way. I said to Dixie, 'One thing, John, is that it's a ritual for new players to give a wee song to the team.'

Dixie, no' being shy, gets up and gets a haud of the mike. So he's up there, giving it 'Band of Gold'. He didn't need a lot of persuasion, by the way. He was a good, wee player. A nightmare to play against.

CATTENACH: He was so strong. Body-wise, you couldn't rattle him about. He would just come back and dae you again.

HAY: Aye, he was brave.

COONEY: What about the backroom heroes of Parkhead?

CATTENACH: The most embarrassing thing for me came when I was in getting treatment for an injury. I was lying on the treatment table with Bob Rooney overseeing things. Frank Haffey was sitting there. I'd only been in the place for about three weeks. Haffey was making faces at me.

'What's up with you?' Bob inquired.

Duncan Mackay couldn't stand Bob. Called him a witch doctor. Haffey once threw two squibs into his room.

CONNELLY: The things I can most mind about Bob was that, if anyone was injured, he was in the Park from nine in the morning till nine at night. I mean he was a great servant to Celtic – no doubt about that. The other thing was when I was on the ground-staff, he told me that, if I ever wanted a cup of tea, I should just go into his wee room and take one.

HAY: So you'd make him a cup?

CONNELLY: Aye, that's whit it would be, Davie.

CATTENACH: He was a really nice man, though. Just a smashing, lovely man.

CONNELLY: He was a brilliant servant to Celtic.

CATTENACH: Talking about brilliant servants, what about Sean? Anyone shaking his hand would suffer from broken bones. What a strength!

HAY: He's no' changed that much.

CATTENACH: He looks great.

CONNELLY: He was a good guy to look up to.

HAY: Sean was for us.

CONNELLY: He wasn't coming in there shouting, or trying to unnerve you. He had a nice way about him.

CATTENACH: We beat Rangers 3–1 in that Glasgow Cup final on a Monday night. Quinn scored. Oh, what a goal he scored! We were all there that night. Alex Macdonald was playing for Rangers – he could be a dirty so-and-so. The ball came between us on the halfway line and we were both going for it. I did him up high, at the top of his neck. He was carried off on a stretcher. Stein went ballistic at half-time. 'Oh, you f***** bastard!' he screamed. He called me for everything. I was shattered.

Sean comes up and says, 'All right, Catt? That was one of the finest tackles I've ever seen in my life!'

That lifted me – no mistakes. Mind you, about six months later, we were playing against Hibs at Celtic Park on a Friday night. I was playing at the back with you, Geordie. Kenny Dalglish had just been there for a short while and, to be honest, he wasn't doing that well. He'd been playing in about five positions before Stein got his true position. This night, Willie Hunter was booting Kenny repeatedly. It wasn't really bad or malicious but he was still doing it. Big Jock asked to see me for a minute at half time; we went through to the showers. He told me he was switching me to the middle of the park to go and sort out Hunter for what he was doing to Kenny.

I'm looking at Stein, who had been screaming at me not long since, and I'm thinking to myself, 'Will I or will I not?' In the end, I never said a word. I just went out and done him, then I went back to join my pal Geordie as sweeper.

Job done!

CONNELLY: Sean used to say to me, 'If anyone hits you, don't let them see you're hurt. Just get up as if nothing has happened.' I was tackled by Davie Holt one day – what a whack it was! I got up and it seemed to be all right. See the following week, I had to get taken off the park. My back was still f****** sair. That's no joking. Another thing Sean used to say to me was to start the game fast. If you started in lower gear, you would never get up. So you ran to take throw-ins, ran to take corners. In some of the Celtic games in recent years – especially that one against Motherwell where they should have won the championship when Martin O'Neill was the manager – they were walking to take shies. To me, they should have started that game off quick.

CATTENACH: What do you think of this Scott Brown? I've never seen him play live.

HAY: Aye, he's good. He's aggressive but he's controlled himself without losing the aggression.

CATTENACH: I've not actually met Gordon Strachan; it's as if he's trying to get them to play at pace all the time.

HAY: You'll see that maybe more next season. I think when he had Neil Lennon there, Neil had a style that had the modern-day game in it. It was kinda knock it here, knock it there, get it back, progress through there. Scott Brown's not that type of player. He's more direct.

CATTENACH: Strachan was like that. So you could be right, Davie – he's trying to get that type of player. Do you not think it's unfair that a lot of the supporters are still not convinced about Strachan?

HAY: I don't know if it's because sometimes how his manner comes across – he can be a bit abrupt – or whether it's because the team's not done well recently. The funny thing is I remember they were trying to say in one article that

Strachan was going to play a better style of football than Martin O'Neill. I didn't agree with it. Martin O'Neill's style was good. A lot of people were trying to say that Strachan wanted to play a more passing game, but Neil Lennon and Paul Lambert played with Celtic and they were passing players. I don't know if it's how he comes across sometimes and people maybe take a dislike to him because of that.

CONNELLY: The impression I get sometimes is that he's playing certain players to please people.

HAY: I think, to make a stand sometimes, he might pick somebody from his point of view. Sometimes you can be stubborn and do that.

CONNELLY: I feel that Aiden McGeady is one of the best talents in Britain and I feel he should be the first name on the team sheet.

HAY: Yeah, you're right but, if you watched him in the cup final, he had a poor game. There was nothing going for him that day. And I think what happens, see when you're younger, is that people give you the benefit of the doubt. I like him. I think he's direct. Nakamura was poor as well. Not many Celtic players actually played well.

CONNELLY: I think they stopped playing well after AC Milan.

HAY: Aye and they had won the league. Mind you, Lennon's substitution in the cup final could have been Strachan's way of making a point. Just before he got taken off, he was run by one of their players. It was still nothing each. It wasn't as if it was the last ten minutes. Yeah, I think Strachan was making a statement. Lennon was not amused.

CONNELLY: That was his platform. He should have just given the crowd a wave and got a cheer and that would have been it. He should have turned it into a positive for himself.

HAY: I think he did that at the end when he kinda milked it a wee bit. Think of yourself as a player. It's your last game, it's nothing each, your team is no' playing well but you are not playing that badly, you're not the one that's thinking, 'It's going to be me!' But, I think with Lennon there was surprise. He was shocked. Then he went up the tunnel before realising he'd better go back.

CATTENACH: He said later that he had gone to phone his mother and father – to tell them that was it.

HAY: There were nae mobiles in our time but I think that would have been the last thing I would have done.

The reunion of the Quality Street Gang was over. This one was never destined to be riotous like the old days at Davie Cattenach's house but it has been a joy for all that. We have dipped liberally into the memory bank and the withdrawals have made us all think, laugh and cry. In deference to my fight against alcohol, we drank nothing stronger than tea, coffee and diet Irn-Bru. Promises were made to make this a regular event on the football calendar. But will those promises ever be kept?

17

BACK IN PARADISE

My life is all about extremes. In fact, I'm such a regular commuter between heaven and hell that I should join a frequent-flyer scheme and save myself a few bob. Hell was certainly the destination I was heading for around the time of my fifty-eighth birthday on 1 March 2007. Of course, such a negative thought didn't enter my mind at the time when I was addressing the small matter of celebrating my special day.

But, before I go there, let me try to explain my form of alcoholism. There, I've said the word – that's an achievement in itself. I have always attempted to hide away from the truth – just closed the shutters and pretended certain things didn't exist. Now, I'm prepared to look the truth straight in the eye, if not to spit in it. Yes, I am an alcoholic – indeed, as the man from the local branch of the AA puts it, an alcoholic with a capital A. I've been struggling with the addiction and its terrible side effects for years. I cannot tell you how much it interferes with all aspects of my life. Drinking is not an everyday occurrence and I suppose, in that respect, I'm lucky. But, every so often, this horrible illness creeps up on me and puts me out of the game for more time than I care to think about. It leaves me senseless and incapable of rational thought or deed. Everything else stops when I'm on the sauce – my part-time job on the taxis, my marriage, my relationship with my kids, my diet, my fitness routine . . .

When I've been struggling with the devil drink and its temptations and I wake up lying next to the one woman who has made me truly happy in this life, I often wonder how she puts up with me. Helen Blackadder – I say her name and love the sound of it. We have lived together for thirty years and, during that time, we've shared every emotion there is – happiness, sadness, disappointment, pride, we've experienced them all. We've fallen out and then made up just as quickly and it's all because of the way I live and have chosen to live my life. But we have the wonderful common denominator they call love. That love is probably stronger than it was when we met in 1977. It has needed to be that way. When I'm sober, we fall for each other all the time. It's just one of those attractions. She's always been there for me. You know by now that Helen hates the abuse of alcohol. She'll take the occasional drink herself but seeing what it's done to me has made her despise it.

The format of my binges is predictable: I go out and drink till it's coming out of my ears and then I seek some form of sobriety before going back to Helen and apologising. Yes, I apologise humbly for my misbehaviour and position myself so that I don't fall down when the earbashing comes my way. And there's no escaping it – it's as inevitable as tomorrow and it comes with the accuracy of laser beams. Then my words spill out like sugar from a bag, 'That's me. That's it. Finished! Never again!' I suppose, if I was really on the honesty kick, I should add, 'There will now be a short intermission – till the next time.' And there always is a next time.

Anyway, when I get back after a session, Helen will sort of celebrate my return – keeping it pretty much to herself, mind. My ear will have had its bashing and I'll have been deposited in the bad books for a wee while. It's screwball stuff – sure it is – but I take the earache for a couple of days then, inch by inch, I gradually worm my way back in to her affections. And that affection never wavers.

Helen's a friend, a great friend, to me and, boy, do I need friends! She's done countless things that should put her in line for a sainthood and I'm not the only one to recognise it. Some years ago, I was in a pub in Kincardine which is now a nursing home and, by the way I was behaving that day, I belonged in some kind of home or other. I was steaming – feeling absolutely no pain at all – and Helen had come down for me, to make sure I didn't get into any bother. It was the week after Hill O'Beath won the Scottish Junior Cup but I wasn't celebrating that – no, this was more of a private celebration. Probably it was a good, clear day and I wanted to raise a glass to the fact. Who needs an excuse? Anyway, John Brownlie, the former Hibs player, was in the pub and, when Helen was taking me out the door, he said to her, 'You've got a big heart! You're a brave woman!'

Now, I suppose, in my deluded little world, I probably think that no one outside my own protected patch knows what I'm about but, in my sober moments – and, trust me, I have many – I know that's simply not true. People know exactly what I'm like. Brownlie certainly did and he was right – Helen is a brave woman with a great big heart and that's why I love her so much.

When I fall out with Helen over my drinking, I usually land up in my own place in Alloa that I've had for the last few years. I call it the Jimmy Greaves house because, apparently, he was said to have kept a place where he could go during his bad drinking times. So I have my place and she has hers – we need our own space when the mechanism of marriage fails. I can't blame Helen or anybody else for all the times I've found myself in the Alloa house. I've got to face up to the reality that there's only one person who is responsible for all the nonsense and that's me.

But what is that reality? Well, I suppose it's when one of Helen's pals – Laraine was a nurse in an alcoholic unit – tells me that I need to watch myself, that maybe I'm using up too many chances and my next bender could be my swansong in this life. Laraine had been coming to the house a lot but, when I've got a 'numb heid' on, I don't bother listening to her – in fact, nothing gets through to me at those times. And I'm an expert on numb heids – I've been putting them on for thirty-odd years. The time to bother, to fret, to worry, is when you're free of the demon, when you're as sober as any of the judges who sit in our courtrooms. So what do I think of myself at times like that? I can only admit that I cringe. I ask myself all the usual questions – 'What did I do?' 'Why did I do it?' But these are difficult and embarrassing questions so the temptation is, of course, to say, 'Oh, for f***'s sake, just give me another drink!' and that's what I used to do all the time.

Now I know that reaction was entirely the wrong one and, for the most part, I'm trying my best to live sensibly. I'm trying my hardest not to drink and, by doing so, maybe add a few extra years on to my lifespan. Only a fool thinks he's invincible and, at my age, I'm no fool. So, instead of putting numb heids on, I'm analysing everything and trying to put things into context.

And when I do this, there's no getting away from the shame side of drinking and there's plenty of *that* going about. For example, I'm barred from a certain pub for annoying people about drink. I think I need another drink to help me to forget the discredit that a ban brings. No, what I really need to do is go back to see the publican and tell him that I'm sorry but, no doubt, I'm still barred so that wouldn't work. And apologies, after all, don't turn the clock back. I must admit that, when I get too drunk, I do start blethering a lot of rubbish. I tend to pub hop – I like to get out and see everybody, distribute myself all over the place. Pubs can be braw, can't they? You meet all kinds in there – nice folk, sometimes not-so-nice folk and sometimes downright dangerous folk. Oh, you've got to watch yourself – if someone puts a glass in your face, that could be it! But they still draw you in.

I've also been barred from a pub in Kincardine for drinking a bottle and a half of sherry in the morning, hammering the whisky in the afternoon and then annoying and pestering people. I remembered being barred after my dad died too. Then it was sherry in the morning, whisky in the afternoon and annoyance all round. Nobody knows what I can consume. Look, I'm not trying to boast about it – it is nothing to be proud of – but, when I am really on it, it's something else. I don't share the same planet as most other people. I've learned at the feet of the masters – something I addressed in depth earlier in this book.

An old guy up at the AA once said to me, 'You may know a lot about fitba but you don't know anything about drink.' Maybe he's right. Maybe I'm just trying to kid myself on. Maybe I should body-swerve it completely. Whatever, I'm trying my best but you've got to remember that this opponent is not an out-of-condition footballer – this is a thing that is equal to all the guile you can muster. It doesn't give you up without a fight so you need weapons if you're going to beat it.

Anyway, back to my fifty-eighth birthday . . . Deep inside my stubborn head, I look on my birthday as a day for celebration and not even the love of a good woman is going to get in the way of it. Get thee behind me, Saint Helen. But this year there were other considerations, weren't there? Of course there were – particularly this book. What about my responsibilities to the publishers? Ach, the publishers wouldn't mind – let's face it, they would never know. Besides, I had my needs. I'd been off the mad lotion for weeks and my mouth was desert-dry. I was getting the message that a few down my throat would do me no harm at all. So I got a couple of bottles of Magners inside me, just to get the taste. I know everything I need to know about drinking cider. It's quite harmless – doesn't put you up or down. Naturally, Helen makes a fool of me when I come out with something like that, as if there won't be any repercussions. She tells me people will laugh at me for saying such things. There are always repercussions, she says – it's inevitable that one or two ciders will lead to something else. She's right, of course, and it was no different that time.

Fifty-eight years old or not, I was skint and had just about enough to buy myself a half pint of lager but money is not an issue on the streets where I live. It never is when your name is George Connelly. I know everybody and everybody knows me. There have been times when I've gone into the Auld Hoose in Kincardine and there would be about ten people standing at the bar and I'd get them all a drink – and not just the one, either. I like to see people with a smile on their faces, see people happy. So that day, as I advanced on Alloa with two bottles of cider under my belt, I had a confident smile on my face.

In the first pub I entered, I spotted a guy I knew from AA meetings. I shouted him over and told him I was struggling in the cash department. There was no hesitation in his response and his hand-to-pocket co-ordination was quite extraordinary. 'Look, I've got forty-five quid so here's forty,' he said, handing over the money – true generosity, if I wasn't mistaken.

I took it without a shred of guilt and, right at that moment in time, I was as happy as Larry. It was like returning to my youth – the little boy being taken on a picnic. But this was never going to be a picnic and there was to be no turning back either. I was all set for a bender. I got another twenty off a guy from Sauchie and was already planning the next swoop for readies. I was on the Magners and doubling up their effect with whisky chasers. What do they say about two's company? Anyway, I knew I could get money off a guy in a chip shop in Kincardine if I was desperate. I owed him £20 already but that was no problem. I owed somebody else a tenner and someone else a fiver but I'd pay it all back – I always do. Well, Helen pays it back and then I pay her. When I'm working, I've got enough money to make sure no one ever goes squinting.

That day I wasn't concerned for the future – I'd just bought myself a ticket for the present. I'd had four or five Magners and half a dozen halves and now someone was telling me to take a nice malt whisky. The sequence changed from cider, whisky and now it seemed to be malt, blend, malt, blend. They really shouldn't be mixed but who was caring? Certainly not me by this time. With the best part of forty quid in my pocket I had enough to go on my travels and soon I was in another pub, one in Kincardine. Anyway, having drunk the drink that does nothing to upset a man's reason or equilibrium and tossed various whiskies into the equation, I was steaming. I was talking to some guys about fitba and one particular guy – somebody I'd never met before – asked how I was getting on and I responded as if I'd known him all my life. When you belong to the fraternity of drinkers, all sorts of odd things like that happen. I mean guys, strangers, can come up to you and, for no good reason, just hand you some money. And it's a fraternity that embraces people from all walks of life. In the same pub, you can get the highly educated type whose conversation could turn you inside out if you started to talk to them and, at the other extreme, there's the dour guy who you can't get a word out of. The serious drinker doesn't fall neatly into particular categories and, in pubs, all men and drinkers are equal. There really is no class system – you just talk to whoever is available and is willing to listen to you and tolerate your gibberish.

Anyway, as I almost remember it, this guy and I started exchanging gibberish and soon the daylight was being replaced by darkness. It was time for me to hit the road but which road was I going to hit? I knew I'd crossed the line so there was no point in going back and knocking on Helen's door so where was I to go? I'd got through all the money and was too drunk to even think about how I might borrow more. Besides, the donors had disappeared – it was long past their bedtimes. Ideally, I would have taken a taxi over to my bolthole in Alloa but taxis cost money. So, there I was stranded in Kincardine and then came some inspiration – maybe I could get a bed in one of the high-rise flats just along the road from the last pub I'd been in. I've got relations who stay there so surely I could stagger that far.

As it happened, I could and I did – just. But, when I got to the high-rise flats, I decided I couldn't go knocking folk up at that time of night. Maybe the walk in the cold night air had punched some sense into me but, whatever it was, it seemed unreasonable to present myself to them at that hour and in such a horrible drunken state. Then I had another idea – a real brainwave this time – and I made my way into one of the chute rooms (there's one on every floor for the rubbish) and I found that my luck was in. There was an old settee in a corner – someone must have chucked it out of their flat and it was waiting to be uplifted by the council. I had found a bed for the night. No blankets, no central heating and, as usual in Scotland in the month of March, it was absolutely freezing but it wasn't all bad news – I at least had a bed of sorts. I got my head down and waited for sleep to claim me. With the amount I'd had to drink, I didn't have to wait long.

I was out for the count and I'm sure I could easily have frozen to death but human kindness was at hand and, at around five o'clock, I was wakened by a man called Vincent Cardwell.

Every muscle in my body was screaming, my neck felt as if one of the superstars of wrestling had been practising with it and there was a Kango hammer starting up inside my head. Vincent took me into his neighbour's flat – a guy called Willie Logan – and they gave me a couple of duvets and a hot-water bottle to warm a body that was as cold as a corpse. I then got my head down. I'd been saved again and, on this occasion, help had probably arrived just in the nick of time.

Later, if there had been a brain in my head instead of a pound of mince, I would have hightailed it up the road and started playing that old tune of regret to Helen but there was no grey matter on that March day. I had survived day one of a bender, having slept semi-rough, but there was still some running left in me. That place called home would have to wait awhile for the arrival of Mr Connelly. The taste was on me and there was a drinks marathon to be run.

After a few days, Helen came over to my Alloa house with my possessions in a bin bag. She was going to a funeral but she had another funeral sitting right in front of her. She was so sick of me that she wouldn't even talk to me. I knew then that the bender had to end. I felt so bad it was as if someone had punched a hole in the bottom of my life and all the contents were strewn on the ground.

Happy birthday, George!

You've accompanied me to the hell of last March and there was to be another huge binge in July that I won't bore you with. Instead, come and sample my kind of heaven. On 4 October 2007, I was sitting in my favourite chair, trying to make some kind of sense to what had happened to me the night before. But let's start by going back over the few weeks leading up to that moment.

After I'd got my head together in March and then again in

July, I really started screwing the nut. With some great difficulty, I managed to stop the bingeing. I smartened myself up and began to put my life back on an even keel. I started dieting again, cutting out all the fatty foods and chocolate that had begun to alter my shape. There was a book launch to be addressed so I needed to be professional and get fit. I began power-walking again – it was a case of small distances at first, followed by marches that Don Thompson, the diminutive Olympic race-walker, would have approved of. More than thirty years after that nightmarish time when I left my career at Celtic behind me, I suddenly realised that I didn't want to be letting people down any longer. Gradually, bit by painful bit, I was putting myself back together again – becoming a human being again. The weight dropped off and, at last, I began to feel that life was worth living without a drink in my hand. In fact, the very thought of drinking began to disappear into the distance. The real world was beckoning me over and, for once, I didn't resist its call.

Celtic's publicity man, Tony Hamilton, rang and asked me if I would take part in a DVD that's due to come out around Christmas 2007 and I amazed myself by saying I'd be happy to do it. I think it must have gone well because Tony then asked me if I would do the half-time draw during Celtic's Champions League match against AC Milan on 3 October. I shocked myself again and agreed to do it – I mean, I hadn't been at the Park for over thirty years.

So now we come to what happened on the night of that Celtic v AC Milan match. Our friends, Andrew and Linda Connor, were going through to the Park for the big game and they said they'd give Helen and me a lift there in their Voyager people carrier. We felt like royalty because the Voyager had darkened windows so it acted as a dress rehearsal for the royal welcome I was to receive at the Park.

I had wondered how I should dress for the occasion and, eventually, I chose a dark blue suit. Helen told me that I looked a million dollars and I certainly felt that way when Peter Lawwell, the Celtic chief executive, came up to talk to us. He was so warm and welcoming. 'Don't ever be a stranger again,' he said and he made me feel like a giant. As far as drink was concerned, I behaved myself impeccably. Helen had three gin and tonics and I was so pleased that, at last, she could enjoy herself without having to worry about me. As I sipped my diet Irn-Bru, alcohol was the furthest thing from my mind. I was intent on taking in all the sights and sounds – and there were plenty of them to take in. We met Gordon Strachan, who was in his customary effervescent mood, and we had our photographs taken together. God, I felt so proud. We also met Bobby Lennox and Joe McBride and I think I frightened wee Bobby when I told him the distances I was now walking.

Just before half-time, we were taken from our VIP seats and led down to the tunnel, prior to the draw ceremony. As I watched myself on the big screen scoring three of the best goals of my career, my previous life with Celtic came to me in flashbacks and thirty-odd years were compressed into thirty seconds. I swear I saw myself doing that keepie-uppie display and I glimpsed Jock Stein, the greatest football manager on earth, and then Big Billy, the best centre half in the world. You will never know the size of the lump that came into my throat as I prepared to walk out on to that centre circle, a Celtic scarf draped around my shoulders. A lump? It was more like a boulder! At one moment, I thought that I was going to spoil it all by breaking down but I knew I had to hold myself together. The roar from the crowd was phenomenal and the fans were fantastic. It was like I had never been away. What a sensational few moments! Why, oh why, had I stayed away for so long?

I took a firm grip of my emotions and got on with the job I

was there to do. Strangely enough, I thought I might be full of nerves but this wasn't the case. Cameras were clicking in my face and people were asking me questions but nothing could faze me on the night. I just took it all in my stride.

Helen and I were invited to go for some drinks and tapas after the match but, what with my return to Paradise and Celtic's magnificent victory over AC Milan, we decided we'd had enough excitement for one night – a night that was only slightly marred by a Celtic fan running on to the pitch after Scott McDonald scored the winning goal.

I suppose I was fairly silent as we went back home but I was just savouring an occasion that, for once, had not overwhelmed me. I was also thinking about my situation concerning alcohol. The last binge had been almost three months ago and it had taken some amount of recovering from, I can tell you. Now I had found a friend in the form of the Antabuse tablets I'd been taking. I'm determined to put myself right, determined to get the better of this thing that's been beating me around the head for so many years. I had Antabuse tablets years ago but these ones seem to be more powerful. They are intended to take the glamour away from drinking – that's assuming there is any glamour in the first place. I've been through everything but this latest course of treatment is designed to stop you thinking about drink. Now I can't touch a drop unless I stop the tablets for three to four days. If I did take alcohol, it might give me a heart attack and I could die. My doctor has told me that, if I do drink when I'm on them, then I will end up in hospital for certain. Now, is there any glamour attached to that little lot? Tell me if you see any. Whatever, the glamour seems to be away at the moment, in a far, distant place. Please God, it stays there. Now I'm not licking my lips and thinking everything is going to be sweet if I could only get my hands around a glass of cider.

You know, in an ideal world, I think professional footballers should all be like Bobby Charlton or Billy McNeill. They should get married and have a lovely wife, beautiful children and an altogether great life – end of story. Aye, right! But what makes people like George Best and Jim Baxter? What makes a man like George Connelly? What makes him climb almost to the top of the mountain and then want to go back down long before he's actually put a foot on the summit? I don't really want to place myself in the same category as Best and Baxter because they were touched with genius and I will never really know what I had – I was away out of it at the age of twenty-six – but at least I did share some characteristics with them. I'm trying so hard to play the good guy now. I'm taking the tablets and attempting to walk a steady line. But will this new drugs regime last? Will it present me with the answer to this addiction? Is there any cure for the condition that haunts me and terrorises me? Can there be any long-lasting peace in my life? Right now, I'm so happy I feel as if I'm in heaven but I know hell could be just around the corner.

But I'm not going to dwell on the negatives. I'm so high that I need oxygen because something that's better than anything I could imagine has just happened. It came in the shape of a text from my son David, who is now in Australia. He had been listening to the Celtic v AC Milan match on the Internet and his message read, 'Guan, yersel', Dad. I'm proud of you!'

It just doesn't get any better than that.

18

GETTING THE JOB DONE

The mobile phone, everyone's umbilical cord to immediacy, stayed resolutely and almost truculently silent whilst my wife and I were on holiday in France. Thus, rested and rejuvenated, I was preparing to return home and resume writing the book upon which I embarked in March – the story of perhaps one of the most fascinating, if complicated, characters I had ever encountered in professional football or, indeed, professional sport. Down the years, my job has inclined me to concentrate on human conundrums like George Best, Alex Ferguson, Alf Ramsey, Diego Maradona, Severiano Ballesteros, John McEnroe and Alex Higgins. A new kid has joined them on the block, however – joined them and perhaps even elbowed them out of the way. For sheer raw complexity, George Connelly challenges any of them.

This day, on the way to the airport, I was day-dreaming of that book. As far as authorship was concerned, I was in the home straight and, yes, my eyes offered confirmation that there was a little chap hefting a chequered flag on the horizon. The work was almost complete – only a couple of chapters to go. I had sashayed through the badlands of publishing so expertly that I was prepared to take issue with anyone who said that book writing was a labour of Hercules. Come on, chaps. It's not *that* difficult!

Just as we were making our way into the airport compound,

however, something happened to dramatically alter the land-
scape of that opinion. The mobile suddenly burst into life. It
was David Connelly, George's son. He sounded severely
discomfited, as if he might be tap-dancing on a rusty nail.
I got the feeling he'd rather be doing something else than
phoning me. 'Really sorry to bother you but weren't you
supposed to be coming over tomorrow to see Dad? I'm afraid
. . . er, you'd be wasting your time. He's gone! He vanished
last week.'

It was time to make an admission – time to lay out the
blackjack cards on the table with such a clatter that the
normally impassive croupier registered his surprise. The
writing of *George Connelly, Celtic's Lost Legend*, was never going
to be a facile assignment. Originally, I had suggested to the
publishers that we call it: *George Connelly: Lost and Found*.
Back in that small airport at Tours, I was now tacitly agreeing
that they had been comfortably within their rights to ignore
the suggestion. The word 'found' did not belong in the same
breath as Connelly's name. No one could ever be overly optimistic about this man. He had, by his own admission, a drink
problem that was gargantuan in stature. Over the past few
months, we had addressed that problem for hours on end,
directed searchlights into the darkest recesses of his existence
and unearthed random skeletons. I'd listened to him when
he had what he termed his 'numb heid' on. On those days,
he traded in monosyllables and frustrated the hell out of you.
On those days, the door to his life stayed resolutely shut and
you would have needed to be the world's strongest man to
open it.

Conversely, when his head admittedly was liberated from
the accursed demons, I'd heard him talk about life and its vicis-
situdes in a such manner that you could see him delivering
lectures at university. And yet, so far, I had never actually *seen*

him with a drink in his hand. I'd always tried to avoid imagining that particular scenario. Now, the possibility was staring defiantly at me, challenging me to come outside and confront it on the cobblestones. Several theories rushed into my mind at once and threatened to cause a gridlock – these theories had surrendered their subliminal status. What if this particular Connelly bender went on ad infinitum? Did I have enough material to finish? What if he repeated the vanishing act if and when the book was published? What if he absented himself when he was due to complete the promotional interviews? What if his apprehension turned into terror and he did a runner, just like he did when he once was ostensibly master of all he surveyed at Celtic?

I left Tours in the no-frills but ultra-efficient company of Ryanair. Under normal circumstances, while I am not the type to resort to skittering down aeroplane aisles, chittering with fright, I am rarely in Des Lynam mode when on an aeroplane. I have a healthy apprehension of life at altitude but not that day – that day, flying was the very least of my worries.

However did such an enterprise begin? On a cold day early in 2006, to be precise, I made my way to Firhill to interview the veteran striker Billy Dodds for the *Sunday Herald*. While I was waiting, I encountered Jimmy Bone. Now, if only football was replete with men like him, we all would be in a better place. Jimmy comes from the Stirling area. As I stayed there for three years back in the 70s and one of my sons was born there, we share a common denominator. So, we began to shoot the breeze and, somewhere down the line, George Connelly's name was flagged up. Nice chap, George. Wonderful footballer. Shame what happened to him. So, what had become of him? Jimmy provided some of the answers. The last time they met, George was doing some taxiing over in Fife but the taxiing was only a means to support his heavy drinking. Jimmy and I exchanged our regrets that such a thing should happen to such a great player. But, already, an idea had burrowed its way into my brain and demanded board and lodging.

I was about to record a series for BBC Radio Scotland. It was called *The Pain of the Game* and it explored psychological suffering in sport. The series would feature Faye MacLeod, Zola Budd, Alex Arthur, Tommy Docherty, Damon Hill and Rodney Marsh. It might need another ingredient. Could Connelly supply it? Could I ever find him? My name was not Magellan, after all. There had been more sightings of the yeti than there had been of Connelly in recent years. Bone suggested I tried David Hay, Connelly's closest friend.

Within days I was testing the advice. Hay, possessing the skills of a celebrated social worker, provided me with Connelly's number and offered encouragement. I rang Connelly. He remembered me but, when I suggested that he might take part in a radio show, you could almost see him levitating. 'I could never dae that,' he replied. 'It's just no' me. Mind you, I might agree to do a one-to-one if it was a newspaper.'

It was months before contact was made again. We agreed on an interview for the *Sunday Herald* and that I should travel through to Connelly's home. On that day, you could see immediately that life hadn't exactly rewarded him for all the liberties he had taken with it – his skin was a bit puffy and he perhaps carried an extra couple of stone of ballast – but, considering the drinking he was reputed to have done, he had emerged relatively unscathed. He revealed that he had been on the wagon for months and that he power-walked every day – five miles minimum. The new regime began a month ago. The first day he tried it, he was so close to exhaustion that Helen, his second wife, had to come and pick him up in the car. I shared my own health experience with him. I was a heavy drinker until 1986 when it was diagnosed I had an enlarged heart. Causation? Too much booze! Part cure? No more drinking. Connelly seemed alarmed at such an eventuality. 'That's great,' he conceded, 'but it's a long life when you're not having a drink, eh?'

Indeed. I was beginning to feel I needed one then. He returned to his health kick with even more enthusiasm. 'Sometimes, I do eight to ten miles – about fifteen minutes for a mile. I'm really galloping these days. I weigh about fifteen to sixteen stone – I was nearer fourteen when I was playing. But now I watch what I'm eating all the time. You should watch what you're eating if you've got heart trouble. I never eat anything fried. The worst thing for you is biscuits, I would think. I never have them in the hoose. Today, I'll have half a tin of plum tomatoes, a hard-boiled egg and three pieces of lean meat – no bacon.'

With all this talk of nutritional benefits, I was beginning to feel as if I had joined the Gillian McKeith appreciation society. I wanted to inspect the real deal around Connelly and investigate what caused him to walk away from Celtic when he was virtually licensed to walk on air. I wanted to know the truth about his drinking. He was fairly open about the first question and fed me the line that he hadn't been happily married and that he could not live on the wage paid to him by the Celtic directorship. As for the drinking, he admitted it was a problem but he was as cautious as most boxers are in the first round of a fight.

Deeper into the conversation, he admitted that he drank over the limit of most people's tolerance levels. 'I go on wee benders, mini-benders. I try and stay off it as long as I can. But, aye, I'm strong in the heid the now. I'm too fit and feeling too good to be misbehaving. Besides, I'm dieting for Christmas. I'm going to lose more weight.'

Unfortunately, the feel-good factor was not transferring to me. Earlier that day, I imagined this might just be the best interview of my life. I was sitting in Connelly's lounge thinking that our exchange represented the barest scratch on the surface of his life. Yet I suddenly became aware of a somewhat disembodied voice talking to me from the corner of the room. What it was saying captured so much of my attention that I felt I was in bondage. Connelly suddenly had questions of his own. 'Do you think I have enough stories for a book? Could you arrange it for me? Could you help me?'

I was stunned. I plundered a line from *Fawlty Towers* and adapted it. Was there enough in him for a book? Listen, folks, there was enough for a bloody conference! I further assembled my wits and gave him the best advice that I could muster. 'If you're going to do a book, you should tell the truth. There are far too many life stories on the market that are desperately wide of the mark in this respect. Autobiographies? Do me a favour! They are deluding the public! But, first, you really want to be sure you *want* to do a book.'

The advice seemed to be absorbed. Connelly said that revelations concerning his drinking habits did not concern him. Yes, he was happy to address the truth and nothing but the truth. I told him I'd make the necessary inquiries and get back to him. My job now was to take it on from there and interest the guys who make the publishing world go around. But would they be too busy with the utterly compulsive works of young ladies like Chantelle Houston and Coleen McLoughlin, or could they identify a genuinely cracking story? Three publishers showed interest and asked me to send them a couple of chapters. I visited Connelly again to put some meat on the carcase. The previously sealed envelope began to open in some style. Connelly was generally non-committal about the breakdown of his marriage, but he told me that it actually ended when his first wife, Christine, started going out with another man. 'That was it. But I didn't care by then.'

His mind went off at tangents, several tangents, but these were acceptable tangents all the same. One minute he was discussing his school days and telling me how his writing was so bad that the teacher recommended he write with his more talented feet. The next he was questioning the advisability of an irritating Alex Ferguson habit. 'Down at our pub, they ask why Fergie chews all that gum. I tell them it's so that he can talk and his mouth wouldn't be all dry. He must be tensed up – he'll be dehydrated all the time. I used to keep a sweetie in my pocket during my early time in the game. I was getting that very same thing, ken? I had an Opal Fruit just to ping myself up and stop that mouth gaun dry.'

I had no means of confirmation but I suspected Connelly's mouth had not been inordinately dry recently. He made me a cup of tea and told me that, on occasions, his head was somewhat anaesthetised by the years of drinking. He smacked his lips and revealed that a couple of pints of Magners might just do the trick. Being something of an expert on the subject, I stood on my redemptive platform and offered him advice from the other side, telling him that cider would solve nothing.

We quickly secured a book deal and, by then, the stories were tumbling out of both George and Helen. They were plunging into waters so murky you couldn't see the bottom – if, indeed, they had a bottom at all. I got the feeling that Connelly's second wife, Helen, was the real heroine in this piece of melodrama. Approximately four or five times a year, George embarked on mini and major benders. In between, he stayed sober and fanatical about his eating habits and fitness. This, of course, was to repair the chaos he had caused to the lives and general well-being of those who loved him – his wife, son, two daughters and a dutiful sister called Jane who, apparently, would lend him money during hard times. During these extremely self-centred boozing sessions, Connelly stayed at his own place in Alloa. He might have gone to bed early but that was only because was up early and diving straight into another vat of drink. His consumption was awesome. At one point, a couple of years ago, Helen became so fed up with carrying the empty bottles that she invested in a wheelie-bin.

Everything possible had been tried to stem the tide of alcohol. Alcoholics Anonymous were still trying but I suspected their bailing arms were tiring. Connelly revealed he didn't often attend meetings. 'I got tongue-tied when in company,' he explained. 'I just couldn't talk about it. It's called Anonymous but I just didn't feel anonymous. I could tell them I was an alcoholic and that I identified with them but that was about it. I couldn't take it on and tell them the things that had happened to me in my life. But it let me know that I was an alcoholic – one who was dabbling and intended to go on dabbling. Really, I'm still in denial. I've got one leg across the garden fence but it seems I can't drag the other leg over. It rears its ugly head now and again and I can't do anything about it. But, yeah, I'm a mouse at meetings. My mind has too many branches. There are too many things to say and they get jammed up. As the guy says, "An alcoholic's mind is like a ball of wool that's got all fankled up."'

At this time, Connelly had taken up a new treatment of Antabuse, tablets. Designed to remove the glamour of alcohol, if he drank while under this regime, there was a distinct chance he would be extremely ill. He had been warned it might even end his life.

What, you may ask, do I know about this terrible disease? I have some experience of excessive drinking myself but, more to the point, my dear brother John died an alcoholic's death – a terrible, lonely death – when he was forty-one. He was a master mariner in the Merchant Navy. He had test-driven all sorts of remedies to beat this desperate tyrant and I had watched a few of those test drives. We arrived at the point where he thought he'd smashed its resistance. Then, when he was out with a new command on an oil tanker in the Middle East, his birthday arrived. He celebrated by locking himself in his cabin and filling himself with whisky. He choked on his own vomit. I took leave of absence from my Fleet Street newspaper to go to the funeral. I remember waiting days for the body to be flown home. After some time, the vigil was over as the plane touched down at Aberdeen Airport. I remember going to the funeral parlour and the mortician telling me I could not see the body because it was so badly decomposed. I shall never forget watching my mother, who was a seamstress, sitting by her sewing machine the night before the funeral. That awesomely soulful song 'He Ain't Heavy, He's My Brother' was coming out of the television and my mother's shoulders shuddered with emotion. She disintegrated before my eyes. I joined the general disintegration.

My feelings for George had gradually changed. I had always liked him but now I had begun to like him enormously. He reminded me in some ways of my brother – kind and gentle. I did not wish to see him waste his life in the same manner as John had but the facts needed to be addressed. He had to start helping himself and accept that he had to assist in the load-bearing process. To allow the whole system of AA to work, it is necessary to perfect the art of self-abasement and I did not think Connelly had arrived at that juncture. He said he felt ashamed of himself but how ashamed was that? Possibly not nearly enough.

There was no doubt in my mind that here was a man in possession of a sensitive nature. I saw evidence of it in those visits to his home but I witnessed it evolve rather spectacularly in front of me one specific day. We were discussing the good side of drinking – I suppose you will find one if you are inquisitive enough – but soon we were addressing its alter ego. He told me of the night he threw a glass in a man's face. He was still mortified by the memory of the event. Suddenly, his large fame seemed to collapse. He exited tearfully from the room. You couldn't help but feel empathy towards someone like that. He is not a villain. Indeed, most of the time, he conducts himself far better than the majority of the footballers I know.

There were, however, further glimpses of a guy who knew how to fight his corner. The subject of Billy McNeill came up and David Hay had, tantalisingly, said, 'Did he tell you about Billy?' Hay would say no more. No, indeed, Connelly had not really told me about McNeill. Oh, he liked him, sure. He thought the world of him, even idolised him. He was anxious that Big Billy would agree to contribute to his book and, when he did, George considered it a great honour. But I just felt there was something between them that he had not shared with me. Just as when I'd asked him about religion, he tended to be defensive. 'Look, I was being groomed for Billy's position but it didn't work out because I wasn't good in the air. What did Billy think? I don't know. I never spoke to him. I just did what I was telt. I suppose it kept him on his toes, eh? I suppose, if you look over the archives, I got the reputation of keeping Billy in the game for another two years when I played beside him. But I'm no' wanting to be big-headed. As you get older, you don't want to fall out with anybody!'

Apart from one sideswipe at his brothers and sisters, I never heard him criticise anyone. Autobiographies often present those who fancy the idea of having a go at folk with the ideal platform to do so but not Connelly and that says a lot about his character.

There was less-than-subtle evidence, however, that he possessed an inferiority complex so huge that it simply could not be measured. One example came when Celtic were on tour. Connelly was sitting in a nightclub in the company of a beautiful Canadian girl. According to reports, the girl fancied him like mad but, for some reason, he got it into his head that she was looking at his ears. Suddenly, it is claimed he said, 'So what if I've got sticking-oot ears? You're a skinny besom!'

The ball of wool that is Connelly's head was in disarray when we met a week before I left for France. He was in a strange, preoccupied mood. Contrast this with the previous couple of sessions when only a gag would have stopped him talking. Helen was sitting beside him on the sofa but, for once, he was not drawing any inspiration from this quarter. There was a new eating fad in his life – the Atkins' diet. Carbohydrates were out and bacon, eggs, mushrooms and chicken were in. Strawberries and cream were particularly recommended. He might not be eating all the pies but it was alarming to see him demolishing strawberries with great dollops of double cream. According to Connelly, the cream was part of the diet and it was only later, much later, that the truth dawned on him.

Still, the couple remembered times when they couldn't afford such luxuries. Connelly recalled one Christmas when they didn't have much money and so he went into the supermarket and bought half a turkey. He insisted that the memory of such poverty had no affect on his well-being. 'I'm feeling great within myself,' he enthused. 'Drinking is not in my plans.'

I had a feeling the last remark was for Helen's benefit. When she went out of the room to go and get another massive helping of strawberries and cream for her man, Connelly looked conspiratorial. 'You know, there are clouds scudding across my heid. I've just got this feeling that a couple of Magners would blow them away.'

Alarmed, I said, 'You haven't been taking the Antabuse, then?'

'No, not for a few days.'

'Well, maybe it's not my business, George, but, if I were you, I'd get up those stairs and take them right now.'

He disappeared before returning a few minutes later. A different person was now occupying the sofa. He told me he'd taken the Antabuse and that he was feeling decidedly better. He was now in a mood to speak more coherently. He admitted, for instance, that maybe he had a complex about mixing with the big stars. 'I'm going to be big-headed and say that it was a shame that people never saw the player I should have been. The fans never saw the player I could have been. They saw only two-thirds – maybe even less.'

Just over two weeks later, I returned from France hoping to meet one hundred per cent of George Connelly but the signs weren't encouraging. He had been away from home for days. At least Helen knew he wasn't starving because she'd found the remains of a leg of lamb that had been cooked in what is known as the Jimmy Greaves household. She'd also found the traditional signs of excess – bottles all over the place. It was wheelie-bin time again. When was this particular nightmare going to end?

Suddenly, there was a break in the clouds, a silver lining threatening to turn to gold. I found a Connelly interview that I didn't know existed. Perhaps I wouldn't need to grill my man again. Then, some days later, my home telephone rang. Connelly was back in the world of the living. He was embarrassed about his disappearance, sure, but he sounded ready to resume the ongoing battle with life. I made fresh arrangements see him. 'Next Monday?' I asked. 'Does that sound good?' Anything seemed to sound good to Connelly – he was back where he was appreciated. The agonising process of detoxification lay ahead of him but he was up for it – it would be a fight but one that he'd win.

I arrived at the Connellys' immaculate terraced house fifteen minutes ahead of schedule. George was there to greet me with a wan smile. There was no handshake but no insult was intended. I sensed he was anxious to return to the lounge and put his backside down on his favourite sofa before he fell down. Descending from the heights he had attained over the past ten days was a precariously difficult business. Helen was her usual bright and optimistic self. She always put on such a brave face – she is just amazing. She took heart from the fact that George had poured a bottle of wine down the sink that very morning – a far better option than pouring it down his throat. On the other hand, she admitted that, the day before, her husband demolished a bottle of brandy.

The fight had some way to go. 'I'm so embarrassed,' George conceded. 'I'm dying to get off the drink – I feel like death warmed up – but three different doctors have told me not to come off the drink completely. It would be too dangerous.'

As if on cue, Helen appeared with a tumbler full of a dark-looking liquid. It was vodka and Coke. The emphasis was on the Coke, she revealed quietly. George accepted it gratefully. He sipped the drink and, as he looked at me almost triumphantly, he said, 'Bryan, I'm hot! You've caught me at it!' He was right – in the seven months since we started the project, this was the first time I'd seen Connelly drinking.

His wife urged him to take coffee as a supplement to the vodka but he wasn't keen. The contradictions in his character were more evident. 'I'm making a serious effort to wean myself off the drink,' he said, 'but it's getting harder as I'm getting older. It gets a grip of you. Once upon a time, I could say, "That's it!" and I'd pour the stuff away, get on the walking shoes and sweat it out. I can't seem to do that now.'

Power-walking had been suspended for the last three weeks while Connelly indulged the devil within himself. The diet disappeared. Takeaways had provided him with some sustenance but, according to his wife, he didn't eat that much of them. 'Some of the carryout meals were unopened and it was obvious from the basin beside his bed that he wasn't able to keep down the things that he did eat,' she said.

I wondered where he had got the money for this prolonged boozing session. Had he tapped his way around the locality? Connelly revealed that he had saved up 'a couple of bob' but that couple of bob turned out to be approximately five or six hundred quid which subsequently rose to a thousand pounds plus a couple of 'taps'.

Helen was adamant that her husband's demons always visited when there was pressure. 'He worries about everything – he's worried sick about David going to T in the Park and, after the terrorist attacks, he worried himself daft over me driving through to Glasgow Airport. He even torments himself over simple things, like whether his granddaughter remembers to put her seat belt on when she's out in the car.'

I asked the question that had loitered in my mind ever since I'd taken that call from David on mobile to say that his dad was posted missing. I needed to know whether writing this book had perhaps been too much for George. Might it have been responsible for sending him toppling over the edge this time?

George was admittedly in poor physical shape that morning but he answered without hesitation. 'Listen, it's been brilliant for me. I'm no' worried about that. I've got everything aff my chest. It's only the truth. I promise I won't let anyone down – you, the publishers, my family, myself . . .' This new-found enthusiasm took him to his feet. 'Nowadays, things come back to me just like that. I mean Bridgeton 2710! That's from over thirty years ago.'

'Bridgeton 2710 – what's that?' I asked him.

'That's the Celtic number before the 0141 carry-on. I used to answer the phone at the Park. It was part of your job when you were on the ground-staff. I've probably spoken to a lot of very famous people.'

Helen was back with more vodka and Coke, more coffee and more conviction. 'Listen, he's a good man. I don't want anything we do here today to be at all negative 'cos it's not. He's so easy to live with, normally. He runs the bath for you. You can put your feet up and he'll soon be through with a cup of tea – he learned that from Bob Rooney. He was always making tea, wasn't he, George? Attentive – that's George. If the daylight is getting in your eye and it's difficult to see the television, he jumps up and draws the curtains. He supports me when he's strong. Some of my friends' husbands disappear away to their beds without saying goodnight. George wouldn't dream of doing that. My mother, as you know, is in the late stages of dementia but, whenever I go to see her, the very first thing she asks is, "Where's George?" It's simple. If you know him, you love him.'

That was a fact and so was her next statement. She revealed that she found her husband putting on his shoes and preparing to head out for the great unknown again only a couple of days after he had returned. She had seen the performance before so she knew what had to be done – she quickly raised the drawbridge and lowered the portcullis.

The much-loved Connelly suddenly looked forlorn. 'I wonder what's around the corner for me. Sometimes I say to myself, "Am I going to land in the loony bin? Or will I end up with dementia?" Oh, I hope not. I'm no' really bad. I think I'm quite a kind person. When I was on my travels the other day, I met a guy with no hands who asked me for a pound. I gave him a tenner. When I see things like that, it lets me know how really lucky I've been in life. Speaking about lives, Bryan, I hope you have a long life.'

I left that small, neat terraced house that day thinking that, if his problem is indeed an illness, then Connelly may be right in the middle of his very own epidemic. The point is that, in this beleaguered year with so much going wrong with the world, have we still got the ability to cure epidemics?

Three days after that visit, Helen and I talked on the phone, ostensibly to discuss any changes to the book. There were very few although she worried whether she may have betrayed him in her own particular chapter. Then she remembered what Al-Anon teaches and she knew she should not be beating herself up in such a fashion.

George had not come near the telephone, which was unlike him, so I asked her for an update on him. The answer appeared a sombre one – the drawbridge and portcullis at Castle Connelly were still in the same position as they'd been in when I left. Helen's optimism belonged to the past. She feared her husband was not yet equipped to stop drinking. She had been entertaining her niece and her baby from Australia recently. Not always comfortable with visitors, George had used this an excuse to go out to buy some crisps but he'd returned with wine. Helen took some comfort in the fact that he had at least returned. However, she feared he might be about to abscond again and, this time, he'd wander far further than the local shop.

I told her I was just completing the last chapter of the book and would send it to her. She laughed. 'Have you got a title for it? Perhaps you should call it "The Bird Has Flown"!'

Helen confided that she didn't think he had even read the manuscript. Perhaps he never will read it. But, when she challenged him about this, she stumbled across a small oasis of hope. He smiled and said, 'Listen, it'll be bullet-proof! Tell Bryan I'll see him at the book signing!'

Almost three weeks after that, I had first-hand evidence that the bird was back in the nest. The man so dearly beloved by Helen was sitting on his usual settee in the lounge, having completed his fair share of apologising and ritualistic foot-kissing. Earlier in this chapter, I pointed out what a struggle detoxification was for George. This proved to be a serious under-statement. In effect, when Connelly finally emerged from that binge – with the exception of those few days when he came home to honour his commitment to his book – it had lasted six weeks. More money had been spent and in all likelihood, if you accepted the premise that hard drinking destroys brain cells, more memory had been squandered.

Connelly, however, did not look any the worse for it. He was clearly sober and in command of his faculties. I told him how pleasantly surprised I was by his appearance and he said he was in the pink. He'd be going power-walking later in the day and publicity man Tony Hamilton was coming to see him that week to record a contribution for a Celtic Christmas DVD. He'd had to cancel the Hamilton appointment a couple of times but it would be kept this week. He also reported that he'd stopped taxiing – at least for the time being. 'I've been daen it for fifteen years now and I wonder how much can a human brain haud! All that fitba, all that drinking, all that taxiing. But, in saying that, since I stopped, I'm feeling a whole lot better. I think I was taking a stutter on the taxis and that was bothering me. I was starting to forget as well – at one time, I actually thought I was taking dementia. It must have been with thinking all the time about the route I was taking, and talking to folk at the same time. But dementia? I soon knew better. My speech is fluent now. Everything's fine now.'

The words were spinning out of him. 'Helen tells me I first departed around the time of Father's Day, before coming back after three weeks. I thought to myself, "Christ, I've got a book coming out, let me get a wee bit of bloody pleasure oot of it." You know whit makes me a drink a lot? The people. I like mixing with the folk. The fact is I know too many people and I like gaun roon them all. But I know I'll need to stop it. If I do go round to see them in the future, it'll need to be a can of Irn-Bru or something like that.'

There was no mistaking the sincerity in Connelly. Trust me, if he was looking to be elected for the local council, you would vote for him. But it was when he announced that the days of the Antabuse were over that my trust began to fragment. Then, before that trust disappeared altogether, he added that he had transferred to Campral. 'They're the same as Antabuse but you can drink with them. They are supposed to kill the craving for alcohol.'

Helen suddenly registered her concern. 'Have you been taking them, George?'

Her concern was vindicated. 'No, not right now. I'll need to start taking them again. The thing is, if you're going to drink, you'll drink. But me? I'll stop for ages. That's a promise. I'll need to look after her.'

I expressed my concerns, asking him why he has banished one tablet which is designed to stop you drinking altogether and replaced it with another which virtually condones it.

'Well, it was the doctors who changed it – I never changed it. They maybe would be worried that I would drink with Antabuse and maybe they weren't wanting the responsibility.'

So, I wondered, how long did he think he would stop this time? 'I'll stop indefinitely. I know I'm not going to drink for a long, long time now. I cannae. This book is coming out and I've got to look after it. I'm no' daft altogether like. I cannae say this in front of Helen . . . aw, well, OK, it'll be Christmas at the very, very earliest. I'll do all my power-walking now that

I'm not taxiing. I think I'll stay away from the taxis. Once it was therapeutic for me but then I began to overload.'

I told him that, in some ways, it had been good to see the other side of him that day when he'd been struggling to come off the drink. 'I was glad you saw me like that, tae. It must have given you an insight into me.'

I also remarked how forlorn he had looked. 'Aye, right. I can remember an old guy at Torness tell me that I suited a thing called sobriety. And that was 1980. But there are always reasons, maybe. I can mind, for instance, when I was a kid and there was always people gaun about drinking. It was a hobby for them. People were going over to that Valleyfield Miners' Club every day. People were brought up on drink.'

I wanted to find out if he was back on the health kick again. 'Yeah, I'm power-walking. I really wrap up and get a good sweat. Helen says that I look mad when I go out. I put on a T-shirt, a jersey, a fleece and then a big, green jaicket!'

Much to Connelly's embarrassment, Helen went out of the room and came back with the clothes worn on these fresh-air extravaganzas. She pointed to the green garment. 'I call this "the dead man's jacket" – a man who died left it to George. He is the only one who it fitted. He wraps himself up in that and, when he comes back, you could ring out the T-shirt and swim in the perspiration. George likes that feeling.'

George then went on to outline the dynamics of his power-walking routine. 'I left the hoose at twenty past five yesterday and came back at ten tae seven – aboot six miles, maybe more. I took one of the neighbour's dogs for a walk. The dog's name is Buster. I've got the keys to the hoose. I just open the door, whistle and away we go.'

The exercise certainly seemed to be doing Connelly good. He looked far more svelte than the last time we met. But he was anxious to point out that his new look owed more to his recent bender than it did to exercise. 'I lost two stane in those few weeks. Really, I didn't eat and I got a shock when I weighed myself. It's a lot, eh? But I'm eating again and eating well.'

The detox caused an even greater shock to the system, however. Helen revealed that there had been wine in the day and through the night. There was, however, no mention of vodka or any spirits this time. But there was a confession from Helen, 'In some ways, I like to see him suffering because then you know that it's working. I don't know why he ever goes back to it when he knows it's so hard to get off it. The retching, the shaking . . . it's not nice by any standards.'

George looked at her, hoping to see some understanding. 'The trouble with drinking, Helen, is that you forget. You forget how bad it is.'

Helen brightened as if she'd remembered something good. 'Mind you, within two days of coming back here, he was talking of going for a walk. Maybe, though, it was too soon for walking. Maybe he bit off a bit more than he could chew. He came back. He didn't go as far as he thought he would.'

It's easy to find yourself being won over by their enthusiasm. Like his wife, Connelly was in a very positive frame of mind and I too had learned to appreciate times when they were as good as this. Normally, he was pumped full of fears but not that day. He put his remarkable recovery down to a solid constitution. 'I had an MOT quite recently on about four different parts of my body. There were blood tests too and everything was A1.'

The response from Helen was immediate. 'Yes and so was that comedian who died recently. What's his name? Mike Reid.'

Connelly was undaunted. 'But he had a bad heart. Mine is all right.'

This didn't warrant a comeback from his wife but she was

keen to explain what the medical people thought about George's latest foray into craziness. 'The doctor said that it was normally always a pleasure to see George but she just couldn't say such a thing this time. He got two types of tablets but the thing is there's no real cure for it. He should just avoid pressure.'

Connelly was unimpressed by this advice from the touch-line. He didn't see anything as an insurmountable problem – not even book writing. 'Look, if I hadn't done this, I would always have had it on my mind. Imagine trying to do something when you're seventy – nae good. Too late! Whatever they throw at me, I'll be all right – nae bother. See what I always say is that it's the thought of things rather than anything else that puts you off – just the thought. See the taxis? In the old days, I used to sit in the hoose on a Friday and imagine what the night would be like. I'd think, "Aw, no, not again!" But, when I went oot and had a bit of a chat with them all, I decided it was better oot there than sitting in the hoose. I mean no disrespect to Helen by that. The taxiing, apart from overloading my heid, was OK, really. It was OK. As long as they weren't shooting or stabbing you, it was OK. Now that's gone. I'll be OK with this book, see if I'm not.'

My job was complete. If it took a little longer than expected, who cares? I had made a friend in perhaps the most enigmatic sportsman of all. Forget the epidemic for one minute. I had the privilege of helping to write the life story of a very gifted man – one who, generally speaking, would say nothing at all rather than speak badly of someone. How many of us can say that?

The last time I was at the Connellys' house, George and Helen escorted me to the door and I swear there was a tear in the eye of the man who likes to be categorised as unemotional. I knew there was in mine. That time, he walked me to my car and there were smiles and handshakes. He told me he was ready for anything. There are far worse people in this world than George Connelly. And that's a fact.

EPILOGUE

George Connelly and I walked up the steps of the rather pictur-
esque Dunblane Hydro on the second of November 2007, with
Helen and her friend Linda just ahead of us, *writes Bryan Cooney*.
We had walked this way many times before, always inde-
pendently, of course, for we scarcely knew each other on those
1970s Saturday nights when Jim McLeod and his country dance
band set the foot-tapping agenda. But, on this, the far more
formal occasion of Connelly's book launch, we were very much
a team. We had welded together through months of hard work,
chiselling out the memories of a past life that sometimes had
difficulty in tolerating exploration. Considering the man's myriad
difficulties and the bizarre way he had chosen to live, we had
scaled a veritable cliff face, now we could sit back on the summit
and relish the benefits, even if it was for one night only. The
thought occurred that we were ridiculously early. We had four
and a half hours to spare before the function, which would be
attended by over two hundred people. What were we to do? I
was soon to learn that a man with time on his hands can be a
dangerous man. The climb up those steps, while not requiring
the use of breathing apparatus, was fairly demanding for all
that. Suddenly, however, the demands proved too much. Where
was that oxygen mask? A speech from Connelly, distinguished
not only by its brevity but its content, had made it so. 'What
do you think might happen if we had a drink?' he asked.

275

In life, when you arrive at moments like these, uncomfortable visions enter your head; visions which provide you with an escort to the X-certificate zone. Right then, I felt I only had to walk through that door and I'd find not only Dante but his accursed inferno! Could Connelly, a man of several illogical acts, really be contemplating such insanity? Was all the discipline and good behaviour executed over the past couple of months going to be despatched in a miasma of drunkenness? For that's how it would have ended, one drink begetting two, two begetting four and so on until we had reached the perimeter fence of the Wild West Show. I stopped him right there and looked into eyes that almost had forgotten what it was like to be bloodshot. 'If we have a drink, George, then it'll be time for the nonsense to begin. We may not regret it tonight or even in the early hours of tomorrow morning, but when we wake up, you can bet that we'll regret it for the rest of our lives!' George nodded his head slowly as if his brain had engaged obedient gear. The issue was put to rest there and then. We went up those stairs and ordered nothing more potent than tea and sandwiches.

When he later went for a nap in the room put at our disposal by the publishers, I analysed our day up until this point. The press launch of *Celtic's Lost Legend–The George Connelly Story* had gone far better than anyone could have envisaged or predicted. Our hero had emerged, suited and booted, from his Clackmannan lair and travelled the twenty-five miles or so to that accursed destination to face the media. Accursed? Connelly likes the city of Glasgow and loves the people, but he's forever frightened of them; frightened that they will smother him in kindness, and fail to accept a negative response when they offer him the one last drink for the road. George has been down that road before. But if Glasgow encouraged an apprehension in him, so, too, did the media. Apart from the odd occasion, he had never really reached any accommodation with many newspaper reporters. He'd been on more than nodding terms with the legendary Ian Archer and, indeed, had borrowed the odd fiver from him when times were necessarily hard. But Archer was the exception. Connelly was a lone wolf as far as the press was concerned. He couldn't face them when he was twenty-four and still stretching out for the stars, so how would he deal with them now that he was fifty-eight years old and grey? But this day, mercifully, he was standing up to his demons. It was too important not to. Of course he had a template for such confidence; he had returned to Celtic Park on 3 October to complete the half-time draw in the Champions League match against AC Milan. It was the first time he had been there in thirty years. He confessed he had been replete with fears on the night, but the roar of the crowd acknowledging his name had provided him with reassurance that he had been forgiven for leaving the 'family' all those years before. He and Helen had met manager Gordon Strachan and chief executive Peter Lawell, and the latter had told him 'not to be a stranger'. Well, here he was back for a second visit within a month. Now, he was back where he always felt he had belonged, desperately nervous inside, of course, but outwardly looking as if he'd never been away.

As the book launch media conference began – with George and I sitting on a dais normally occupied by the manager – I surveyed the compact band of pressmen and felt sanguine about the immediate future; they looked almost as nervous as my immediate neighbour would have been feeling. As they were entitled to be in the presence of a player who had more talent in his toenails than most of today's contemporaries have in their whole bodies. No complaints there. They were respectful and no-one came out with anything approaching impertinence. Indeed, they looked like soldiers tiptoeing around an incendiary device. Now, unsurprisingly, Connelly was scarcely as skilled in the art of communication as a Strachan or a Walter Smith, but he held his head high and answered every question lobbed at him. There were moments when he even managed a bit of levity . . . which later earned him inclusion in the quotes of the year roster. Reflecting on changing times and the inflated pay packets of today's players, he said: 'We were on £65 per week. I always say that if I was on £25,000 a week, they could put a box of tomatoes around the track and they (the fans) could throw them at me if I had a bad game!' Helen, standing in the background, laughed at that. Her man was doing well. His performance didn't disappoint, either, when the main press conference ended and he was taken down to the park for individual interviews. If he had spotted the ghosts of a distinguished past, he didn't allow them to deflect him from his task. He metamorphosed back into being the professional as he talked quietly and sensibly to anyone who wanted to listen. He seemed, outwardly, anyway, just as composed as the night he, as a sixteen-year-old, transfixed 65,000 people with his accomplished ball skills.

Back at the Hydro, Connelly had surfaced from his short siesta and seemed anxious to talk. But I couldn't erase that question from my mind. Had he been serious about it or had it just been the product of his sense of humour? So I asked him outright. The response was immediate: 'Look, the thought of drink will haunt me until the day I die. Yeah, the monkey was on my shoulder. See, I was letting you read my mind. If your mind was going to carry out the orders, I'd have accepted them. If you'd gone away and brought two glasses back, I'd have drunk one of them. But can you imagine what it would have been like if I'd started drinking? I'd have been a laughing stock. I'd no' been eating and a bottle of that good champagne would have knocked me sideways. Drinking makes you dae silly things. It would have been chaotic. Thank Christ I'm sober and remained that way!' What gave me additional cause for concern was the revelation that Connelly's body was a tablet-free zone. Over the years, he had taken tablets in his bid to body-swerve alcohol, the first being Antabuse and latterly Campral. But he immediately assuaged any anxiety: 'I don't need them while I'm on this high. Does it tell you anything about me that when Celtic were down at Leeds in 1970 and I scored that goal in the European Cup semi-final that I never drank after the game? I was in a couple of nightclubs but I was so bloody high that I didnae want to start bevvying!'

George was not alone in thanking God that he had not surrendered to the temptation. There was no point in trying to apply a coat of gloss to things and blame it all on one man who had tumbled into the clutches of rampant binge drinking; we as a unit had almost toppled into the abyss. Nowadays, my drinking is rationed to perhaps one day a year. Then, I can demolish a few bottles of champagne which, according to those who profess to know, is the least harmful of all alcoholic drinks. It is, of course, a potential summons to chaos. It's not that I'm a fall-about drunk, but there is a history of escapades and misfortunes. I'm a far better, nicer person sober than I am when the drink's in. And before Connelly had even spoken, there had been a temptation, if only a tiny one, in me to have a glass and settle the nerves which were threatening to riot in my belly. But we had survived that crisis. I looked at George and he, too, seemed becalmed. His words reinforced that assessment. 'Look, I'm in a beautiful place and decent company. I'm wanting to be known as myself, the ex-Celtic player who is well dressed, has a book out, and has his respect back again. Yes, I am enjoying myself and, to be honest, I'm still feeling like that. I've got a huge build-up in my heid about myself again.'

The feel-good factor remained resolutely in place when I

visited Castle Connelly in the second week of December, to write an interview piece for the *Sunday Herald*. That evening launch at the Hydro had been a considerable success, with over two hundred books sold and Connelly putting in a marathon stint at the signing table. Lots of drink had been consumed that night but, significantly, none of it by the man who would have appreciated it more than most. So here we sat, reflecting on his progress since the launch. I noted that the respectable representative of that split personality was sitting in front of me. Others had noted this, too. Setanta Television had been over to Clackmannan to record a programme and had certainly been impressed. Producer Steve Myles telephoned to say that an hour-long show, entitled *Lost Bhoy*, would be shown on Christmas Evening. Myles told me that the interviewer, Margot McGuaig, had been delighted and amazed at the demeanour of our complex friend. I looked at the rejuvenated man sitting across the room and tried to imagine Setanta being similarly impressed had they attempted filming him a year previous to this; in all probability, they would have had to direct their camera through a letterbox! As ever, though, there were qualifications as far as he was concerned. Connelly, having rejoined the world of sobriety, had also rejoined the world of respect. He'd discovered the resident real man behind the inebriate. But you suspected there was always an innate ability within him to thumb his nose at such promotion.

It wasn't long before we were debating the whys and wherefores of temptation. 'I had the flu a couple of weeks back and it put me on a bit of a downer,' he said. 'I wisnae that fit guy that I'd been for the past few months. While I was driving my taxi, people were saying that I might be better with a couple of halfs down me. That was their recommendation: a couple of halfs and straight to yer bed. To tell the truth, I felt like it. If Helen hadn't been there, I would have taken them. Oh, aye, that's 100 per cent. Yeah. When I was sitting there, with my sinuses playing up and feeling so low, I could have had a couple. Mind you, having said that, I don't think I would gone on a bender because, with all this publicity and the book coming out, I feel as if I've found myself. I mean, all of a sudden I'm George Connelly of the Celtic again, and I'm feeling too good aboot myself to be standing about bars, exchanging the gibberish with folk, and maybe staggering around streets. I feel too good for it today.'

I was still attempting to analyse the emphasis he placed on the word 'today' when he was off again with another torrent of words – this time an endorsement of the human being who, in his book, represents the last word in therapy. 'See when you're bingeing, like I was daen, it's hard to remember things. You forget to pay your rent, your electricity, your gas. Before you know where you are, you're up to your neck in debt. Mind you, I've always had Helen there. She's always been my banker that way. She's always helped me oot.' Helen is, of course, the life force behind him. She's had to deal with all the legacies of the alcoholism. At that moment, however, he felt she might have been applying too much force:

'Listen, Helen has been the most fantastic scout to me. Oh, aye, I might have died without her. If I was staying on my own, I would drink 'cos there would be nothing to stop me. But I have a sense of responsibility with her. The trouble is she's locked onto me now.

'It cannot be healthy sitting about in the hoose with a woman all the time, sitting there with her arranging your life for you. There's times you need men's company to appreciate women's company, otherwise you get to that stale way. A lot of me does think that having a drink provides an outlet. I'm no' gaun to dae it, like. But it's an outlet, a change. You appreciate your wife better when you've been out mixing with roughnecks and scallywags. But Helen doesn't see it that way. She's got every-thing in the world; the hoose is hers, it's in her name, there's money in the bank, but that's not enough. She's wanting me under control. She would give all this up, I think, if I was completely under control and wisnae going to drink again in my life. That's the trouble; you cannot tell. That's been five months I haven't touched it. I've done all right, but I cannae tell if I'm no' gonna drink again. I mean, I've no' had a chance to enjoy the book. If you were coming into a few bob, you'd celebrate, wouldn't you? But, Christ Almighty . . .'

Right then, if Connelly had gone into the back garden, lit a bonfire and started sending smoke signals into the dull skies, there could not have been a clearer or concise message of intent. Of course there was no chance of him exiling alcohol from his life. Not at that moment. Not, perhaps, ever. I watched him closely as he returned to a place that has never known the bene-fits of electricity. 'I can understand how people can go doon and doon; they've no' got what I've got. There's nae opening for them. I feel sorry for them. They end up in depression and they drink on top of it again. I've been there often enough myself. This place has nae light, and nae exit door. It's a black hole. Someone comes in (the pub) and asks you if you want to come to their hoose. So you're away, sitting in someone's hoose, drinking all night, and just guaranteed to be drunk again the next day. You hear a voice, saying, "You got money for the carry-oot the morra?" Aye, you've got money. So you're away again to the store, early doors, for mair drink. When I'm sober like this, I think of those times and I'm ashamed. I dinnae really want to think about them. I've built a wall in my mind so that I cannae think about the things I've done. Listen, I want to preserve this person who's sitting before you today.'

Connelly managed a smile which was so weak it could scarcely force its way onto his lips. No, he didn't wish to remember the shame. 'There are things we couldnae go into. I mean, an alcoholic will no' tell you everything. I was lucky because I had fitba to fall back on for the book, to beef it up, but the stories I got from other guys . . . you widnae want to hear them, surely to God. I can tell you this one, though. There was this guy one night, he was a hard man, a real hard man, and I was a wee bit scared of him. He telt me: "When I wis drinking, I wid have killed you for a can of beer!" Now the point of this is that he meant it. He meant it all right. Thae kind of things frighten me about drinking and there's nae doubt, I went over the top with alcohol. I always say aboot myself that I would love to be chained to two miners. They'd say to me: "We're going to have a drink, four or five pints, and that's it. Then we're away! Home!" That's the only way I could have a social drink; to have been chained to a couple of sensible miners. There would have been nae option but to leave and go hame. A lot of it I put down to my lack of education. It's a funny thing. I mean, if I knew more about life, I wouldnae drink. It's been said about me that although I may know a lot about football, whit I know about drink you could put on a postage stamp. I mean, I don't even know the strength of alcohol on the bottles. Just give me it and I'll drink it; that's always been my philosophy.'

As he talked, there was a question forming on my lips about the man who, before his career hit black ice in 1975, effected more disappearing acts than Harry Houdini. I was wondering how long it would be before he put his hands around a glass of cider or worse. 'I'm gonna be honest here. The whole book-writing exercise has been 100 per cent therapeutic. It's done mair for me than all the (AA) meetings in the world. Look, I'll never go back to what I was like before. I'm that confident. I've said that to Helen, although she tends to laugh at such statements. Even if I was going out for a drink, I widnae let myself

. . . there again, the drink might take me, but I don't think so. Naw, naw, I'm too strong for it and have too much respect for myself.'

POSTSCRIPT

George Connelly returned to those desolate wastelands of drink just before Christmas 2007. The session lasted two weeks, followed by another great swathe of sobriety which was (temporarily but worryingly) broken again in April 2008. Then, he confessed he could not bear to look into the mirror. 'I didnae want to see the reflection – a face like a big watermelon – full o' drink. It makes me ashamed.' At time of writing, he has reunited himself with normal life. He's trying to cope with the death of his beloved sister, Jane, who succumbed to pancreatic cancer; he's still running messages for those who cannot do it for themselves; he's cutting grass for those who find that beyond them; he's occasionally wearing a panama hat ('it makes me feel good'); on a less sartorial note, he's back in his 'deid man's jacket' walking once more for Britain; and he's making Helen remember why she fell in love with him. Importantly, at times like these, he is no longer terrified to look in the mirror.

POSTSCRIPT 2019

George Connelly is reaping the rewards of sensible living. He still power walks every day; he has added cycling to his fitness regime. And, probably most importantly, he has been sober since 2014.

ACKNOWLEDGEMENTS

I would like to thank Bryan Cooney for all his help, patience and understanding during the writing of this book.

My appreciation also goes to all the folk I've met in football, at both professional and junior levels – you'll never know how much every one of you means to me.